CURRICULUM STRATEGIES
FOR
TEACHING SOCIAL SKILLS
TO THE DISABLED

CURRICULUM STRATEGIES
FOR
TEACHING SOCIAL SKILLS
TO THE DISABLED

Dealing With Inappropriate Behaviors

By

GEORGE R. TAYLOR, Ph.D.

Coppin State College
and
Core Faculty
The Union Institute

CHARLES C THOMAS • PUBLISHER, LTD.
Springfield • Illinois • U.S.A.

Published and Distributed Throughout the World by
CHARLES C THOMAS • PUBLISHER, LTD.
2600 South First Street
Springfield, Illinois 62794-9265

© *1998 by* CHARLES C THOMAS • PUBLISHER, LTD.
ISBN 0-398-06790-2 (cloth)
ISBN 0-398-06791-0 (paper)
Library of Congress Catalog Card Number: 97–20088

With THOMAS BOOKS *careful attention is given to all details of manufacturing
and design. It is the Publisher's desire to present books that are satisfactory as to their
physical qualities and artist possibilities and appropriate for their particular use.*
THOMAS BOOKS *will be true to those laws of quality that assure a good name
and good will.*

Printed in the United States of America
OL-R-3

Library of Congress Cataloging-in-Publication Data

Taylor, George R.
    Curriculum strategies for teaching social skills to the disabled:
dealing with inappropriate behaviors / by George R. Taylor.
        p.   cm.
    Includes index.
    ISBN 0-398-06790-2 (cloth) – ISBN 0-398-06791-0 (pbk.)
    1. Handicapped children–Education–United States. 2. Social
skills–Study and teaching–United States.   3. Behavior modification–United States.   4. Socialization–United States.   5. Curriculum planning–United States. I. Title.
LC4031.T35 1997
371.9–dc21
                                                                97–20088
                                                                CIP

CONTRIBUTORS

George R. Taylor, M.Ed., Ph.D.–This distinguished author and noted lecturer is Professor of Special Education and Chairperson of the Department of Special Education at Coppin State College, Baltimore, Maryland. His knowledge and expertise in the area of learning disabilities is both locally and nationally renown. He has made significant contributions through research and publications in the field of special education and has conducted numerous workshops for teachers of disabled children on the local and national level.

Helen Brantley, M.Ed., Ph.D.–Professor of Special Education at South Carolina State College where she has held several administrative positions. She has been actively involved with the education of disabled individuals and has made significant contributions to special education through publications, participation, and conducting local and national workshops and conferences.

Shirley Edwards, M.Ed.–Assistant Professor of Special Education at Coppin State College. She has had extensive experiences working with disabled individuals and actively participates in local and national organizations serving the disabled. She has conducted several federally funded grants concerning training teachers of disabled individuals.

Bernadette Francisco, M.Ed., D.Th.–Adjunct Professor of Special Education at Coppin State College. She is a specialist in developing transitional education curricula for children with autism and is facilitator for the P.A.L. Program (Program for Autistic-Like [students]) at the Lake Clifton–Eastern High School in Baltimore City.

Frances Harrington, M.Ed., Ph.D.–Teacher of multicategorial special education at the Shawtown Primary School, Lillington, North Carolina. She has had extensive teaching experiences on the college level and has been active in local and national organizations that serve the disabled. She has added to the body of research through several publications, curriculum development, program evaluation and participating in and conducting local and national conferences and workshops.

Loretta MacKenney, M.Ed.,–Adjunct Professor of Special Education at Coppin State College where she instructs undergraduate students. She has taught students with disabilities in grades K–3 in Baltimore County public schools for several years.

Lois Nixon, M.Ed., Ph.D.–Professor of Special Education at Coppin State College where she is also Coordinator of the undergraduate program. She is responsible for the development and evolution of the program and has had extensive experiences working with disabled individuals. Dr. Nixon has contributed to professional literature in special education through publication and curriculum development.

Thaddaus Phillips, M.Ed., Ph.D.–Assistant Professor in the Department of Special Education at Coppin State College. In addition to his teaching responsibilities, his research interests lay in learning disabilities in urban schools, and assessments for inclusion and technology. He has published several articles associated with disabled and minority individuals.

Richard Rembold, Ed.D.–Currently serves as an Assistant Vice President for Academic Affairs at Coppin State College. His past experiences with disabled individuals include teaching in Baltimore City Public Schools and other local colleges and was Coordinator of Alcoholism Services at Sinai Hospital. He is active in community and professional organizations and has made significant contributions to the field of special education through publications.

Lavania Lee Rice-Fitzpatrick, M.Ed.–Assistant Professor and Coordinator for two grant programs at Coppin State College. These grant programs focus on training teachers to effectively work with programs for disabled individuals. She has worked with the developmentally disabled population for over twenty-five years while providing direct hands-on classroom instruction. She has held the position of Chief of Training for the Developmental Disabilities Administration of the Maryland State Department of Health and Mental Hygiene.

PREFACE

This social skills curriculum has been developed as a guide to assist instructing disabled individuals in determining what behaviors are acceptable and what behaviors are not acceptable in our society. It is also designed to assist individuals working in community agencies with responsibilities for working with disabled individuals. Parents and other family members will find the strategies useful for follow-up activities from the school.

Socialization skills which are assessed as necessary for disabled individuals to function successfully in society are highlighted. Social skills outlined in the text stress strategies needed to: (1) show respect for the rights of privacy of others; (2) learn how to handle anger; (3) learn how to act in public places; (4) demonstrate ability to show good sportsmanship; (5) take responsibility for one's actions; (6) encourage self-control; (7) present alternatives to using profanity; (8) learn how and when to apologize; (9) present alternatives to telling lies; (10) deal with individuals who hit or threaten others.

This book is written with this point of view in mind. It presumes that a basic understanding of instructional methods and procedures have been attained. It does not address all of the dimensions of a functional curriculum, neither does it overview all of the possible instructional activities to employ in teaching social skills to disabled individuals. Rather, the book simply provides a framework for innovative educators to extrapolate additional methods and procedures for teaching appropriate social and interpersonal skills to disabled individuals.

Much of the materials contained in this book are a direct result of inservice presentations, consultancies with public schools and empirical research projects dealing with improving social skills of disabled individuals. Additional research studies are included for the reader's assessment and review.

George R. Taylor

ACKNOWLEDGMENTS

Methods and procedures outlined in this social skills curriculum have been developed over a period of years. It was developed to address the critical issue of providing early social skills training to disabled individuals. It was the view of the authors that a functional systematic approach to teaching social skills was needed in order to equip disabled individuals to function successfully in society.

It would have been impossible to complete such an awesome task without the assistance of others. A deep sense of gratitude is extended to the Baltimore City Public Schools and the graduate students at Coppin State College. The authors are appreciative to **Dr. Bernadette Francisco** for her commitment and efforts in proofing and typing the manuscript.

CONTENTS

	Page
Preface	*ix*

Chapter

1. The Disabled, Classified and Defined   3
  Introduction   3
  Mildly to Moderately Disabled   4
  Severely to Profoundly Disabled   4
  Impact of Federal Legislation and Definitions
    and Classificationof Disabled Individuals   5
  Overview of Social Skills Development for the Disabled   8
  Causes of Social Deficits   10
  Social Competency   11
  Summary   13

2. Social Learning Theories: An Overview   16
  Theoretical Framework   16
  Social Cognitive Theory   17
  Same Behavior   19
  Matched-Dependent Behavior   19
  Copying Behavior   19
  Modeling and Imitation   23
  Self-Efficacy   25
  Summary   27

**3. Behavioral, Social and Academic
Characteristics of Disabled Individuals**   30
  Introduction   30
  Behavior Disorders   33
  Deaf and Hard-of-Hearing   35

Mental Retardation   37
Orthopedic and Health Impairments   39
Learning Disabilities   41
Visually Impaired   44
The Speech and Language Impaired   47

4. Behavioral Styles of Disabled Individuals   53
Introduction   53
The Effects of Behavioral Styles   54
Correlating School Activities   55
Learning Styles   56
Cognitive Dimension   56
Affective Dimension   56
Physiological Dimension   56
Phychological Dimension   57
Evaluating Learning Styles   57
Assessment Techniques   59
The Learning Channel Preference Checklist   59
  Auditory Learning Style   59
  Visual Learning Style   59
  Haptic Learning Style   60
The Relationship of Culture to Learning Styles   61
The Relationship Between Learning and Instructional Styles   62
Implications for Education   62
Summary   63

**5. Application of Social Learning Theories
   to Social Situations**   66
Vzygotsky's Theory   67
Commonality Among Theories   76
Implications for the Disabled   68
Application of Modeling Techniques   68
Aggression   69
Anger and Hostility   70
Social Skills Teaching Strategies   71
  Teaching Apology Strategies   71

Teaching Self-Regulation Skills 72
Be Aware of One's Thinking Patterns 72
Making a Plan 72
Develop and Evaluate Long-Term Goals 72
Integrative Aspects of Social Skills Development 74
Social Skills Models of Disabled Individuals 76
Summary 77

6. Practical Application of Social Learning Theories
to Educating Disabled Individuals 80
Introduction 80
Types of Social Skills Deficits 81
Effects of Social Skills Deficits 81
Assessing Social Skills Deficits 84
Self-Evaluations 84
Portfolio Assessment 85
The Pediatric Evaluation of Disabilities Inventory 85
The Preschool Checklist 86
Application of Behavioral Intervention Strategies 87
Summary 89

7. Direct Intervention Techniques for Teaching
Social Skills to Disabled Individuals 91
Introduction 91
Direct Instruction 91
Skillstreaming 92
Cognitive Behavior Modification 92
Proximity Control 95
Coaching 95
Cuing 95
Modeling 96
Role Playing 97
Videotape Modeling 98
Cooperative Learning 99
Cooperative Learning vs. Peer Tutoring 101
Special Group Activities 100

Group Play Activities   102
Social-Cognitive Approaches   102
Making Better Choices   102
Role Of The School In A Behavior Setting   103
Summary   104

8. Parental Roles in Social Skills Development   109
Introduction   109
Parental Guidelines for Promoting Social Growth   111
Summary   115

9. Social/Interpersonal Skills Curriculum
For Disabled Individuals   117
Curriculum Development –An Overview   117
A Proactive Approach   120
A Functional Approach   121
Curriculum Development   121
Assessment of Social Skills   122
Social Skills Unit.   123
General Objective 1   123
Specific Objectives   123
Recommended Activities   123
General Objective 2   128
Specific Objectives   128
Recommended Activities   129
General Objective 3   135
Specific Objectives   135
Recommended Activities   136
General Objective 4   141
Specific Objectives   141
Recommended Activities   141
General Objective 5   146
Specific Objectives   146
Recommended Activities   146
General Objective 6   149

Specific Objectives 149

Recommended Activities 150

General Objective 7 152

Specific Objectives 152

Recommended Activities 152

Evaluation of Social Skills 156

Specific Evaluation Techniques 156

Sample Evaluation Checklist for Evaluating Social Skills 158

Summary 159

10. **Summary** 160

Early Environmental Experiences 162

Home Environment 163

Transforming the Environment 165

Enhancing Self-Esteem of Disabled Individuals 167

Personality Development 168

Parental Involvement 168

A Holistic Approach 170

Transforming the School Environment 171

Appendices 177

Glossary 201

Author Index 203

Subject Index 209

CURRICULUM STRATEGIES
FOR
TEACHING SOCIAL SKILLS
TO THE DISABLED

Chapter 1

THE DISABLED CLASSIFIED AND DEFINED

GEORGE R. TAYLOR & J. RICHARD REMBOLD

INTRODUCTION

An analysis of definitions, criteria and diagnostic procedures in the classification of disabled individuals must be predicated upon an understanding of the interrelationships among the various disabling conditions. Others avoid categorical definitions describing disabled individuals. The classification system used by the various states are designed to facilitate identification, evaluation, placement and programming for disabled individuals.

Most states provide a written description of characteristics for each categorical type for whom they provide an education. These descriptions usually follow the P.L. 94-142 categories which include deaf, hearing impaired, mentally retarded, orthopedically impaired, other health impaired, seriously emotionally disturbed, severely learning disabled, speech and visually impaired. Most states have added two additional categories not found in P.L. 94-142 and they are: (1) multiple disabled and (2) homebound and hospitalized.

A few states use generic classifications. The State of Maryland is one state employing this classification system. The State frequently categorizes disabled individuals as mildly to moderately or severely to profoundly and by age levels, regardless of their disabling conditions. Regardless of their classification system in use, all disabled individuals can profit from social skill training and intervention.

MILDLY TO MODERATELY DISABLED

This group of disabled individuals consist of the largest group of disabled individuals. They make up approximately 90 percent of all students with disabilities based on the federal categories. This large group includes students who have disabilities in the following areas: (1) speech and language, (2) learning disabilities, (3) emotionally disturbed, (4) mental retardation, (5) hearing impairments, (6) orthopedic impairments, (7) other health impairments, (8) visual impairments, and (9) deaf-blindness.

These children are very similar to their normal peers, displaying a variety of behaviors, social, physical, motor and academic and learning problems. A highly structured and functional program is needed in order to reduce and minimize their disabling conditions. Many of their educational needs can be met in the regular classroom, providing adaptations and modifications are made in their school program. Early identification and assessment and curriculum adaptations for mildly to moderately disabled children appear to be the key elements in successful school experiences. If properly instructed, many mildly to moderately disabled individuals can become independent and productive adults in our society. Detailed classification and characteristics of mildly to moderately disabled children are beyond the scope of this text. The reader is referred to any basic textbook in exceptionality.

SEVERELY TO PROFOUNDLY DISABLED

Students who are classified as severe to profound make up approximately 10 percent of all students with disabilities. Collectively, these students have wide and diverse abilities. Most of them can profit best from highly structured and individualized programs. Many skilled professionals are required to attend to the many disabling conditions in the cognitive, physical, mental and social areas. Frequently, related services are needed to provide the most basic services.

Children classified as mildly to moderately disabled, if conditions are severe enough, may be classified as severe to profound. Appropriate assessment will determine the classification. In addition,

P.L. 101-476 lists autism and traumatic brain injury under the severely to profoundly disabled.

These children are markedly different from their normal peers, displaying noticeable differences in mental, physical, and social characteristics. Many of their needs cannot be successfully met in the regular classroom. Special placements and treatment and interventions are essential for these children. Many of them will need adult supervision for all of their lives, they seldom will be independent adults. Detail classification and characteristics of severely to profoundly disabled children are beyond the scope of this text. The reader is referred to any basic book in exceptionality.

Impact of Federal Legislation and Definitions and Classification on Disabled Individuals

Public Law 94-142

The systematic identification of disabled individuals is required of states receiving federal aid under Public Law 94-142. States are mandated to develop procedures resulting in the identification of all children who may be disabled, regardless of type or severity of disabling conditions, as well as making a determination of special education needs in terms of children currently being served or children not currently being served.

The law made available a free and appropriate public education to all school-aged students with disabilities. It directed that students with disabilities must be educated in the least restrictive environment, and mandated that an individualized education program (IEP) be developed for all disabled students using nondiscriminatory evaluation techniques. Additionally, a due process provision was outlined which was designed to protect the rights of the family and the child. Finally, the law stated that no student may be excluded from public education because of a disability, and that each state must take action to locate children who may be entitled to special education services.

Public Law 94-142

The emphasis on P.L. 94-142 and subsequent revisions are the requirements that parental consent be obtained for any decision made in the IEP process. Also that parents always be informed of any steps in the IEP process, whether they concern pre-referral, referral, evaluation, service, treatment, progress, annual review, and modifications of the IEP. Parental consent is the voluntary agreement of the parent or guardian after being apprised of all information in a comprehensible form. Parent awareness and approval is essential.

Public Law 99-457

Public Law 94-142 was amended in 1986 and became the Education of the Handicapped Act, P.L. 99-457. This act extended the authority of P.L. 94-142 in the following ways:

1. Provided a free and appropriate education to preschool children.

2. Disability categories were not required to be reported by the states.

3. The law provided for the development of cost-effective method of service delivery in early childhood.

4. A grant program was developed to provide financial incentives for states to establish programs for infants and toddlers who were developmentally delayed.

Public Law 99-457 (Part H Infants and Toddlers Program) is designed, in part, to assist states in setting up early intervention programs for children from birth through age two who need special services. Early intervention services include the following: physical, mental, social and emotional, language and speech, and self-help skills. The total family is involved, the focus for service is on the total family (Baily, Buysse, Edmondson & Smith, 1992). Special education services may be provided to children from birth through age two who have special needs, such as a physical disability, partial or total loss of sight, severe emotional problems, hearing or speech impairment, mental handicap, or learning disabilities. The key is early intervention, which should be designed to treat, prevent and reduce environmental factors associated with disabling conditions and the impediment of social growth and development.

The P.L. 99-457 piece of legislation was greatly needed due to the public dissatisfaction with earlier legislation created for the disabled. There was also a need for early care and education for not just the disabled child, but also for the normal child. Two factors also contributed to educators searching for early child care services: (1) the increase in the number of mothers who were working outside the home and, (2) the realization that many of these children were disadvantaged. Many disabled individuals are not developmentally ready for school. Early intervention can reduce or eliminate many of the conditions attributed to development delays. Public Law 99-457 places the family in the center of the early intervention process. The major thrust of the law is to develop meaningful parent-professional partnerships to support the development of infants and toddlers (Summers, 1990). Hanson (1992) wrote that the issues of which families and professionals focus in providing services for infants and toddlers are closely related to the families' beliefs, values and childrearing practices. Consequently, when working with families from diverse backgrounds, professionals should be culturally sensitive. This is particularly true when developing the IEP. Family preferences should be respected and included when legally possible. Objectives and outcomes should be written in terms familiar to the family.

Public Law 101-476

In 1990, the Congress of the United States amended the Education of the Handicapped Act (P.L. 99-457) and renamed it the Individuals with Disabilities Act (IDEA), P.L. 101-476. Specific changes in the act included:

1. The term "handicapped" was removed and the term "disabled" was substituted.

2. Autism and traumatic brain injury were added to the list of disabling conditions.

3. The definition of special education was broadened to include instruction in all settings where disabled individuals are educated including work places and training centers.

4. Related services were expanded to include rehabilitation counseling and social work services.

5. The IEP was modified to include a transition planning statement for students by age 16 or younger.

6. Assessing, identifying, and placing disabled individuals require the use of nondiscriminatory and multidisciplinary assessment in constructing the IEP.

7. Parental involvement in the total process was mandated. Procedure safeguards (due process) were reinforced to protect the

child and family.

8. The rights of all children to learn in the least restrictive environment with nondisabled peers was affirmed.

These federal laws have had widespread implications for educating disabled individuals in this country. These laws have revolutionized education for disabled individuals. The acts have made it possible for millions of disabled individuals to receive a free and appropriate education in the public schools. The recent impact of federal legislation has extended special education to include all instruction in all settings, including the workplace, rehabilitation centers and shelter workshops. See Appendix G for additional information on federal laws.

These laws were specific in many areas. One of the areas indicated was that disabled individuals must be educated in the least restrictive environment. For many disabled individuals, this meant that many of them would be educated with their normal peers. Research findings have shown that many disabled individuals do not display appropriate social skills (Gresham, 1993; Hanson, 1990; Odom, 1988; Peck, 1983; Sasso, 1990). With this mandate, disabled individuals must be instructed in several areas of social development. Many social experiences may be integrated into the regular curriculum. Early intervention is necessary in order to reduce the amount of isolation and rejection experienced by many disabled individuals in regular classes.

OVERVIEW OF SOCIAL SKILLS DEVELOPMENT
FOR THE DISABLED

An individual's personality is organized around various aspects of self-awareness and self-concept. What a person believes about himself/herself affects what he/she does, what he/she sees and hears, and his/her ability to cope in the environment. It may be concluded that self-concept is significantly influenced by life experiences (Taylor, 1992). Many of the life experiences of disabled individuals are negative and do not provide opportunity for the self to emerge successfully, consequently many disabled individuals' self-concepts are lower than their normal peers.

Social skills should be taught to disabled individuals who need them, and in some instances, should supercede academic skills.

Appropriate social skills must be taught and modeled for many of these individuals before a meaningful academic program can be pursued.

The first and foremost instruction in the mastery of social situations involve the interactions of parents with their disabled children. The notion of modeling and imitative learning should be provided. This approach is consistent with Bandura's Social Learning Theory (1977). Unconsciously disabled individuals model social skills demonstrated by their parents and family members. They also instruct their children on appropriate responses, such as saying "please" and "thank you." If the parents are poor role models, their children will imitate and model what they see and observe in social situations.

Not only are social skills important in academic areas, but they are also related to socialization. Several behaviors are necessary in the socialization process, including the emergence of self-identity and self-concept. Social skills are developed through the interactions with family, school, and the community. Disabled individuals' social skills are shaped by the reinforcement received as a result of the individuals reacting with their environments. Disabled individuals should have as much social contact with their normal peers as necessary. This type of involvement appears to facilitate social skill development (Odom & McEvoy, 1988; Peck & Cooke, 1983; Fox, 1989).

Disabled individuals not exposed to the aforementioned strategy will often have difficulties with social behavior throughout the developmental, childhood, adolescent and adulthood years.

Disabled individuals are frequently rejected by their peers because of inappropriate behaviors. Rejection may lead disabled individuals to display aggressive behaviors when responding to certain social acts. The schools have not developed effective programs directed toward developing social skills of disabled individuals. Traditionally, social skills training has been directed toward those disabled individuals who respond aggressively to conflict situations or toward those who are isolated and withdrawn. There is an urgent need to expand social skills training to disabled individuals regardless of personality traits and characteristics. Due to the lack of social skills training, many disabled individuals' behaviors may be inappropriate. This may be attributed to them not being able to predict a social situation in advance because they have not been provided with appropriate social role models. Not understanding the dynamics of social encounters, disabled individuals cannot organize their behavior effectively. Frequently, they may take an excessive amount of time to process the interaction and lose the essence of the ongoing social activity. Thus, their reaction to the social activity may be assessed as awkward, clumsy or impulsive. Total integration of social skills training throughout the curriculum will minimize inappropriate responses of disabled individuals to social behaviors.

Causes of Social Deficits

Impoverishment of a child's early environmental experiences, including any major restrictions on play activities or lack of feedback from older individuals is suspected of retarding his/her social development and learning. Lack of adequate adult stimulation in the early years can lead to the disabled individual's developing negative social behavior which may be irreversible.

An increasing number of disabled individuals are failing to succeed in school because of their inadequate social skills (Gresham, 1989). It has been suggested that social skill deficits interfere with success to the peer group and educational behavior patterns. Social skill deficits place students at risk for failure in the educational and cultural mainstreams. The acquisition of social communication skills is extremely important for these individuals, primarily because social communication skills are at the foundation of interpersonal competence. The inclusion of social skills training in curriculum and specific lesson plan design, provides the classroom teacher with the opportunity to effectively address social skill deficits.

Gresham (1993) concluded that social skills deficits do not necessarily constitute a specific learning disability. The same analogy may be applied to other types of disabilities. Normal children may also exhibit social skill deficits. Regardless of the type of classification or disabling conditions, all children with identified social skill deficits, regardless of eligibility criteria, should receive remediation.

Social skill techniques and interventions designed to correct or reduce social deficits among disabled individuals have proven to be effective in structured and well-controlled environments, such as schools, workshops, vocational centers and other agencies serving the disabled. However, recent findings have shown that the transfer of these social skills over time to the home, neighborhood, and employment settings is difficult to achieve (Sasso, Melloy & Kavale, 1990; Schloss, Schloss, Wood & Kiehl, 1986; Simpson, 1987).

In order to improve transferring social skills outside of well-controlled environments, a total integrated approach is recommended. This approach should involve, including the disabled child's total ecological environment, his family, and community. Experiences offered in the school should include participation by families and communities.

Generally, disabled individuals have some or all of the following characteristics which may produce interpersonal difficulties: (a) poor self-esteem, (b) oppositional behavior, (c) isolation, (d) poor peer interaction, and (e) learning difficulties. An intervention program stressing pro-social skill development is needed (Greene, 1987; Hallowell, 1994; Levine, 1993; Silver, 1992; Smith, 1988).

Social Competency

Social competency is an important aspect of interrelationships. The experience of interacting with others is necessary for existence. Disabled individuals need to be acknowledged, noticed, valued, respected and appreciated by others and to be aware that others want these things from them. Social competency is the sum total of one's ability to interact with other people, to take appropriate social initiatives, to understand people's reactions to them and to respond accordingly. This process of learning and practicing social skills lasts a lifetime. Social skill strategies include employing eye contact, using facial expressions, gestures and tone of voice, saying the right thing, using humor, exhibiting appropriate body language, and respecting boundaries, to name a few. Successful interaction is automatic once it is learned. Opportunities should be provided whereby inappropriate social behaviors of disabled individuals can be remediated.

Many of the behaviors of disabled individuals contribute directly to social failure. Disabled individuals with social skill deficits lack an awareness of other viewpoints and may attempt to impose their inappropriate view because they have no appropriate model to use. These types of behaviors frequently lead to rejection and social isolation.

Individuals with disabilities grow up to become adults with disabilities. By adulthood, many of the psychosocial aspects of this disability are manifested in dysfunctional behaviors such as social isolation and/or poor judgment in selecting friends–a carryover from previous difficulties in sustaining interpersonal relationships. Low self-esteem is another characteristic of the disabled individual who failed to achieve success in school or with friends. Many disabled individuals become increasingly isolated and are often the objects of ridicule and humiliation (Smith, 1988). Appropriate social skills and verbal and nonverbal responses are frequently absented. A certain degree of verbal and nonverbal responses are necessary for effective communication and interpersonal development. Many disabled individuals do not develop these skills appropriately for their ages (Olivia & LaGreca, 1987). Woeppel (1990) supported the notion that disabled children should have as part of their curriculum social skills instruction designed for specific ages and grade levels. He further related that the teaching of social skills and problem-solving has increased in our nation's schools, it has not been institutionalized. According to Woeppel (1990) social skills instruction should be part of a total integrated curriculum, including strategy. Disabled individuals may have great difficulty improving skill deficits (Olivia & LaGreca, 1987).

Social conditions involving conflict posed the greatest challenge to disabled children's appropriate use of social skills. They tend to be either aggressive or passive rather than negotiable (Woeppel, 1990). In a comparison of disabled individuals' and nondisabled individuals' social behaviors in two school districts, the disabled individuals rated themselves higher than their peers on social-desirability behaviors. The findings were interpreted as an indication that disabled children want to be like other children despite their actual performance. Self-esteem and self-perception play a significant role in the mastery of social skills as well as the expectations and/or negative perceptions of others (Woeppel, 1990).

In a study conducted by Olivia & LaGreca (1987), disabled boys and nondisabled boys were asked to formulate goals and strategies in problem-solving social situations, the disabled boys generated significantly less sophisticated goals than the nondisabled boys. In addition, the younger boys, as a group, generated less friendly strategies than the older boys. Their goals were strongly correlated with their social skillfulness. These results imply that disabled children may be deficient in cognitive skills necessary to formulate general social rules.

Olivia & LaGreca (1987) postulated that, when performing academic activities, disabled children encounter problems with developing appropriate goals and strategies. Consequently, the same conclusion may be drawn when disabled individuals develop goals and strategies for peer interactions. Research findings by Bryan (1991) suggested that disabled individuals are at risk for experiencing problems in the social domain. Her findings were based upon reviewing 30 studies, 24 of those studies indicated disabled children to be at greater risk than nondisabled children with regard to social rejection. Additionally, Bryan (1991) indicated that disabled children have difficulty gaining social acceptance across a wide age range. They also have problems relating to rejection by peers and others.

Bryan (1991) found learning disabled individuals to be less tactful than nondisabled individuals. This study focused on using language as a social tool. Learning disabled individuals were required to (a) take into account the characteristics of the audience, (b) understand what is already known and what information is new to the listener, and (c) understand and adhere to the rules that govern conversation. Learning disabled boys were more polite to their peers than they were to adults. They did not simplify things for younger children. On the other hand, learning disabled girls were overly differential to everyone. It was found that learning disabled children were less persuasive, agreed more, disagreed less, asked fewer questions, were less likely to argue their positions, and were less likely to ask open-ended questions.

Children with learning disabilities do not differ on fundamental skills but the subtle differences include persuasiveness, tact, and the ability to sustain a conversation, to make a good impression, to disagree and argue a contrary position, and to give positive and negative feedback. As Bryan (1991) stated, "It is our responsibility as learning disability specialists to take their social problems seriously and to treat them as we would academic difficulties with the best technology we have."

SUMMARY

We have not done a satisfactory job in providing quality education for disabled individuals. The schools have failed in educating the "whole child." According to a recent report by the National Association of State Boards of Education (1992), it was voiced that a holistic view that is attuned to the student's nonacademic needs must be included as part of his/her instructional program, which includes social, emotional, personal and citizenship training. A holistic integrated approach is needed in educating disabled individuals.

To avoid fragmenting school experiences, disabled individuals' social and emotional well-being must be integrated and infused into a total program emphasizing social and interpersonal needs, communication needs, and academic needs (Bauer & Sapona, 1991). The schools must begin to use the vast amount of research present to experiment with various ways of including social skill development into the curriculum if disabled individuals are to achieve up to their maximum potentials. Radical intervention models are needed stressing social skills and interpersonal skill development. This text is designed to accomplish such a purpose.

REFERENCES

Baily, D.B., Buysse, V., Edmondson, R., & Smithe, T.M. (1992). Creating family center services in early intervention: perception of professionals in four states. *Exceptional Children, 58*, 298-309.

Bandura, A. (1977). Self-efficacy toward a unifying theory of behavior change. *Psychological Review, 84*, 191-215.

Bauer, A.M., & Sapana, R.H. (1991). *Managing Classrooms to Facilitate Learning.* Englewood Cliffs, N.J.: Prentice Hall.

Bryan, R. (1991). *Assessment Of Children With Learning Disabilities Who Appear To Be Socially Incompetent.* Paper presented at the annual conference of the council for exceptional children. Atlanta, GA.

Fox, L.C. (1989). Peer acceptance of learning disabled children in the regular classroom. *Exceptional Children, 56*, 50-59.

Greene, L.J. (1987). *Learning Disabilities and Your Child.* New York: Ballantine.

Gresham, F.M., & Elliott, S.N. (1989). Social skills assessment technology for LD students. *Learning Disability Quarterly, 12*, 141-152.

Gresham, F.M., & Elliott, S.N. (1989). Social skills deficits as a primary learning disability. *Journal of Learning Disabilities. 22*, 120-124.

Gresham, F.M. (1993). Social skills and learning disabilities as a Type III error: Rejoinder to Conte and Andrews. *Journal of Learning Disabilities, 26*, 154-158.

Hallowell, E.M., & Ratey, J.J. (1994). *Driven to Distraction.* New York: Random House.

Hanson, M.J. (1990). Ethnic, cultural, and language diversity in intervention settings. In E.W. Lynch, & M.J. Hanson (Eds.). *Developing Cross-Cultural Competence: A Guide For Working With Young Children and Their Families.* Baltimore: Paul H. Brookes.

Levine, M.D. (1993). *Developmental Variation and Learning Disorders.* Cambridge, MA: Educators Publishing Service.

Odom, S. & McEvoy, M. (1988). Integration of young children with handicapped and non-handicapped children: Mainstreamed versus integrated special education. In S. Odom & M. Karnes (Eds.). *Early Intervention for Infants and Children with Handicaps:* An Empirical Base (pp. 241-267). Baltimore: Paul H. Brookes.

Olivia, A.H., & LaGreca, A.M. (April, 1987). *The Strategies and Goals of Learning Disabled Children in Social Situations.* Paper presented at the biennial meeting of the society for research in child development. Baltimore, MD.

Peck, C.A. & Cooke, T.P. (1983). Benefits of mainstreaming at the early childhood: level: How much can we expect? *Analysis and Intervention in Developmental Disabilities, 3*, 1-22.

Sasso, G.M., Melloy, K.J., & Kavale, K.A. (1990). Generalization, maintenance, and behavioral in variation associated with social skills training through structured learning. *Behavioral Disorders, 16*, 9-22.

Schloss, P.J., Schloss, C.N., Wood, C.E., & Kiehl, W.S. (1986). A critical review of social skills with behaviorally disordered students. *Behavioral Disorders, 12*, 1-14.

Silver, L.B. (1992). T*he Misunderstood Child: A Guide for Parents of Learning Disabled Children.* New York: McGraw-Hill Book Co.

Simpson, R.L. (1987). Social interaction of behaviorally disordered children and youth: Where are we and where do we need to go? *Behavioral Disorders, 12*, 45-53.

Smith, S. (1988). Preparing the learning disabled adolescent for adulthood. *Children Today, 2*, 409.

Summers, J.A., Dell, O.C., Turnbull, A.P., Benson, H.A., Santelli, E., Campbell, M., & Siegel-Clausey, E. (1990). Examining the individualized family service plan process: What are family and practitioner preferences? *Topics in Early Childhood Special Education, 10*, 78-99.

Taylor, G. (1992). Impact of social learning theory on education deprived/minority children. *Clearinghouse for Teacher Education.* ERIC 349260.

The National Association of State Boards of Education (1992). Alexandria, VA: p.13.

Woeppel, P. (1990). *Facilitating Social Skills Development In Learning Disabled and/or Attention Deficit Disordered Second to Fifth Grade Children and Parents.* Ed.D. Practicum: Nova University.

Chapter 2

SOCIAL LEARNING THEORIES: AN OVERVIEW

GEORGE TAYLOR & FRANCIS HARRINGTON

D uring the last two decades we have witnessed the rediscovery, creation, or the validation of a great diversity of social learning theories. These theories have provided us with a common language learning theories on academic performance of disabled and other individuals.

The study of social learning theories enables the school to better understand both how disabled and other individuals think about school-related processes and how the children are likely to be feeling about themselves in relation to the process. The school's understanding of both the cognitive and the affective characteristics of disabled individuals may be termed as "empathic." One way of showing empathy to children is through designing effective classroom environments that considers the cognitive and affect levels of the children (Butler, 1988; Hilliard, 1989).

THEORETICAL FRAMEWORK

Throughout the latter half of this century, during the years following World War II, social learning theory emerged as an integral part of behaviorism. As researchers defined learning paradigms, while the opponents of classical and operant conditioning offered a lawful relationship of behavior and the environment, social learning theory postulated that an individual could acquire responses by observing and subsequently imitating the behavior of others in the environment (Rotter, 1966; Bandura, 1963; Coleman, 1986).

Social learning theory is defined as a psychological theory that emphasizes the learning of socially expected, appropriate and desirable behavior (Kahn & Cangemi, 1979; Rotter, 1966). Social learning theorists view behavior as an interaction between an individual and the environment. From its inception, social learning theory was an attempt to integrate the stimulus-response and the cognitive theories. Advocates of this school of thought felt that theorists must include both behavioral and internal constructs in any theory of human behavior and learning (Rotter, 1966; Bandura, 1963).

Social Cognitive Theory

By 1986, Bandura, defined his position by using new terminology. Social learning theory was replaced by the term social cognitive theory (Bandura, 1989; Ronestock, 1988; Corcoran, 1991).

Social cognitive theory is an attempt to explain human behavior from a natural science perspective by integrating what is known about the effects of the environment and what is known about the role of cognition. It suggests that people are not merely products of their environment nor are they driven to behave as they do by internal forces. Social cognitive theory presents a cognitive interactional model of human functioning that describes behavior results from reciprocal influences among the environment, social, physical, personal, thoughts, feelings, perceptions and the individual's behavior itself (Kauffman, 1993). In summation, social cognitive theory reconceptualizes that thought and other personal factors, behavior, and the environment all operate as interacting determinants. Because of the reciprocal causation, therapeutic efforts can be directed at all three determinants. Psychosocial functioning is improved by altering faulty thought patterns, by increasing behavioral competencies and skills in dealing with situational demands and by altering adverse social conditions (Bandura, 1986). Bandura uses the term triadic reciprocality to describe the social cognitive model. Because we have systems with which to code, retain, and process information, several human attributes are incorporated into social cognitive theory.

Social learning theory is concerned with acquisition of new behaviors that occur as unlearned or previously learned responses that are modified or combined into more complete behaviors. This process, according to social learning theory, is speeded up by direct reinforcement or expected reinforcement through imitation (Miller & Dollard, 1941).

Miller & Dollard

N.E. Miller & E. Dollard (1941) were influenced by the earlier work of Hull. Theories developed by Miller & Dollard investigated the circumstances under which a response and a cue stimulus become connected. Accordingly, both a cue and a response must be present in order for social learning to exist. Four factors of psychological principles are outlined by Miller & Dollard: drive, cue, response and reward.

DRIVE: Drive is defined as the first factor in learning that impels action or response. It is the motivating factor which allows the individual to view a situation and react toward stimulus. Individuals have primary or innate drives and secondary or acquired drives. The behavior that the drive leads to will be learned if results in a reduction of drive (Miller & Dollard, 1941). Reinforcement always results from reduction of drive (Kahn & Cangemi, 1979).

CUES: Cues determine when the individual will respond where and which response he or she will make. In social learning, the individual waits for cues from society and then responds to those cues. Society can control the individual by sending out various cues and rewarding the response, either positively or negatively. The presence or absence of cues, number of cues, and/or types of cues can determine the resulting amount and type of learning that occurs.

RESPONSE: The response is the most integral part of assessing whether or not the individual has learned, and to what degree learning exists. It is the result of the individual's reaction elicited by cues.

REWARD: Reward determines if the response will be repeated. If a response is not rewarded, the tendency to repeat that response is weakened. Similarly, responses that are rewarded are likely to be repeated. Moreover, a connection can be made between the stimulus and the reward, thereby strengthening the response. Rewards may be positive or negative and can themselves become a motivating factor or drive.

Miller & Dollard (1941) outline the following phrases to describe imitation.

Same Behavior

Same behavior is created by two people who perform the same act in response to independent stimulation by the same cue. Each has learned independently to make the response. The behavior may be learned with or without independent aides.

Matched-Dependent Behavior

Matched-dependent behavior primarily consists of leadership by which followers are not presently aware of the consequences of their action, but rely totally on the leadership of others, and follow without question. The individual is controlled by the cues which the leader exhibits and the response from the individual becomes a predictable source for the leader to maintain. Most crowd behavior is demonstrated in this matched-dependent mode. No immediate reward criteria need be present at this time. The actions of the individual can become motivating within themselves. The participation and interaction the individual is allowed to take part in becomes the rewarding factor.

Copying Behavoir

Copying behavior is demonstrated when an individual duplicates his or her attitudes and responses so that it matches that which has been deemed socially acceptable by the peer group of the individual. The individual is rewarded for modeling after a select group of peers and the acceptance of their norms. Miller and Dollard (1941) have suggested that the child's tendency to copy is an acquired secondary drive that can account for the psychoanalytic concept of identification.

Julian B. Rotter

Julian B. Rotter (1954, 1966, 1990) combined a social learning framework and behavioral approaches with applications for clinical, personality, and social psychology. While Rotter was inspired through his work with his former teacher Kurt Lewin, he rejected Lewin's and Hull's position because he felt that they did not conceptualize past experiences. Thus, they did not explain and predict all behavior. According to Rotter (1966),

> Cognitive approaches were of little value in predicting the behavior of rats; and approaches that did not take into account the fact that human beings think, generalize along semantic lines, and are motivated by social goals and reinforced by social reinforcements, were extremely limited in their explanations or predictions.

Rotter turned to the learning theorists, wherein his thinking was strongly influenced by Alfred Adler. Beginning in 1946, immediately following World War II, Rotter culminated work from his masters thesis and his doctoral dissertation and published the work in Social Learning and Clinical Psychology in 1954.

From a construct point of view, Rotter (1966) outlined seven principles of social learning theory as follows:

1. **The unit of investigation for the study of personality is the interaction of the individual and his/her meaningful environment.** This principle describes the social learning position of an interactionist approach.
2. **Personality constructs are not dependent for explanation on constructs in any other field.** Rotter contends with this principle that scientific constructs should be consistent across all fields of science.
3. **Behavior as described by personality constructs takes place in space and time.** According to Rotter, any constructs that describe events themselves are rejected because constructs must describe physical as well as psychological variables.
4. **Not all behavior of an organism may be usefully described with personality constructs.** Behavior that may usefully be described by personality constructs appear in organisms at a particular level or stage of complexity and a

particular level or stage of development. This postulate recognizes that events are amenable to specific terms. Likewise, they are not amenable to others.

5. **Personality has unity**. In this context, Rotter defines unity in terms of relative stability and interdependence. The presence or relative stability does not, however, exclude specificity of response and change.

6. **Behavior as described by personality constructs has a directionality aspect.** Behavior is said to be goal directed. This principle is the motivational focus of social learning theory. Social learning theorists identify specific events that have a known effect either for groups or for individuals as reinforcers. Environmental conditions that determine the direction of behavior also refer to goals or reinforcement. When reference is made to the individual's determining the direction, Rotter calls these needs. Both goals and needs are inferred from referents of the interaction of the person with his/her meaningful environment. Learned behavior is goal oriented and new goals derive their importance for the individual from their associations with earlier goals.

7. **The occurrence of a behavior of a person is determined not only by the nature or importance of goals and reinforcements but also by the person's anticipation or expectancy that these goals will occur**. This principle is an attempt to determine how an individual in a given situation behaves in terms of potential reinforcers.

Rotter's expectancy-reinforcement theory stresses that the major basic modes of behavior are learned in social situations and are intricately fused with needs required for their satisfaction (Kahn & Cangemi, 1979).

Internal versus external, i.e., control of reinforcement often referred to as locus of control, is firmly embedded in Rotter's social learning theory (Rotter, 1954, 1966, 1990; Strickland, 1989). Internal versus external control refers to the degree to which persons expect that a reinforcement or an outcome of their behavior is contingent upon their behavior or personal characteristic versus the degree to which persons expect that the reinforcement or outcome is a function of chance, luck or fate or is under the powerful influence of others.

Basic to Rotter's position is the fact that reinforcement acts to strengthen an expectancy that a particular behavior will be followed by that reinforcement in the future. Once an expectancy for a reinforcement sequence is built, the failure of the reinforcement to occur will reduce or extinguish the expectancy. As an infant grows and has more experiences, he differentiates casual events from the events that are reinforcing. Expectancies also generalize along a gradient from a specific situation to a series of situations that are perceived as related or similar (Rotter, 1966).

Albert Bandura

Albert Bandura is considered the forerunner of social learning theory and is most often associated with empirical research in the area (Bandura, 1965, 1989; Coleman, 1986; Evans, 1989; Tudge & Winterhoff, 1991; Bandura & Walters, 1963; Wiegman, Kuttschreuter, & Baarda, 1992).

Because concerns with subjective measurement created skepticism among scientists regarding social learning theory, Bandura insisted on experimental controls. Thus, he was able to transcend from empirical observations to experimental validity (Rotter, 1966; Bandura & Walters, 1963; Tudge & Winterhoff, 1991). Bandura wanted a broader meaning of behaviorism which would include learning from the behavior of others. He too, was dissatisfied with the stimulus response theories who contended that people acquire competencies and new patterns of behavior through response consequences (Bandura, 1986). He could not imagine how a culture could transmit its' language and mores through tedious trial and error (Evans, 1989).

Bandura's major concern was in the social transmission of behavior. Two prevailing principles support the theory. The first is the element of observational learning and second is the inclusion of a model or an individual who might serve as an example for another (Kahn & Cangemi, 1979; Bandura, 1966). Learning through imitation is called observational learning (Bandura & Walters, 1963). Modeling is a process of teaching through example that produces learning through imitation (Charles, 1985). The basic assumptions underlying Bandura's position is that behavior is learned and organized through central integrative mechanisms prior to motor execution (Bandura, 1971).

Modeling and Imitation

Bandura believed that the basic way that children learn is through imitation of models in their social environment and the primary mechanism driving development is observation (Bandura, 1966). Imitation is to copy, to follow a model or example or to repeat, rehearse, or reproduce (Bandura & Walters, 1963).

Two kinds of processes are identified by which children acquire attitudes, values and patterns of social behavior. Direct imitation is described as explicit directives about what adults, most often parents and teachers, want the child to learn and they attempt to shape the child's behavior through rewards and punishes and/or through direct instruction. Active imitation, through which personality patterns are primarily acquired consists of parental attitudes and behaviors, most of which the parents have not attempted to teach (Bandura, 1967; Kahn & Cangemi, 1979).

Bandura pointed out that human subjects in social settings can acquire new behaviors simply by seeing them presented by a model. He maintains that even if the observer does not make the response himself and even if at the time neither he nor the model is reinforced for the behavior, the observer may learn the response so that he can perform it later. The observer acquires internal representational responses which mediate subsequent behavioral reproduction or performance (Bandura, 1969).

According to Bandura (1966), imitative learning comprises three interrelated subprocesses. The first subprocess is attention. The subject must attend to the model and must discriminate among the distinguishing features of the model's behavior. Variables that are related to the characteristics of what is observed include: novelty, interest, variety, competence of the model, sex and age of the model, and models who are observed to be rewarded for the behaviors they perform. Observer variables include dependency, self-esteem, competence, and observers history of reinforcement for attending.

A second subprocess is retention of the observed behavior. Bandura contends that observational learning can be retained over long periods of time without overt response. Retention depends in part upon sufficient coding or mediating the event and upon covert rehearsals.

A third subprocess is motoric reproduction. The observer may be able to imagine and to code behaviors of which he is motorically incapable. Motor responses are most readily acquired when the observer already possesses the competent skills and needs only to synthesize them into new patterns.

Several constructs have been applied to the modeling process. The first construct, imitation, is the process wherein the person copies exactly what he or she sees the model doing. The model's example is repeated, rehearsed or reproduced. The observer's next step is identification, the process that requires incorporation of personality patterns. The observer has to determine how and/or if the behavior-response pattern embodies his or her personality. In most cases, the observer performs the learned behavior embellished with his/her idiosyncrasies rather than imitating the model's actions precisely (Edwards, 1993). Bandura felt that imitation was too narrow; identification, too diffuse. The third construct is social facilitation. In this process, new competencies are not acquired and inhibitions serve as social guides (Bandura, 1963).

Actual performance depends upon incentive or motivation. The absence of positive incentives or negative sanctions may inhibit the response or the individual may have a reason to make the response. For example, parental prohibitions against foul language in their children and/or the young child that is not given an opportunity to talk, dress, or feed himself, may have acquired the necessary responses through observations, but this child will not deem it necessary to actually perform the response.

Bandura acknowledges the important influences of personal factors, endowed potentialities, acquired competencies and stresses reciprocity between internal mechanism and the social environment (Moore, 1987).

According to Bandura (1977), there are three effects of modeling influences. First, modeling can facilitate the acquisition of new behaviors that did exist in the observers repertoire. Second, previously acquired responses can strengthen or weaken inhibitory/responses in the observer (disinhibitory effect). Finally, observation can serve to elicit a response that has been previously exhibited by the model. This response facilitation effect was demonstrated in studies conducted by Bandura (1965) in which children observed aggressive behaviors by models who were rewarded or punished for their aggressive acts (Bandura, 1977).

Literature is voluminous in support of the use of modeling as an effective teaching strategy (Archenback & Ziggler, 1973; Bandura, Ross & Ross, 1963; Norby & Hall, 1973; Travers, 1972; Kazdin, 1980; Manz & Sims, 1986; Mercer & Algozzine, 1977; Cummings & Rodda, 1989; Kuttschreuter & Baarda, 1991; Tudge & Winterhoff, 1993; Schoss, Sedlak & Filips, 1982; Bandura, 1986, 1989; Edwards, 1993; Bandura, Gusec & Menlow, 1966).

During the 1960s Bandura & Walters (1963) conducted a classic group of experimental studies on imitation. By introducing actions of the model as the independent variable, Bandura was able to observe the effects on the behavior of children who had observed the model. Further, by systematically varying the behavioral characteristics of the models (for example, from nuturant to powerful; to cold to neutral) Bandura was able to assert the kinds of persons who were the most effective models (Damon, 1977). He notes specifically, that other adults, peers and symbolic models are significant in the learning process of children. When exposed to conflicting role standards as represented by adults, peers and other observed models, children will adopt different standards than if adults alone provided the model. Peer modeling, however, is not more effective than child-adult interaction. The attitude of the child toward the model, whether or not the model is rewarded for his/her behavior and the personal characteristics of the model are more important to Bandura (1986, 1989).

Vicarious learning as it relates to television viewing has been investigated extensively (Bandura & Walters, 1963; Bandura, Gusec & Menlow, 1966; Bandura & Ross, 1961, 1963). Bandura's work in the sixties and seventies demonstrated the powerful effects of both live and filmed models on young children's behavior. Viewing of television violence was found to correlate significantly with children's aggressive behavior (Eron, 1987).

Self-Efficacy

Bandura's most recent emphasis has been on individual factors in social-interactive contexts. Introduced in 1977, Bandura continued several decades of research regarding the basic source of motivation (Bandura, 1976, 1977). He outlined a theoretical framework in which the concept of self-efficacy received a central role for analyzing the changes achieved in clinical treatment of fearful and avoidant behavior. Because the results of their research showed good maintenance and transfer, the concept of self-efficacy was expanded by adding a program of self-directed mastery (Carrol, 1993). Bandura argued that if individuals are allowed to succeed on their own, they would not attribute their success to the use of mastery aides or to the therapist. This clinical tool restored an individual's coping capabilities. He felt that the treatments that were most effective were built on an "empowerment model." Continued research suggested to the investigators that they could predict with considerable accuracy the speed of therapeutic change and the degree of generality from the extent to which the individuals perceived efficacy was enhanced. Bandura felt strongly that if you really wanted to help people you must provide them with competencies, build a strong belief and create opportunities for them to develop the competencies (Evans, 1989; Bandura, 1995).

Self-efficacy theory addresses the origins of beliefs of personal efficacy, their structure and function, the processes through which they operate and their diverse effects (Bandura, 1995). Four main sources of self-efficacy are cited (Bandura, 1977). The most effective way of creating a strong sense of self-efficacy is through mastery experiences. As individuals master skills, they tend to raise their expectations about their capabilities. Vicarious experiences provided by social models is the second method of creating efficacy beliefs. Seeing people who are similar succeed raises the observers level of aspiration. Bandura (1977) noted however, that this influence is most effective when the observer perceives himself or herself to be similar to the model. Social persuasion, or verbally encouraging persons that they have what it takes to succeed is regarded by Bandura as a weaker influence. Finally, emotional arousal is the source which serves as an indicator to an individual that he or she is not coping well with a situation, the self-regulating capacity.

As Bandura (1977) examined psychological principles as a means of creating and strengthening expectations of personal efficacy, he made a distinction between efficacy expectations and response outcome expectancies. An outcome expectancy is defined as the individuals estimate that a given behavior will lead to specific outcomes. An efficacy expectation is the conviction that one can successfully execute the behavior that is necessary to produce the outcomes.

Perceived self-efficacy is referred as an individual's act of raising or lowering their self-efficacy beliefs. A major goal of self-efficacy research is an investigation of the conditions under which self-efficacy beliefs alter the resulting changes (Gorrell, 1990). The effects of self-efficacy in regulating human functioning are evident in human cognitive motivational effective and selectional processes (Bandura, 1989; 1995). There are three levels of self-efficacy theory that are applied to cognition of interest to educators. The first application is concerned with how children perceived self-efficacy affects their rate of learning. This level of self-efficacy concerns the students' belief in their capacities to master academic affairs. In 1991, Moulton, Brown & Lent conducted a meta-analysis to determine the relations of self-efficacy beliefs to academic outcomes. Results revealed positive and significant relationships between self-efficacy beliefs, academic performance and persistence outcomes across a wide variety of subjects, experimental designs and assessment methods. Moulton, Brown & Lent supported earlier studies of Bouffard (1989) and Schunk (1987). A second level of application examines how teachers' perceptions of their instructional efficacy affects children academically. The classroom atmosphere is partially determined by the teachers' belief in their own instructional efficacy. The recommendation for teachers is to teach children the cognitive tools with which to achieve and enhance their skills of efficacy so that they can use the skills effectively. Bandura (1989) felt that skills are a general rather than a fixed trait. In addition, people with the same skills can perform poorly, adequately or extraordinarily depending on how well the individual uses the subskills that they have developed. The third level of application is concerned with the perceived efficacy of the school. Collective efficacy of the school as a whole fosters academic achievement of the children in the school and creates an environment conducive to learning (Evans, 1989; Ashton, 1986).

SUMMARY

Self-efficacy has been employed to enhance the academic skills of children who are learning disabled (Schunk, 1985), to generate health related action (Bandura, 1995; Rosenstock, Strecher & Becker, 1988), training in self-management (Frayne & Latham, 1987) in achievement predictions in marketing (Kalechestein & Nowicki, 1993), to train self-confidence in sports (George, 1994) career choice and development and addictive behavior (Bandura, 1995) and in many other applications that are too numerous to mention here.

The application of Bandura's social learning principles to social situations have wide implications for the school and other social agencies charged with instructing disabled individuals. Principles outlined has been successfully demonstrated with many groups, including disabled individuals. Applications of these principles do not require extensive training or preparation.

REFERENCES

Ashton, P.T., & Web, R.B. (1986). *Making a Difference:Teachers' Sense of Efficacy and Student Achievement.* White Plains, NY: Longman.

Bandura, A. (1995). *Self-Efficacy in Changing Societies.* Cambridge: University Press.

Bandura, A. (1989). Human agency in social cognitive theory. *American Psychologist,* *44,* 1175-1184.

Bandura, A. (1986). *Social Foundations of Thought and Action: A Social Cognitive Theory.* Englewood Cliffs, NJ: Prentice Hall.

Bandura, A. (1977). Self-efficacy toward a unifying theory of behavior change. *Psychological Review, 84,* 191-215.

Bandura, A. (1976). Social learning analysis of aggression. In Ribes-Inesta, E. & Bandura, A. (Eds.). *Analysis of Delinquency and Aggression.* Hillsdale, NJ: Halsted Press.

Bandura, A. (1971). Psychotherapy based upon modeling principles. In A.E. Bergin & S.L. Garfield (Eds.). *Handbook of Psychotherapy and Behavior Change.* Englewood Cliffs, NJ: Prentice Hall.

Bandura, A. (1965). *Social Learning and Personality.* New York: Holt, Rinehart & Winston.

Bandura, A., Gusec & Menlow (1966). Observational learning as a function of symbolization and incentive set. *Child Development, 37,* 499-506.

Bandura, A., Ross, D., & Ross, S.A. (1961). Transmission of aggression through imitation of aggressive models. *Journal of Abnormal and Social Psychology, 63,* 575-582.

Bandura, A., Ross, D. & Ross, S.A. (1963). Vicarious reinforcement and imitative learning. *Journal of Abnormal and Social Psychology.*

Bandura, A. & Walters, R.H. (1963). *Social Learning and Personality Development.* New York: Holt, Rinehart & Winston.Bouffard-Bouchard, T. (1989). Influence of self-efficacy on performance in a cognitive task. *Journal of Social Psychology,* 130, 353-363.

Butter, O.B. (1989). Early help for kids at risk: Our nation's best investment. *NEA Today,* 7, 51-53.

Carroll, J. (1993). Self-efficacy related to transfer of learning and theory-based instructional design. *Journal of Adult Education, 22,* 37-43.

Charles, C.M. (1985). *Building Classroom Discipline.* New York: Longman.

Coleman, M. (1986). *Behavior Disorders: Theory and Practice.* Englewood Cliffs, NJ: Prentice Hall.

Corcoran, K. (1991). Efficacy, skills, reinforcement and choice behavior. *American Psychologist.* February.

Damon, W. (1977). *The Social World of the Child.* San Francisco: Jossey-Bass.

Eron, L. (1987). The development of aggressive behavior from the perspective of a developing behaviorism. *American Psychologist, 42,* 435-442.

Evans, R. (1989). *Albert Bandura: The Man and His Ideas—A Dialogue.* New York: Praeger.

Frayne, C. & Latham, G. (1987). Application of social learning theory to employee self-management of attendance. *Journal of Applied Psychology, 72,* 383-392.

George, T. (1994). Self-confidence and baseball performance: A causal examination of self-efficacy theory. *Journal of Sport and Exercise Psychology, 16,* 381-399.

Hilliard, A. G. (1989). Teachers and cultural styles in a pluralistic society. *NEA Today, 7,* 65-69.

Kalechstein, A. & Norwicki, S. (1993). Social learning theory and prediction of achievement in telemarketers. *Journal of Social Psychology, 134,* 547-548.

Kauffman, J. (1993). *Characteristics of Emotional and Behavioral Disorders of Children and Youth.* New York: Merrill.

Kahn, K. & Cangemi, J. (1979). Social learning theory: The role of imitation and modeling in learning socially desirable behavior. *Education, 100,* 41-46.

Miller, N.E. & Dollard, E. (1941). *Social Learning and Imitation.* New Haven, CT: Yale.

Moore, S. (1987). *Piaget and Bandura: The Need For A Unified Theory of Learning.* Paper presented at the biennial meeting of the society for research in child development. Baltimore, MD: April 23-26, 1987.

Moulton, K., Brown, S., & Lent, R. (1991). Relation of self- efficacy beliefs in academic outcomes: a meta-analytic investigation. *Journal of Counseling Psychology, 38,* 30-38.

Rosenstock, I., Strecher, V., & Becker, M. (1988). Contribution of HBM to self-efficacy theory. Health *Education Quarterly, 15,* 175-183.

Rotter, J. (1954). *Social Learning and Clinical Psychology.* New York: Prentice Hall.

Rotter, J. (1966). Generalized expectancies for internal versus external control of reinforcement. *Psychological Monographs: General and Applied, 80,* 80.

Rotter, J. (1990). Internal versus external control of reinforcement: A case history variable. *American Psychologist, 45,* 489-493.

Schunk, D. (1987). Peer models and children's behavior change. *Review of Educational Research, 57,* 149-174.

Strickland, B. (1989). Internal-external control expectancies from contingency to creativity. *American Psychologist, 44,* 1-12.

Tudge, R. & Winterhoff, P. (1991). Vzygotsky, Piaget and Bandura: Perspectives on the relations between the social world and cognitive development. *Human Development, 36,* 61-81.

Weignan, O., Kuttschreuter, O., & Baarda, B. (1992). A longitudinal study of the effects of television viewing on aggressive and prosocial behaviors. *British Journal of Social Psychology,* 31, 147-164.

Chapter 3

BEHAVIORAL, SOCIAL, AND ACADEMIC CHARACTERISTICS OF DISABLED INDIVIDUALS

HELEN BRANTLEY

INTRODUCTION

There is general agreement among professionals that disabled children and youth exhibit behavior that causes problems in school (Ysseldyke, Algozzine & Thurlow, 1992; Butler-Nalin & Padilla, 1989; Milich, McAninch & Harris, 1992; Polloway, Patton, Epstein, Cullinan & Luebke, 1986). These behaviors may interfere with employment opportunities (Agran, Salzberg & Stowitschek, 1987l; Butler-Nalin & Padilla, 1989; Baron, Trickett, Schmid & Leone, 1993; Sullivan, Vitello & Foster, 1988; Zetlin & Hosseini, 1989). Additionally, they may serve as the primary factor in dropping out of school (Butler-Nalin & Padilla, 1989; Nelson, 1988).

Behavioral characteristics of pupils who have mild learning and behavior problems indicate that many of these pupils talk out, do not pay attention, do not follow the rules, get angry easily, start fights, use obscene language and sarcasm, interfere with the work of others and frequently engage in temper tantrums and out-of-seat behavior (Farmer & Farmer, 1996; Roberts & Zubrick, 1992; Mercer & Mercer, 1989). In 1991, Forness and Kavale reported that the classmates of children with learning and behavior problems expressed that they actively dislike them. Because social acceptance is closely related to self-esteem (Henley, Roberts & Algozzine, 1993) the peer rejection experienced by pupils with mild learning and behavior problems contributes to a low self-esteem. In addition, academic success and attending behavior are related to acceptance by peers, whereas, disruptive and aggressive behaviors are related to rejection by peers (Roberts & Zubrick, 1992).

Generally, children are expected to regulate and manage their own behavior in school (Farmer & Farmer, 1989). The socially competent individual generates social interaction; that is, the socially competent individual initiates or participates in a reciprocal social exchange which is maintained through natural reinforcers (Nelson, 1988). The lack of social competence is cited as one of the primary reasons that students with mild disabilities have difficulties in regular classrooms (Gresham, 1981; Nelson, 1988). Further, social competence ratings are lower for children with mild handicaps when compared to regular education pupils (Merrell, Merz, Johnson & Ring, 1992). The absence of offers to share, smiling, making eye contact when speaking, asking for help, saying thank you or following directions could potentially nullify a social interaction (Nelson, 1988).

Deficits in appropriate age-level social skills may be a contributing factor in the disabled's inability to get along with peers. Social immaturity is often observed in antisocial behavior and failure to recognize responsibility and the rights of others (Mercer & Mercer, 1989).

A confounding variable that must be considered in examining peer relationships of the disabled is the influence of labels. Milich, McAninch & Harris (1992) reviewed studies that concluded that labels such as learning disability or behavior disorder can lead to peer stigmatization which results in disturbed or disrupted peer relations. These authors concluded that expectancy effects do occur among children and the effects occur in response to even minimal stigmatizing information; the stigmatizing information affects not only how the perceiver feels about the disabled child but also how the disabled child feels about the ensuing interaction. Finally, the authors pointed out that negative behavior of the disabled may have immediate and long-term consequences for peer relations.

According to the International Study of the Center for Health Education and Social System Research (Butler-Nalin & Padilla, 1989) the graduation rates of youths with disabilities (56-59%) are considerably lower than the graduation rates of nondisabled youths (70-74%). Independent variables, namely the youths' behavior and experience and the degree of social integration are examined as particular behaviors and experiences that influence the chances of pupils dropping out directly. These variables were examined on the basis of whether or not students had one or more of the following incidents:

being fired from a job, leaving school of suspension or expulsion, and ever being arrested or incarcerated. Social integration was measured by whether the parent reported that the youth belonged to a school or community group in the past year. The results pointed out two measures of youth behavior as related to many disabled individuals. They exhibit negative behavior and seldom belong. Negative behavior is consistently related to dropping out of school. Belonging to a group is also significantly related to dropout and graduation.

Finally, in 1976, Sirvis and Carpignano analyzed the status of the disabled populations as having a unique social status parallel to what occurs with minority groups including the disadvantages of discrimination and prejudice which accompanies that status. Fourteen years later, in 1990, the Americans Wiith Disabilities Act (ADA 101-336) was passed with an intent to end discrimination against individuals with disabilities in private-sector employment, public services, public accommodations, transportation, and telecommunications. ADA required four years for employers and businesses to make reasonable modifications (Blackhurst & Berdine, 1993). Although the jury is out regarding the effects of ADA, we expect research to report productive changes in the lives of the disabled members of our society.

While the introductory portion of this chapter focused on general behavioral-social characteristics of students who have mild learning and behavior problems, the next section will provide an overview of specific behavioral-social and academic characteristics of specific categories of disabled children and youth. Behavior disorders, learning disabled, mental retardation, communication disorders, visual impairment, orthopedic and health impairments and learning disabilities will be discussed in general terms. (For specific information, the reader is referred to any basic book in exceptionality.)

Please note that within each disability category, conditions may exist in mild, moderate or severe forms. The mild to moderate levels are those pupils who have more contact with regular education programs. Pupils who have severe disabling conditions are most often educated in more restrictive settings with less interaction with the regular education programs. All disabled children should be educated with their normal peers to the extent that their disabilities will permit.

For each disabled group mentioned, there are several types and degrees of disabilities and each type will require a different type of assessment and intervention strategy, as reflected under the short portrait for each group.

BEHAVIOR DISORDERS

Portraits of Behavior Disordered Students

In a self-contained multihandicapped class in a primary school, three boys diagnosed as behavior disordered enter the classroom with the teacher's assistant. One of the boys (Student A) yells, "Good morning everybody," while he throws his backpack onto the floor. The teacher directs the class to begin their seatwork and the boys to put their things away, have a seat, and likewise, get started with their morning work. Student A, removes his paper from his desktop, rolls it into a ball, and throws it and hits Student B on the side of his face. Student B, runs toward Student A and the two begin an altercation. The teacher immediately intervenes while directing Student C to leave for his mainstreaming class. Specific strategies will need to be in place to deal with maladaptive behaviors in the classroom.

Social-Emotional Characteristics

Children with behavior disorders are more likely than any other category of disabled youth to drop out of school. Dropout rates are reported at 55 percent with nearly half of the dropout rate, 26.8 percent, due to behavior problems (Butler-Nalin & Padilla, 1989). The behaviors observed interfere with the establishing and maintaining positive relations with others (Zargota, Vaughn & McIntosh, 1991). Problems in adapting to the school environment and relating socially and responsibly to teachers and authority figures are evident.

In addition, behavior disordered students are skilled at eliciting emotional responses of others (Henley, Ramsey & Algozzine, 1993). These behaviors affect the social climate of the classroom and are of particular concern to the teacher because they require the teacher to take time to arbitrate disputes and encourage appropriate social interaction. Defiance, aggression and noncompliance toward authority figures are likely to alarm the teachers and other school officials (Carr & Pungo, 1993; Blackhurst & Berdine, 1993).

Behavior disordered children and youth are also characterized by distractibility and impulsivity (Carr & Pungo, 1993). Frequently, there are difficulties in listening, asking for teacher assistance, bringing materials to class, following directions and completing assignments. Many behavior disordered students are unable to ignore distractions and often cannot deal with anger and frustration. Introducing oneself, beginning and ending a conversation, sharing social problems solving and apologizing are generally difficult social skills for behavior disordered students to master (Hardman, Drew, Egan & Wolf, 1993).

Some children with behavior problems avoid peer and social relationships (Glassberg, 1994; Henley, Ramsey & Algozzine, 1993). They withdraw and isolate themselves. Others have engaged in asocial behaviors that are unacceptable to their peers and are, thereby, rejected by their peers (Kirkcaldy & Mooshage, 1993). Older behavior disordered students are described as destructive and intractable (Glassberg, 1994).

Zargota, Vaughn & McIntosh (1991) reviewed twenty-seven studies that examined social skills interventions for behavior disordered youth. These studies validate the behaviors discussed previously. The independent variables in the research included: nine studies used interpersonal problem solving, i.e., smiling, conversation skills; following instructions and joining a group were targeted in ten; one study addressed coping with anger, two included one or more of social cognition, coping with conflicts and forming friendships; three addressed peer interactions; one examined moral development, choice, perspective taking and consequences; and finally, a study addressed self-control and coping behaviors.

Academic Characteristics

It becomes obvious from the prior discussion that behavior disordered children will most likely experience academic deficits as an indirect result of their behaviors. According to Heyward & Orlansky (1992) many more children than normal score in the slow learner or mildly retarded range on IQ tests. These authors define a score of about 90-95 as the average score for behavior disordered children and youth. Kauffman (1989) concurs but uses a range of 80-100. He also cites the average IQ score for children who are severely disturbed at around 50.

DEAF AND HARD-OF-HEARING

Portrait of a Deaf Individual

Student E is deaf as a result of a hereditary neurological impairment. She is eighteen, a senior in high school and lost her hearing around the age of three. Her younger brother who is two, also appears to be affected. She is an "A" student enrolled in regular education. Student E sits in the front of the class and is an avid lipreader. She reads the lips of the speaker and responds verbally. Her voice is soft with a slight foreign accent. She has a drivers license and works as Santa's helper during Christmas. A two year follow-up of Student E revealed that she was in college, still an "A" student and engaged to marry a male who can hear.

Student E, along with many other deaf individuals, cast doubt into much of the research regarding deaf individuals. Student E however, came from a middle to upper income family and was enrolled in an enrichment preschool program for the deaf.

Social-Emotional Characteristics

The social-emotional development of children with hearing impairments follows the same basic pattern found among nondisabled peers (Meyen, 1990). Young deaf children are like hearing children in many ways–few differences exist. In language development, the deaf and the hearing child coo, gurgle and babble. However, within eight to twelve months of age, vocalizations cease for deaf children and they withdraw and become silent. Children who are hard-of-hearing continue to vocalize (Moore, 1987). During the next few years of the child's life, parents become concerned and realize that something is wrong. The child, thus, becomes confused and frustrated (Bigge & O'Donnell, 1976). The beginning of school may involve the deaf and hard-of-hearing in mutual play interests that are not impeded by communication differences (Meyen, 1990). However, the social interactions of the deaf and hard-of-hearing child may, because of social immaturity, result in impulsivity (Haring & McCormick, 1990); Greenberg & Kusche, 1989). Throughout the school years, language becomes an important facilitator of socialization and social-emotional growth (Meyen, 1990). Thus, children who are deaf and hard-of-hearing may be characterized by isolation and peer rejection, passive inferiority, and egocentrism (Greenberg & Kusche, 1989). In addition, deaf children may be less capable of interpreting emotional states and situations due to limited opportunities for social interaction (Cole, 1987). Although the graduation rates of deaf and hard-of-hearing children approach the rate of the nondisabled school-aged youth (Butler-Nalin & Padilla, 1989), their estimated rate of behavior problems is high (Greenberg & Kusche, 1989). The social environment of deaf children and youth is dependent upon whether the deaf child has deaf or hearing parents, severity of the loss (severity of the hearing loss is positively correlated with social adjustment) and the family climate (Hardman, Drew, Egan & Wolf, 1993; Greenberg & Kusche, 1989).

Academic Characteristics

Greenberg and Kusche's (1989) review of current research regarding the development of deaf children and adolescents summarized that on verbal tests of intelligence, deaf children scored lower than hearing peers. On measures of nonverbal intelligence, the deaf scored within the normal range. Caution however, is suggested in interpreting these findings because the tests that were used to test the deaf pupils were standardized on hearing children and because the language background of deaf students is different from that of hearing peers (Geers, 1985).

Tests of academic achievement show deficits among deaf children, in part, because achievement is based upon language (Greenberg & Kusche, 1989; Haring & McCormick, 1990).

Intellectual development for individuals with hearing impairments is more of a function of language than cognitive ability. Difficulties in performance appear to be closely associated with speaking, reading and writing the English language (Hardman, Drew, Egan & Wolf, 1993). Children who are hard-of-hearing experience difficulty in reading achievement thereby suggesting that any hearing loss appears to be detrimental with regard to reading achievement (Higgins, 1980). Moore's (1987) interpretation is that deafness imposes no limitations on the cognitive abilities of individuals.

MENTAL RETARDATION

Portraits of Mentally Retarded Students

Student G is a twelve-year-old mildly retarded Down Syndrome female. She had surgery at an early age that removed much of the visibility effects of the syndrome. With the exception of slight obesity, Student G appears normal. She is enrolled in regular education but has speech and occupational therapy twice a week. She spent two years, kindergarten and first grade, in self-contained classes with resource support. From the second grade she has been in regular classes with related services. Student G maintains a "C" average.

Student H is fifteen and severely retarded. Additionally, he has cerebral palsy and is nonambulatory and is nonverbal. He is enrolled in Severe/Profound Handicapped class (SPH). He performs approximately at the three year range. He is enrolled in alternative communication classes. This wide deviation in mental retardation will require alternative instructional strategies.

Academic Characteristics

According to the American Association of Mental Deficiency, mental retardation refers to subaverage general intellectual functioning which interpreted means that a retarded child's intellectual capacity must be at least two standard deviations below the mean (Grossman, 1993). Thus, mentally retarded school-age children are classified according to expected achievement in the classroom. (There will be variations in classifications and nomenclature from state to state). They are usually classified as follows:

Educable - Expected achievement level 2nd to 5th grade.
Trainable - Some academic achievement but primary focus is upon self-help skills
Custodial - Unable to care for their basic needs (Hardman, Drew, Egan & Wolf, 1993).

Readers should be aware that the above expected achievement levels are not intended to be used as ceilings for achievement among mentally retarded students. Some students in each category will exceed expectations-others may not reach the levels of expectations.

Social-Emotional Characteristics

The social skills of the mentally retarded are evaluated as they relate to adaptive behavior. Adaptive behavior, which is included in the current definition of mental retardation, is defined as the ability to adapt to the environment, relate to others and take care of personal needs (Henley, Ramsey and Algozzine, (1993). In other words, impairments in maturation learning and social adjustment, in addition to other specified criteria, must be present in order to classify a student as mentally retarded.

In the classroom, mentally retarded children are socially immature. They usually have a poor self-concept and are thus susceptible to peer influence (Henley, Ramsey and Algozzine, 1993). They are also rejected by their peers (Polloway, Patton, Epstein and Luebke, 1986). Retarded children have inadequate attention levels, therefore, they experience difficulty in maintaining attention (Borkowski, Peck and Damberg, 1983).

The drop out rate for mentally retarded children and youth is listed at 34 percent with behavior accounting for 13.6% of the rate.

Using the educable, trainable and custodial classifications, Hardman, Drew, Egan and Wolf (1993) outline the social skill development of the mentally retarded as follows:

Educable - Social development will permit some degree of independence in the community
Trainable - Social adjustment limited to the home and closely surrounding area
Custodial - Need care and supervision throughout life

Retarded children and youth may not be considered retarded in their home and community environments. Many mildly retarded adults (educable mentally retarded) achieve satisfactory adjustment in the community, marry and have children. There are, however, problems related to getting along with others, maintaining employment and personal frustration (Zetlin, 1988).

In spite of limited social skill development among the trainable, it is still necessary for them to develop appropriate social skills

(Hardman, Drew, Egan, 1993).

It is important to recognize that the social needs of the mentally retarded may be overlooked because they are defined as having subaverage intellectual functioning. The emotions of the retarded are normal. They too want to be accepted, liked and valued (Henley, Ramsey and Algozzine, 1993).

ORTHOPEDIC AND HEALTH IMPAIRMENTS

Student G is twelve-years-old and has spina bifida. He is non-ambulatory and is incontinent. His IQ is in the normal range of intelligence. He is well-liked by his peers because of his attractiveness. Student G is in a self-contained classroom setting, and he is mainstreamed for a part of the school day.

Student K has cerebral palsy. She is hemiplegic. Her speech is slurred and she functions well within the normal range of intelligence. She has speech therapy and one hour of resource assistance. As much as possible, these children should be included with their normal peers.

Social-Emotional Characteristics

Students with orthopedic and health disabilities are a varied population (Heyward & Orlansky, 1993). Researchers use different classifications when referring to this group. For example, Haring and McCormick (1994) refer to this group of disabling conditions as crippled and other health impaired, physically handicapped and physically disabled. Blackhurst and Berdine (1993) group this category of the disabled according to three functional categories: ambulation and vitality; medical diagnosis; and, other disabling conditions. Meyen (1990) used etiology to establish three categories; neurologic, orthopedic and health conditions. Public Law 94-142 used orthopedic and health impairments to describe this group of children and youth (Federal Register 1977, p. 42478).

Children with orthopedic and health impairments include children with cerebral palsy, muscular dystrophy, spina bifida, juvenile rheumatoid arthritis and poliomyelitis. Health impairments include asthma, allergies, epilepsy, juvenile diabetes mellitus, hemophilia, cystic fibrosis, sickle cell anemia, cardiac conditions, cancer and aids. The Individuals With Disabilities Education Act, P.L. 101-476 of 1990 added traumatic brain injury as a separate disability category.

Because this group of children and youth typically have characteristics that do not conform with societal standards for physical attractiveness, they may have problems with being accepted or difficulty with feeling that they are accepted by peers (Meyen, 1990). Antonello (1996) relates secondary physical problems such as atypical mannerisms, self-control, hyperactivity, diminished attention, poor concentration and failure to recognize social boundaries as influential in social interactions.

Undesirable social characteristics such as drooling, incontinence and seizure activity can have a negative effect on the establishment of positive relations. Mobility devices, life sustaining equipment and prosthetics may interfere with the development of positive images (Meyen, 1990).

Academic Characteristics

Research defines three limitations on learning with reference to children who have orthopedic and health disabilities. These include:

1. Limitations on the ability to process information.
2. Limitations on the ability to receive information through the senses.
3. Limitation on the range and nature of interpersonal and environmental interactions (Meyen, 1990).

Children who have conditions that affect their motor skills should have the full range of cognitive abilities. Generally, this group of children encompass the full range of intellectual capacity. Finally, the graduation rates of this group are equal to their nondisabled peers (Butler-Nalin & Padilla, 1989).

Characteristics of specific types of disabilities under the mildly to moderately categories are overviewed. A general portrait is given with strategies for improving social skills development in the social-emotional and academic areas. Chapter 8 addresses these topics in greater detail.

LEARNING DISABILITIES

Portraits of Learning Disabled Students

Franklin is a fourteen-year-old adolescent who enjoys sharing and discussing articles of interest from the *New York Times* with his teacher. In reading, Franklin reads "was" for "saw," "on" for "no," and "b" for "d". He appears quiet and withdrawn at times, highly distractible, and awkward during his gym classes. He also has low frustration tolerance and negative impulse control. His cursive writing consists of large letters that overlap the lines on his paper. However, he thinks critically and engages in complex problem-solving activities.

Loretta is a twelve-year-old who daydreams in her math class and works laboriously through her class assignments. She is inattentive, unmotivated, and shows no interest in classwork. Her school assignments are below grade level, and she performs poorly in all academic subjects. Her creative skills are two grade levels above her current grade placement, and she enjoys working alone. As indicated, there are wide deviations among and between learning disabled individuals.

Social-Emotional Characteristics

Although there is great controversy regarding the nature of children and youth with learning disabilities, there are some generalizable social and emotional characteristics. Researchers (Hallahan & Reeve, 1980; Lloyd, 1980; Loper, 1980; Torgesen, 1988) have documented numerous social processes including rejection, isolation and loneliness. All students with learning disabilities have subject related problems. Franklin and Loretta were experiencing social relations problems. Additionally, any learning disability affects many other areas of the lives of students including relationships with friends, roles in the family, self-image and confidence in the ability to handle social situations.

It is quite apparent that students with learning disabilities display social skills problems in school (Haager & Vaughn, 1995). Their interaction with nondisabled peers is often repulsive and misunderstood. Research (Stone & LaGreca, 1990) shows that students who are constantly isolated and ignored are more likely to be aggressive, hostile, and socially anxious in their classes. These behaviors (emotional intelligence) interfere with the necessary skills and time students need to focus and concentrate on classwork successfully. Emotional intelligences (a concept elaborated on by Goldman, 1996) indicates that to perform at the level commensurate with one's ability requires them to exercise awareness of social deftness, good impulse control, self-motivation, persistence and self-discipline.

Since many learning disabled students often show extraordinary abilities (Thomas Edison, Nelson Rockefeller, Albert Einstein, Pablo Picasso, Hans Christian Anderson et al.) educators should focus on these areas to provide for social acceptance, school success and relevant learning experiences since much of the rejection is due to poor school achievement. Many learning disabled students possess hobbies and areas of interest that are well-respected by significant others. A program where students are exposed to a variety of intellectual, social, and cultural perspectives reflective of students' background needs and interests, will in many instances, address the social skills problems of the learning disabled (Clark, 1983; Kaplan, 1996).

Students with learning disabilities also have low self-esteem, poor self-concept and very low motivation. They usually have little success at school and feel that the effort is not rewarded. In many cases, they apply the learned helplessness approach (even if I try hard, I am destined to fail) to school-related situations and tasks. Students with learning disabilities often rely on an external locus of control. That position does not permit them to become self-directed learners (internal locus of control). The attitude of learned helplessness (Hallahan & Kauffman, 1994; & Seligman, 1992, Bender, 1995) impedes their social, cognitive and emotional abilities.

Research shows that 36 percent of these students drop out of school due to academic and social problems and 14.4 percent drop out because of behavioral problems. During the high school years, social and behavior problems often take precedence over academic problems. These students, usually at this point, have had repeated failures in school, little encouragement and little motivation, social rejection by peers and viewed as troublemakers.

Kaplan (1996) detailed several studies that have been conducted failing to demonstrate significant discrepancy between the classroom behavior of students with learning disabilities and those labeled as mild mental disabled, slow learners or other mild disabilities (Vaughn et al., 1992; Oakland, Shermis & Coleman, 1990; Stone & LaGreca, 1990). These researchers concluded that the social difference in learning disabled students may be a pattern that occurs in students who fall within the low-achieving category. This category, in many cases are evidenced during the school hours where acceptable communication skills, acceptable class behaviors and acceptable social perceptions are part of the norm of the school climate (Brantley, 1989).

Academic Abilities

Students with learning disabilities usually have a disorder in one or more of the basic psychological processes involved in understanding or in using language-spoken or written, which may manifest itself in an imperfect ability to listen, think, speak, read, write, spell or to do mathematical calculations (Kaplan, 1996).

Students with learning disabilities tend to vary from average to above average intellectually. The range is 90-130 or two or more standard deviations above the mean. That range includes those students who are classified as gifted and talented with learning disabilities. Many of these students do not differ from the average in terms of their characteristics.

A multiplicity of characteristics have been associated with the significant discrepancy between what a learning disabled student is capable of learning and academic achievement in reading, science, mathematics, social studies, vocabulary, and writing. Yet, there is great confusion concerning a great number of negative characteristics and traits these students receive. However, students with learning disabilities tend to demonstrate specific thinking deficits (cognition) more commonly than the average students. Substantial evidence indicates that students with learning disabilities are very poor reflective thinkers. They also portray auditory and visual processing deficits. These difficulties often impede the smooth learning of classroom skills associated with school related subjects.

Many of the strategies to succeed in school related subjects require active participation and the employment of a host of problem-solving and critical thinking skills. Students with learning disabilities experience difficulty in the application and strategies necessary for memorization and generalization of these skills. However, when memory strategies are taught and apply in meaningful learning situations, learning disabled students perform as well as others in reading, writing, and other communication skills.

The academic performance of such students is poor. They usually possess problems in reading and writing. Achievement is some subjects may be average, but achievement in others are below-average and in many cases, at the failure level, which is not indicative of their potential (Scott, 1993). There is great variation among this population in school subjects also. Many of these students perform quite successfully and are classified as having areas of gifts and talents, but a great percentage of them possess basic academic and social problems.

Generally, students with learning disabilities experience severe problems in reading. Commonly noted observational characteristics include: accuracy, fluency, and normal rate in reading; omissions, substitutions and mispronunciation of words; inadequate auditory closure and sound-blending skills; a deficit in phoneme-grapheme relationships; poor decoding and comprehension skills; vocabulary deficits, poor spelling skills and inferential reading skills. Reading skills are necessary for success in all aspects of the student's school life and are correlated with psychological success (Norris, Haring, McCormick, 1994).

Difficulties with language is also common among the learning disabled population. They frequently have problems with impaired discrimination of auditory stimuli; slow language development; difficulty imitating statements; a mastery of automatic rules of language; difficulty in expressive and receptive language and problems with phonological production or speech. Learning disabled children and youth with oral language problems often manifest these problems in written assignments in all subjects.

THE VISUALLY IMPAIRED

Portraits of Visually Impaired Students

Ashanti was born with a moderate visual impairment. She is now 14 and will be attending high school in a regular class setting. Ashanti reads braille fluently but is not performing well in reading-related classes. She loves math and science, enjoys solving complicated math problems and conducting science experiments. Her attitude toward school work is positive but she is constantly alone and is very unsure of herself.

Wanda is a blind thirteen-year-old who is in a regular class placement and receiving assistance from the resource room. She is intellectually above average and demonstrates outstanding academic work. Despite her high ability in academic subjects, she cries frequently and cannot sustain her ability in completing many of the class assignments. Wanda is very withdrawn and finds it difficult to interact with her sighted peers.

Social-Emotional

The development and embellishing of social skills are very much depended upon vision. Children and youth with limited vision find it difficult to rely on visual cues or signals to communicate with significant others in the social environment (Sacks & Reaedon, 1989). In a research study conducted by Kekelis and Sacks (1992) and MacCuspie (1992) on the social interaction of children who were blind and their nondisabled peers, it was pointed out that the behaviors of these children were void of creativity, flexibility, and elaboration. Visually disabled children and youth with severe visual loss, or the nonexistence of vision, are deprived of the opportunities to emulate social role models and engage in meaningful social interactive experiences (Norris & McCormick, 1990). These situations may cause social isolation, negative attitudes, and school anxiety (Leonhardt, 1990). These behaviors can have a significant impact on the social and academic learning of the visually impaired student.

The self-esteem of visually impaired learners is not significantly different than that of their sighted peers (Ubiakor & Stile, 1990). "If learners with visual impairments have had significant verbal interaction with others, such as participating in games and friendships, they do not differ from their sighted peers in social/cognitive tasks (Schwartz, 1983)."

The classroom teacher plays an important role in helping the visually impaired students to develop good self-esteem and to feel good about their settings. Tuttle (1984) concluded from his analysis that the lack of self-confidence in the visually impaired is due to their limited interaction and attitudes of sighted people. The positive interaction of sighted others will provide a sense of confidence and further opportunities to develop social competencies for school, home, and community independence.

Academic Characteristics

The difference between the development of language of children who are visually disabled compared to sighted children is not significant. Research (Civelli, 1983; Matsueda, 1984) into the language of the visually impaired indicated that these students do not differ from their sighted peers on verbally related activities. The visually impaired students may even have a higher auditory acuity than the nondisabled visual peers. The auditory channel is the major link between the visually impaired student's language and the outside world, and many researchers have highlighted its' importance.

Studies highlighting the impact of this missing sense with the visually impaired have indicated that the quality of word meaning has deficit due to the lack of or an impairment of vision. Gallagher & Anastasiow (1993) indicated that visually impaired students had less understanding of words as vehicles and were slower to form hypotheses about word meaning. Warren (1984) concluded after studying the literature on the language of the visually impaired that the new work of the past several years strongly suggests that while blind children may use words with the same frequency count as sighted children, the meanings of words for the blind are not as rich or as elaborated as for the sighted child.

Research also shows that there is much variation among the cognitive development of children and youth with visual impairments when compared to their nondisabled peers (Ittyerah and Samarapungavan, 1989). Because of the absence of visual information and experience, visually impaired students generally have difficulty with projecting positions in space, including recognition of shapes, construction of a projective straight line conceptualization of right and left in absolute and mirror image orientation (Birns, 1986).

Learners with visual impairments have difficulty in determining and relating right to left to others although they are able to discriminate orientation to themselves. The concepts of spatial relationships is particularly important to the visually impaired due to personal mobility.

The development of concepts for the visually impaired student is quite different since many of them are learned through the visual modality. Researchers (Davidson, Dunn, Wiles-Kettenmann & Appelle, 1981; Stephens & Grube, 1982) using concepts based on the developmental theory have concluded that children who are blind lag behind their sighted peers. The tactual and auditory channels assist the visually impaired students in seeing the world. They must take great care in focusing their mental attention to gain the most from their social interaction environment and their experiences with significant others (Groenveld & Jan, 1992).

THE SPEECH AND LANGUAGE IMPAIRED

Portrait of a Language Impaired Student

Timothy says "wabbit" for "rabbit" and "poch" for "porch." His articulation problems also interfere with his classwork. When he attempts to speak out in class, his peers tease and kid him. He has a difficult time making friends and purposely stays away from girls. Since he has entered high school, he fights often and is constantly isolated because of his behavior.

Academic Characteristics

Speech, language, and communication problems may result from input problems: hearing or visual disability; processing disability; problems related to central nervous system dysfunction or output disability; cleft palate disorders appear single or in clusters. They may result from articulation, voice, and fluency which are the various types of speech disorders.

When a child fails to acquire the semantic aspects of language, this interferes greatly with communicative skills and can result in acquiring other components. Children with language difficulties in semantics either do not learn the meaning of words or are unable to interpret the meaning of a series of words collectively or convey meaning. Expressive language problems may result from semantic difficulties from the lack of symbols to partial deficits.

Pragmatics involves the functional use of language as a social tool for communication, learning, directing behavior, or generating new ideas (Bernstein & Tiegerman, 1993). As children master the structural and content component of language, they also must learn to use language in appropriate and functional ways in various contexts. A great percentage of children with language disorders lack skills in pragmatics or language use (Haring & McCormick, 1990). Problems in expressive intentions and difficulties in maintaining a flow of conversations are the most common difficulties children experience. Some children are restricted communicatively because they use language in limited ways.

Social Problems

Communication disorders may interfere with the social interaction and cognitive development of language disabled learners throughout the school day. However, research indicates that it is important that learners with speech and language deficits be educated in settings with nondisabled peers (Schiefelbush & McCormick, 1981). Many language delayed children do not understand how to take turns or engage in reciprocal interactions necessary for conversation. Still others may not attend to the contents of the speaker's remarks or understand their role in continuing the discussion. The context in which the disabled students must function is the best place to practice the art of communication.

REFERENCES

Adelman, H.S., & Taylor, L. (1993). Enhancing motivation for overcoming learn ing and behavior problems. *Journal of Learning Disabilities, 16,* 384-392.

Antonello, S. (1996). *Social Skill Development: Practical Strategies for Adolescents and Adults With Developmental Disabilities.* Boston: Allyn & Bacon.

Agran, M., Salzberb, C., & Stowitscheck, J. (1987). An analysis of a social skills training program using self-instructions on the acquisition and generalization of two social behaviors in a work setting. *Journal of the Association of Severe Handicaps, 12,* 131-139.

Baron, C., Trickette, E., Schmid, K., & Leone, P. (1993). Transition tasks and resources: An ecological approach to life after high school. *Prevention in Human Services, 10,* 179-204.

Bender, W. (1995). Teachers' attitudes toward increased mainstreaming: Implementing effective instruction for students with learning disabilities. *Journal of Learning Disabilities, 28*, 87-94.

Bigge, J. & O'Donnell (1976). *Teaching Individuals With Physical and Multiple Disabilities.* Columbus, OH: Charles E. Merrill.

Blackhurst, A.E., & Berdine, W.H. (1993). *An Introduction to Special Education* (3rd ed.). Lexington, KY: Harper Collins College Publishers.

Borkowski, J., Peck, V. & Damberg, P. (1983). Attention, memory and cognition. In J.L. Matson & R. Milich, *Handbook of Mental Retardation*, p. 479.

Brantley, H. (1989). Creating an academic climate in rural schools. Doctoral dissertation, Teachers College, Columbia University.

Butler-Nalin, P. & Padilla, C. (1989). Dropouts: The relationship of student characteristics, behaviors and performance for special education students. Washington, DC: U.S. Department of Education, Office of Special Education Programs.

Carr, S. & Pungo, R. (1993). The effects of self-monitoring of academic accuracy and productivity on the performance of students with behavior disorders. *Behavior Disorders, 18*, 241-250.

Civelli, E. (1983). Verbalism in young children. *Journal of Visual Impairment and Blindness, 77*, 61-66.

Cole, P.R. (1987). Recognizing language disorders in F.N. Martin (Ed.), *Hearing Disorders in Children.* Austin, TX: Pro-Ed.

Davidson, P.W., Dunn, G., Wiles-Kettenman, M. & Appelle, S. (1981). Haptic conversation of amount in blind and sighted children: Exploratory movement effects. *Journal of Pediatric Psychology, 6*, 191-200.

Farmer, T. & Farmer, E. (1996). Social relationships of students with exceptionalities in mainstream classrooms: Social networks and hemophilia. *Exceptional Children, 62*, 431-450. Federal Register (1977). 42 (163) 42474-42518.

Feldheusen, J.F. (1966). How to identify and develop special talents. *Educational Leadership, 53*, 66-69.

Forness, S.R., & Kavale, K.A. (1991). Social skills deficits as primary learning disabilities: A note on problems with the ICLO diagnostic criteria. *Learning Disabilities Research & Practice, 6*, 44-49.

Gallagher, K. & Ansastasiow, N. (1993). *Educating Exceptional Children.* Boston, MA: Houghton-Mifflin.

Geers, A. (1985). Assessment of hearing impaired children: Determining typical and optimal levels of performance. In F. Powell, T. Finitzo-Heiber, S. Friel-Patti & D. Henderson (Eds.). *Education of the hearing impaired child* (pp. 57-83). San Diego, CA: College Hill.

Glassberg, L. (1994). Students with behavior disorders: Determinants of placement outcomes. *Behavior Disorders, 19*, 181-191.

Goldman, D. (1995). *Emotional Intelligence: Why It Can Matter More Than IQ.* New York: Bantam Books

Greenberg, M.T., & Kusche, C.A. (1989). Cognitive personal and social development of deaf children and adolescents. In M. Wang, M. Reynolds, & H. Walberg (Eds.). *Handbook of Special Education: Research and Practice, 3*, 95-129.

Gresham, F.M. (1981). Social skills training with handicapped children: *A review.* *Review of Educational Research, 51,* 139-170.

Groenveld, M. & Jan, J.E. (1992). Intelligence profiles of low vision and blind children. *Journal of Visual Impairment and Blindness, 86,* 68-71.

Grossman, H. (1993). *Manual of Classification of Mental Retardation.* Washington, DC: American Association of Mental Deficiency.

Gross-Tsur-Varda (1995). Developmental right-hemisphere syndrome: Clinical spectrum of the non-verbal learning disability. *Journal of Learning Disabilities, 28,* 80-86.

Haager, D. & Vaughn, S. (1995). Parents, teachers, peers, self-reports of the social competence of students with learning disabilities. *Journal of Learning Disabilities, 28,* 205-215, 231.

Hallahan, D.P. & Reeve, R.E. (1980). Selective attention and distractibility. In B.K. Keogh (Ed.). vs Advances in Special Education: Vol. 1. Basic constructs and theoretical orientations (pp. 141-181). Greenwich, CT: JAJ Press.

Hardman, M.L., Drew, C.J., Egan, M.W., and Wolf, B. (1993). *Human Exceptionality: Society, School and Family.* Needham Heights, MA: Allyn & Bacon.

Haring, N. & McCormick, L. (1990). *Exceptional Children and Youth.* (5th ed.). Columbus, OH: Charles E. Merrill.

Henley, M., Ramsey, R. & Algozzine, R. (1993). *Characteristics of and Strategies for Teaching Students With Mild Disabilities.* Needham Heights, MA: Allyn & Bacon.

Heyward, W. & Orlansky, D. (1992). *Exceptional Children,* (4th ed.). New York: Merrill.

Higgins, D. (1990). *The Challenge of Educating Together Deaf and Hearing Youth: Making Mainstreaming Work.* Springfield: Charles C Thomas.

Kaplan, P. (1996). *Pathways for Exceptional Children.* West Publishing Company: Minneapolis (pp. 504-505).

Kauffman, J. (1989). *Characteristics of Behavior Disorders of Children and Youth.* (4th ed.) Columbus, OH: Merrill.

Kauffman J., Cullinan, D. & Epstein, M. (1987). Characteristics of students placed in programs for the seriously emotionally disturbed. *Behavior Disorders, 12,* 175-184.

Kekelis, L., & Sacks, S.Z. (1992). The effects of visual impairment on children's social interactions in regular education programs. In S.Z. Sacks, L. Kekelis & R.J. Gaylord-Ross (Eds.). The development of social skills by blind and visually: impaired students: Exploratory studies and strategies (pp. 59-82). New York: American Foundation for the Blind.

Kirkcaldy, B.D. & Mooshage, B. (1993). Personality profiles of conduct and emotional disordered adolescents. *Personality and Individual Differences, 15,* 95-96.

Leonhardt, M. (1990). *Stereotypes: A Preliminary Report on Mannerisms and Blindness, 78,* 54-55.

Lloyd, J. (1980). Academic instruction and cognitive techniques: The need for attack strategy training. *Exceptional Education Quarterly, 1,* 1-8.

Loper, A.B. (1980). Metacognitive development: Implications for cognitive training of exceptional children. *Exceptional Education Quarterly, 1,* 1-8.

MacCuspie, A.P. (1992). The social acceptance and integration of visually impaired children in integrated settings. In S.Z. Sacks, L. Kekelis, & R.J. Gaylord-Ross (Eds.). The development of social skills by blind and visually impaired students: Exploratory studies and strategies (pp. 83-102). New York: American Foundation for the Blind.

Matsueda, M. (1984). A comparative analysis of blind and sighted children's communication skills. *Journal of Visual Impairment and Blindness, 78,* 1-4.

Mercer, C.D. & Mercer, A.R. (1989). *Teaching Students With Learning Problems* (3rd ed.). Columbus, OH: Merrill.

Merrell, K., Merz, J., Johnson, E., Ring, E., (1992). Social competence of students with mild handicaps and low achievement: A comparative study. *School Psychology Review, 21,* 125-137.

Meyen, E. (1990). *Exceptional Children in Today's Schools.* Denver, CO: Love.

Millich, R., McAninch, C., Harris, M. (1992). Effects of stigmatizing information on children's peer relations: Believing is seeing.

Moore, D.M. (1987). *Educating the Deaf: Psychology, Principles and Practices.* (3rd ed.). Boston, MA: Houghton-Mifflin.

Nelson, C.M. (1988). Social skills training for handicapped students. *Teaching Exceptional Children.* (Summer).

Norris, G., Haring, L., & Haring, T. (1994). Exceptional children and youth, (6th edition), New York, MacMillan.

Polloway, E., Patton, J., Epstein, M., Cullinan, D. & Leuebke, J. (1986). Demographic, social and behavioral characteristics of students with educable mental retardation. *Education and Training of the Mentally Retarded, 21,* 27-34.

Raine, A., Hulme, C., Chadderton, H. & Bailey, P. (1991). Verbal short-term memory span in speech-disordered children: Implications for articulatory coding in short-term memory. *Journal of Child Development, 62,* 415-423.

Roberts, C. & Zubrick, S. (1992). Factors influencing the social status of children with mild academic disabilities in regular classrooms. *Exceptional Children, 59,* 192-202.

Sacks, S. & Reardon, M. (1989). Maximizing social integration for visually handicapped students: Applications and practice. In R. Gaylord-Ross (Ed.) *Integration strategies for students with handicaps* (pp. 77-104). Baltimore, MD: Paul H. Brookes Publishing Co.

Sacks, S.Z. & Wolf, K. (1992). The importance of social skills training in the transition process for students with visual impairment. *Journal of Vocational Rehabilitation, 2,* 46-55.

Schiefelbush, R.L. & McCormick, L. (1981). Language and speech disorders. In J. Kauffman & D. Hallahan (Eds.), *Handbook of Special Education.* Englewood Cliffs, NJ: Prentice Hall.

Schwartz, T. (1983). Social cognition in visually and sighted children. *Journal of Visual Impairment and Blindness,* 77, 377-381.

Seligman, M.E. (1992). *Helplessness: On Depression, Development and Death.* San Francisco: W.H. Freeman.

Silverman, F. (1995). *Speech, Language and Hearing Disorders.* Allyn & Bacon, Needham Heights, MA.

Sirvis, B.O., Carpignano, J. (1976). Psychosocial aspects of disability. In J.L. Bigge (Ed.) *Teaching individuals with physical and multiple disabilities.* Columbus, OH: Charles E. Merrill.

Stephens, B. & Grube, C. (1982). Development of Piagetian reasoning in congenitally blind children. *Journal of Visual Impairment and Blindness, 76,* 133-143.

Stewart, D. (1994). Distinguishing learning disabilities in postsecondary settings. *Guidance & Counseling,* (1994-1995), *52,* 12-17.

Stone, W.L. & LaGreca, A.M. (1990). The social status of children with learning disabilities: A reexamination. *Journal of Learning Disabilities, 23,* 32-47.

Sullivan, C.A., Vitello, S. & Foster, W. (1988). Adaptive behavior of adults with mental retardation in a group home: An intensive case study. *Education & Training in Mental Retardation, 23,* 76-81.

Torgesen, J.K. (1988). Studies of children with learning disabilities who perform poorly on memory span tasks. *Journal of Learning Disabilities.*

Tuttle, D. (1984). Self-esteem and adjusting to blindness. Springfield, IL: Charles C Thomas.

Ubiakor, F. & Stile, S. (1990). The self-concepts of visually impaired and normally sighted middle school children. *Journal of Psychology, 124,* 190-200.

USA Today (April 1994). Fostering creativity in youngsters, Vol. 114, (12).

U.S. Department of Education (1988). To assure the free and appropriate public education of all handicapped children: Ninth annual report to congress on the implementation of the education of the handicapped act. Washington, D.C.

Vaughn, S., Hogan, A., Kouzekanani, K. & Shapiro, S. (1990). Peer acceptance, self-perception, and social skills of LD students prior to identification. *Journal of Educational Psychology, 82,* 101-106.

Warren, D. (1984). Blindness and early childhood development. New York: American Foundation for the Blind.

Wehmeyer, M. (1995). A career education approach: Self-determination for youths with mild cognitive disabilities. *Intervention-in-school-and-clinic,* (1995), *30,* 157-163.

Ysseldyke, J. & Algozzine, B. (1990). *Introduction to special education.* (pp 132-145). Boston: Houghton Mifflin.

Ysseldyke, J.E., Algozzine, B., Thurlow, M. (1992). *Critical issues in special education.* Dallas: Houghton Mifflin.

Zargota, N., Vaughn, S. & McIntosh, R. (1991). Social skills interventions and children with behavior problems: A review. *Behavior Disorders, 16,* 260-275.

Zetlin, A. (1988). Adult development of mildly retarded students: Implications for educational programs in M.C. Wang, M. Reynolds & H.J. Walberg (Eds.). *Handbook of special education* research and practice. New York: Pergamon, pp. 77-90.

Zetlin, A.G. & Hossein, A. (1989). Six postschool case studies of mildly handicapped young adults. *Exceptional Children, 55,* 405-411.

Chapter 4

BEHAVIORAL STYLES OF DISABLED INDIVIDUALS

GEORGE R. TAYLOR & THADDAUS PHILLIPS

INTRODUCTION

As indicated earlier, many disabled individuals have not mastered the social skills needed to be successful at school and within the larger community. There are frequently conflicts between the children and school on what is considered to be appropriate behavior. Much of this confusion can be attributed to the school's lack of understanding specific characteristics of disabled individuals as outlined in Chapter 3 and the value and impact of various cultural styles on learning. Cultural values influences the behavior of individuals. According to Hyun and Fowler (1995), culture understanding and awareness may be expedited by employing the following strategies:

1. Exploring one's own culture heritage;
2. Understanding and examining the attitudes and values associated with one's cultures.

Specific strategies were suggested to improve culture awareness, such as interviewing family members, examining official records, clarifying one's attitudes toward diverse cultures, reading and reviewing resources about various cultures, and associating with various groups and members of diverse culture groups.

The powerful influence of cultural systems on cognitive style and behavior should be recognized and integrated into the instructional program of disabled individuals. Curriculum planners must be cognizant of the fact that no one behavioral instructional strategy will be appropriate for intervention. Rather, strategies selected should be based upon children's abilities and assessed needs as presented in Chapter 3.

Consideration should be given to cultural factors when planning instructional programs for disabled individuals. Each cultural style is different, however, there are similar characteristics which operate across specific cultures. It is of prime importance to recognize cultural styles and how styles impact and influence learning. All curricula should reflect the richness and contribution of each culture, thus promoting the self-perception of disabled individuals.

THE EFFECTS OF BEHAVIORAL STYLES

Style is learned, learned patterns can be either changed or augmented, but cannot be ignored. Style tends to be rooted at a deep cultural level and is largely determined by prior experiences and motivation. Hilliard's (1989) research indicated that educational dialogue in recent years has given substantial attention to the question of the importance and precise meaning of style in teaching and learning, particularly for minority groups. Style differences between teachers and students and between students and the curriculum have been cited as explanations for the low academic performance of some disabled individuals.

Misunderstanding of behavioral style can lead to misjudging disabled students' language abilities and intelligence. Establishing rapport and developing communication (Hyun & Fowler, 1995). Style is directly associated with cultural values. Modifying style is a slow and arduous process, and may never be fully realized. A proper sensitivity to style can provide a perspective for the enrichment of instruction of all children for the improvement both of teacher-student communication and of the systematic assessment of students. The schools must become more sensitive to style out of basic respect for children, and for their tremendous potential for learning (Hilliard, 1989). Additionally, a person can use more than one style and can be taught to switch styles when appropriate. A climate for growth depends upon healthy, fertile, social relationships where the styles and experiences of disabled individuals are recognized and respected. The notion that each culture has made significant contributions to mankind should be highlighted by the school and integrated into the curriculum (Bennet, 1988; Bank, 1991; Obiakor, 1990).

CORRELATING SCHOOL ACTIVITIES

Upon entering school, children are regimented and required to follow specific school rules, which often conflicts with their styles and modes of learning. In many instances, the child and school conceive learning differently. The school is mostly concerned with verbal and written expressions and standardized tests results. Accordingly, many of these activities are strange to some disabled individuals and many have not developed sufficient background or skills to master them. Consequently, behavior problems frequently occur when different standards of behaviors are expected between the children's abilities and the expectations imposed by the school. If the school is to be successful in meeting the needs of children, especially disabled individuals, children must be given an active role in their own learning by structuring activities which are relevant and meaningful to them. Additionally, teachers must be free to experiment with various models of instruction (Taylor, 1992).

The role of the school should not be to fill disabled children with information, but to help them construct understanding about what they are doing. Disabled children's competence, their ability to make meaning from their environments to construct knowledge to form generalizations, to solve problems and to associate and transfer knowledge, is seldom encouraged by the school.

The concept that style requires a pedagogical response, especially at the point of applying special teaching strategies, appears to be a sound approach. It is widely believed that such an approach ought to be attempted and that when they are made, teaching and learning will be more successful. Student's cultural and learning styles appear to be inseparable, therefore, matching these styles with appropriate instruction appears to be a sound instructional strategy for disabled individuals.

LEARNING STYLES

Children receive and order information differently and through a variety of dimensions and channels. Mason and Egel (1995) implied that teachers frequently find it difficult to assess an individual's learning style preference. Making sense out of the world is a very real and active process. During early childhood, children master complex tasks according to their own schedules without formal training or intervention, the structured environment of the school appears to impede the personal learning styles of many disabled individuals are not exceptions.

There is no one common definition of learning styles, however, researchers have considered learning styles from four dimensions: cognitive, affective, physiological, and psychological.

Cognitive Dimension

The cognitive dimension of learning styles refers to the different ways that children mentally perceive and order information and ideas.

Affective Dimension

The affective dimension refers to how students' personality traits–both social and emotional–affect their learning. This dimension refers to how the student feels about himself/herself? What way can be found to build his/her self-esteem (Butler, 1988)? These research findings tend to indicate that learning styles are functions of both nature and nurture. Learning style development starts at a very early age.

Physiological Dimension

The physiological dimension of learning involves the interaction of the senses and the environment. There are several channels under the physiological dimension and they are: visual, auditory, tactile/kinesthetic, and a mixed combination of the five senses. The physiological dimension involves the senses and the environment. Does the student learn better through auditory, visual, or tactile/kinesthetic means? And how is he/she affected by such factors as light, temperature, and room design?

Psychological Dimension

The psychological dimension involves the student's inner strengths and individuality.

Research findings strongly suggests that the dominant qualities of a learner's style are unchangeable (Guild, 1994). Teachers can help learners be successful if they will recognize their own styles and use their strengths to teach toward their styles. A teacher that is aware of his/her own style that is most comfortable plus the style most comfortable for the learner can foster growth within the child. Flexibility in working in the context of many styles within the classroom can offer the teacher the opportunity to reach a variety of children with different learning styles. The benefits of the flexibility in teaching is immeasurable.

Finally, the issue of nature vs. nurture controversy has surfaced in the study of learning styles, unlike Meyers (1990), some researchers promote the impact or environment, others promote the impact of heredity, and many are neutral. There are advantages in using all approaches. The salient point is to keep the individual needs in mind as well as the modality favored.

Evaluating Learning Styles

Pupils learn through a variety of sensory channels and have individual patterns of sensory strengths and weaknesses. Teachers should capitalize on using the learning styles of pupils in their academic programs. Disabled individuals go through the same development sequence, however, due to developmental problems, some progress at a slower rate. Several aspects are recommended in considering factors characterizing a pupil's learning style:

1.   The speed at which a pupil learns. This is an important aspect to consider. A pupil's learning rate is not as obvious as it may appear. Frequently, a learner's characteristics interfere with his/her natural learning rate. Although the learning rate is more observable than other characteristics, it does not necessarily relate to the quality of a learner's performance. Therefore, it is of prime importance for the teacher to know as much as possible about all of a learner's characteristics.

2.   The techniques the pupil uses to organize materials he/she

plans to learn. Individuals organize materials they expect to learn information by remembering the broad ideas. These broad ideas trigger the details in the pupils memory. This method of proceeding from the general to the specific is referred as deductive style of organization. Application of this principle may be applied in many situations. Other pupils prefer to remember the smaller components which then remind them of the broader concept, an indicative style of organization. In utilizing inductive organization, the pupil may look at several items or objectives and form specific characteristics, develop general principles or concepts. Knowing a disabled individual's style of organization can assist the teacher to effectively guide the learning process by presenting materials as close as possible to his preferred style of organization (Mason & Egel, 1995).

3. The pupils need for reinforcement and structure in the learning situation. All learners need some structure and reinforcement to their learning, this process may be facilitated through a pupil's preferred channels of input and output.

4. Input involves using the five sensory channels-auditory, tactile, kinesthetic, olfactory and gustatory. These stimuli are transmitted to the brain. In the brain, the sensory stimuli are organized into cognitive patterns referred to as perception. The input channel through which the person readily processes stimuli is referred to as his preferred mode of modality.

5. Similar differences are also evident in output which may be expressed verbally or nonverbally. Verbal output uses the fine motor activity of the speech mechanism to express oral language. Nonverbal output uses both fine and gross motor activities. Fine motor skills may include gesture and demonstration. Pupils usually prefer to express themselves through one of these outputs.

6. A pupils preferred model of input is not necessarily his strongest acuity channel. Sometimes a pupil will transfer information received through one channel into another which he/she is more comfortable. This process is called internodal transfer. Pupils differ in their ability to perform the internodal transfer. Failure to perform this task effectively may impede learning.

The differences in learning styles and patterns of some pupils almost assures rewarding educational achievement for successful completion of tasks. This is, unfortunately, not true for many disabled individuals. The differences reflected in learning can cause interferences with the disabled individual's achievement. The educational environment of disabled individuals is a critical factor. The early identification, assessment and management of disabled individual's learning differences by the teacher can prevent more serious learning problems from occurring.

Some children are concrete learners while others are abstract learners, others focus on global aspects of the problem while others focus on specific points. Since schools traditionally give more weight to analytical approaches than to holistic approaches, the teacher who does not manifest analytical habits is at a decided disadvantage (Hilliard, 1989).

Assessment Techniques

Assessment is the pupils preferred mode of input and output may be conducted through formal and informal techniques. A commonly used instrument is "The Learning Channel Preference Checklist." This checklist is divided into three major sections as outlined.

The Learning Channel Preference Checklist

The learning channel preference checklist is designed for assessing learning styles. Teachers can administer this checklist and follow-up with interpretive discussions. Some modification and adaptation will be needed for disabled individuals depending upon their disabilities.

Students are asked to rank each statement as it relates to them. There are no right or wrong answers. Students rate each item often (3), sometimes (2), and never (1), on three broad categories: visual, auditory and haptic. The highest score indicated preferred learning style is the aforementioned categories.

AUDITORY LEARNING STYLE: This is the least developed learning channel for most children, including disabled individuals. Most children do not report this channel as their strongest, using the checklist.

VISUAL LEARNING STYLE: Many children learn best when they can see information. High scores in this area denotes that they prefer text-books over lectures and rely on lists, graphs, charts, pictures and notes and taking notes. Significantly, a higher number of children rate this area higher than the auditory channel.

HAPTIC LEARNING STYLE: This is the highest learning channel reported by children. In essence, most children prefer this style. Haptic students show a cluster of right-brained characteristics. They learn best from experimenting rather than from textbooks and reading textbooks.

The combined scores in the three areas usually range from 10 to 30. Usually two areas will be close. Scores in the high 20s indicate that the student has satisfactorily developed all three channels and is able to use the modality that best fit the task. Scores below 20 indicate that the student has not yet developed a strong learning channel preference.

Usually students scoring in the 20s have great difficulty with school because they do not have a clearly defined method for processing information. These students should be treated as haptic learners because the haptic style is much easier to develop than the others.

According to O'Brien (1989), the checklist is a diagnostic tool for the teacher and pupil. The checklist will indicate areas of strengths and weaknesses in sensory acuity. Teachers can then adapt or modify the instructional program to include activities to support the strongest modality. Information from the checklist should be shared with the student. O'Brien (1989) stated that, "All students benefit from knowing their learning styles, as well as how to use and manipulate them in the learning process."

Another well know instrument for assessing learning styles is the Myers-Briggs Type Indicator. Learning styles are assessed from basic perceptual and judging traits. The Swassing-Barbe Modality Index assesses auditory, visual, and tactile acuity by asking individuals to repeat patterns using the above modalities. Results also show differences in cognitive strengths, such as holistic and global learning in contrast to analytical, part to whole approacher (Guild, 1994).

These tests are culture and language specific. Individuals respond and interpret self-reporting instruments through their cultural experiences. These responses may be in conflict with established norms and yield conflicting results. Consequently, caution is needed when interpreting results, especially from disabled individuals.

THE RELATIONSHIP OF CULTURE TO LEARNING STYLE

Individuals from certain cultures have a preference for specific learning styles and this preference may effect classroom performance. Schools must also recognize that disabled students from diverse backgrounds have a favored learning style which may affect academic performance. When teachers fail to accommodate students' favored learning style in their instructional delivery, they may not meet their individuals needs (Guild, 1994).

Hilliard's (1989) point of view supported the above analysis. He indicated that the lack of matching cultural and learning styles in teaching younger students is the explanation for low performance of culturally different minority group students. He contended that children, no matter what their styles, are failing primarily because of systematic inequities in the delivery of whatever pedagogical approach the teachers claim to master–not because students cannot learn from teachers whose styles do not match their own.

Guild (1994) provided us with three cautions to observe when attempting to match learning styles with cultural styles:

1. Do students of the same culture have common learning styles? If so, how do we know it? What are the implications for instructional intervention and individual student learning. Care should be taken when matching learning and cultural styles; not to make generalizations about a particular group based upon culture and learning styles. An example would be to conclude that most disabled individuals have the same traits as the targeted group.
2. Caution should be taken in attempting to explain the achievement differences between disabled individuals and nondisabled individuals; this being especially true when academic differences are used to explain deficits.
3. There is come controversy between the relationship of learning and cultural styles due chiefly to philosophical beliefs and issues. Such issues and philosophical beliefs such as instructional equity versus educational equity and the major purpose of education, all combine to confuse the controversy. The relationship between learning style and culture may prove to be divisive, especially as related to students in elementary

and secondary schools. It may result in generalizations about culture and style and result in discrimination in treatment. It may be used as an excuse for student failure. There is also an implication that some styles are more valuable than others even though learning style should be neutral. Properly used, matching learning and cultural styles can be an effective tool for improving learning of disabled individuals.

THE RELATIONSHIP BETWEEN LEARNING AND INSTRUCTIONAL STYLES

There is some indication that teachers choose instructional styles closely approximating their learning preferences. The key to the learning/instructional style theory is that students will learn more effectively through the use of their preference in learning styles (Hilliard, 1989).

The matching of instructional style and learning style may also have implications for student achievement. The best way for schools to adapt to individual differences is to increase their effect by differentiated instructional techniques (Guild, 1994). According to Hilliard (1989), learning styles and instructional styles matching may not be the only factor in student achievement. The reason younger students do not learn may not be because students cannot learn from their instructors with styles that do not match their learning styles. Additionally, he articulated that there is not sufficient research or models to relate specific pedagogy to learning styles. He concluded by stating that a better perspective may be for teachers to provide more sensitivity to learning styles in the instructional programs until appropriate instructional models are developed.

Implications for Education

By keying teaching and assessment techniques to the diverse ways people think and learn, teachers will be surprised at how much smarter their students get. Traditionally, teachers teach and assess students in ways that benefit those with certain learning styles, but place many other children at a marked disadvantage.

Disabled individuals, as well as all individuals, favor a preferred style, however, they may vary their styles, depending upon the situation. Teachers should be flexible in their teaching and use a variety of styles to assure all students' needs are met. Teachers are generally best at instructing children who match their own style of learning. Consequently, the more students differ from the cultural, socioeconomic, or ethical values of the teacher, the more likely that the learning needs will not be met. Studies have shown that students receive higher grades and more favorable evaluations when their learning styles more closely match those of their teachers. Most students begin to experience success when they are permitted to pursue an interest in their preferred learning style.

SUMMARY

The preponderance of research on cultural and learning styles of disabled individuals, has demonstrated the value of matching these two styles in order to facilitate the learning process. There is widespread belief that this matching can facilitate classroom instruction and provide disabled individuals with the skills necessary to succeed in cultural, learning and teaching styles when applied to educating disabled individuals. However, there is little disagreement in the professional literature concerning the relationship between learning and cultural styles and their impact on academic and social success in school.

Research, conducted over the last decade, has revealed certain learning patterns characteristic of certain disabled and diverse groups (Hilliard, 1989; Shade, 1989; Vasques, 1991; Bert & Bert, 1992; Hyun, Jinhee & Fowler, 1995). Some cultural groups emphasize unique patterns and relationships. The implications for instructional intervention for these individuals should be self-evidence.

As indicated earlier, there is no universal agreement relevant to the application of cultural and learning styles to instruction. Some advocate the the application of cultural and learning styles to the instructional process will enable educators to be more sensitive toward cultural differences. Others maintain that to pinpoint cultural values will lead to stereotyping (Guild, 1994). Another controversy revolves around what extent does culture and learning affect achievement. Research findings have consistently shown that there are serious inequities when the school does not value or accept certain cultural values. Others studies have shown that by incorporating cultural and learning styles in the learning process will not significantly increase achievement, unless inequities in delivery/instructional procedures are improved (Hilliard, 1989; Bennett, 1986, 1988).

A third controversy centers around how teachers operating from their own cultural and learning styles can successfully teach diverse and disabled populations. Most of the research show that the day to day rapport, caring teachers who provide opportunities for children to learn are more valuable than matching teaching and learning styles (Taylor, 1992; Guild, 1994).

The major issue at hand in this controversy is not whether learning and cultural styles should be incorporated in the instructional plan for the disabled individuals, but whether using cultural and learning styles information will assist teachers in recognizing diversity and improve delivery of educational services for them.

REFERENCES

Bank, J. A. (1991). Multicultural education: For freedom's sake. *Educational Leadership, 49*, 22-35.

Bennett, C. (1986). Comprehensive multicultural education. *Theory and Practice.* Boston, MA: Allyn & Bacon.

Bennett, C. (1988). Assessing teachers' abilities for educating multicultural students: The need for conceptual models in teacher education. In C. Heid (Ed.) *Multicultural Education: Knowledge and Perceptions.* Indianapolis: Indiana University Center for Urban Education.

Bert, C. R., & Bert, M. (1992). The Native American: An exceptionality in education and counseling. ERIC. 351168.

Butler, K. (1988). How kids learn: What theorists say. *Learning Styles,* 30-34

Guild, P. (1994). The cultural learning style connection. *Educational Leadership, 51,* 16-21.

Hilliard, A. G. (1989). Teachers and culture styles in a pluralistic society. *NEA Today, 7,* 65-69.

Hyun, K. K., & Fowler, S. A. (1995). Respect cultural sensitivity and communication. *Teaching Exceptional Children, 28,* 25-28.

Obiakor, F. E. (1990). Development of self-concept: Impact on student's learning. *The Journal of the Southeastern Association of Educational Opportunity Program Personnel, 9,* 16-23.

Obiakor, F. E. (1992). Self-concept of African-American students: An operational model for special education. *Exceptional Children, 59*, 160-167.

O'Brien, L. (1989). Learning styles: Make the student aware. *NASSP Bulletin.* October, 85-89.

Mason, S., & Egel, A. L. (1995). What does Amy like? Using a mini-reinforcer in instructional activities. *Teaching Exceptional Children, 28*, 42-45.

Meyers, I. B. (1990). *Gifts Differing* (2nd ed.). Palo Alto, CA: Consulting Psychologists Press.

Shade, B. J. (1989). The influence of perceptual development on cognitive styles: Cross ethnic comparison. *Early Child Development and Care, 51*, 137-155.

Taylor, G. (1992). Impact of social learning theory on educating deprived/minority children. *Clearinghouse for Teacher Education.* ERIC. 349260.

Vasques, J. A. (1991). *Cognitive Style and Academic Achievement in Cultural Diversity and the Schools: Consensus and Controversy.* Edited by J. Lynch, C. Modgil and S. Modgil. London: Falconer Press

Chapter 5

APPLICATION OF SOCIAL LEARNING THEORIES TO SOCIAL SITUATIONS

GEORGE R. TAYLOR

The major emphasis of social learning theories is primarily on environmental learner interaction. The learning of behaviors that are socially accepted, as well as learning ones that are not, is social learning. This view is supported by Stuart (1989). He maintained that social learning theories attempt to describe the process by which we come to know what behaviors should or should not be projected when we are in different types of social situations. The theories themselves are learning theories that have been applied to social situations. These theories have been generally behavioristic rather than cognitive (Bandura, 1970). These theories do not separate the parts from the whole; instead, they have as a major underlying concept the holistic and interactive nature of development. Various areas of development of the self do not exist separately from one another, and that movement toward maturity in one area can affect movement and learning in another area. Social learning theories also address individual differences and how such factors as personality temperament and sociological influences may interact with the developmental process.

They assist us in identifying how different individuals may manage, delay, progress through, or retreat from developmental tasks. These theories also suggest that there are persistent individual differences such as cognitive style, temperament, or ethnic background which interact with development. Additionally, these theories are a source of knowledge about individual types and styles that may be critical to our understanding of differing sources or reward and punishment for students. Vzgotsky's theory gives support to the interrelationship of natural properties with psychological and social development.

Vzgotsky's Theory

Vzgotsky's theory, according to Moll (1991), lends support to the concept that natural properties as well as social relations and constraints make possible the social construction of a child's higher psychological processes. Three major components of Vzgotsky's theory were overviewed: (1) the internalization of culture means; (2) the interpersonal, or social process of mediation; (3) a child's knowledge is formed within the zone of proximal developmental cognitive space defined by social relational boundaries.

One of the major postulates of Vzgotsky's theory, according to Moll (1991), is that there is a functional relationship between the affects of the culture on cognitive development and biological growth. The physical, biological, and neurological determinants are more readily understood and generally agreed upon. However, the impact of the cultural determinants are not as easily understood. The cultural determinants include social processes which transforms naturally through the mastery and use of cultural signs. In essence, the natural development of children's behavior form the biological conditions necessary to develop higher psychological processes; on the other hand, culture provides the conditions by which the higher psychological processes may be realized.

Commonality Among Theories

The common threads uniting these theories and concepts are imitation, modeling, and copying behaviors (Bandura & Walters, 1963). Disabled individuals, as all individuals, imitate, model and copy behaviors directly from their environments. These models and techniques are recently inappropriate and create conflict and tension between children, society and the school. Learning, culture, and behavioral styles of disabled individuals should be, as much as possible, incorporated and integrated into a total learning packet. Social learning theories provide a concrete framework for society and the school to begin to implement additional social skills strategies into the curriculum for disabled individuals.

Social skills is a term used to describe a wide range of behaviors varying in complexity and is thought to be necessary for effective social functioning and academic success. Behaviors which constitute social skill developments may vary depending upon the situation, role, sex, age, and disabling conditions of disabled individuals.

IMPLICATIONS FOR THE DISABLED

Research is congruent in the fact that observational learning offers an important vehicle in teaching disabled youth and adults (Kazdin, 1980). According to Charles (1985), special education was the first segment of public education to recognize the power of Bandura's work. Modeling, when used in conjunction with behavior modification, produced results that surpassed those of any previous technique. The early evidence summarized by Bandura & Walters (1963) indicated that children with a history of failure, and institutionalized children, are all more prone than other children to social influence. Thus, special educators have applied modeling procedures to teach new behaviors, to increase behaviors and to reduce or eliminate undesirable behaviors. Zaragoza, Vaughn & McIntosh (1991) reviewed twenty-seven studies that examined social skills intervention for children with behavioral problems. The most frequently used intervention was one or more of coaching, modeling, rehearsal, feedback or reinforcement. Twenty-six of the twenty-seven studies reported some type of improvement in the social behaviors. The results of this research yielded positive changes in the self, teacher, and parental perceptions.

Application of Modeling Techniques

Charles (1985) believed that the powers of modeling are even more notable in the regular classroom. Modeling, Charles contended, is their most effective method of teaching many of the objectives in the three domains of learning: psychomotor, cognitive, and affective.

Bandura expanded the concept of modeling to include symbolic modeling (Bandura, 1971). Bandura concluded that images of reality are shaped by what we see and hear rather than by our own direct experiences. We have images of reality that we have never experienced personally. A theory of psychology should, thus, be in step with social reality.

During the years that followed, Bandura (1989) identified internal processes that underlie modeling. These processes are referred to as self-efficacy (self-efficacy has been alluded to earlier in the chapter). Bandura (1995) identifies information abilities as mediating links between stimulus and response. Observers function as active agents who transform, classify, and organize meaningful stimuli.

Aggression

Aggression is defined as behavior that results in personal injury and in destruction of property (Bandura, 1976). In reference to the theories of aggression, Bandura's first position, one in which he remained, was that the instinct theories did not explain how children from high risk environments develop pro-social styles. Conversely, they did not explain how children from advantaged backgrounds and disabled individuals develop serious antisocial patterns of behavior. The drive-reduction theorists view was that aggression had cathartic effects. Conditions that were likely to be frustrating to the child, heightened the drive level, thereby leading to aggression. This is especially true for many disabled individuals. Once the aggressive drive was reduced, the belief was that the likelihood of participation in aggressive behavior was abated (Eron, 1987; Evans, 1989; Bandura, 1971). According to Bandura, a complete theory of aggression must explain how aggression develops, what provokes aggression, and what maintains aggressive acts. He points that individuals can acquire aggressive styles of conduct either by observing aggressive models or through direct combat experience-individuals are not born with repertories of aggressive behavior. Contrary to existing theories, Bandura's research showed that frustration could produce any variety of reactions and one does not need frustration to become aggressive. Moreover, he demonstrated that exposure to aggressive models tended to increase aggression (Evans, 1989). These findings have significant implication for reducing aggressive behaviors in disabled individuals. Social forces determine the form that aggression takes where and when it will be expressed and who is selected as targets (Bandura, 1996).

The different forms of aggressive elicitors are delineated to include modeling influences, aversive treatment, anticipated positive consequences, instructional control and delusional control (Bandura,

1976). Geen (1994) regarded aggression as a reactive behavior. In search of a common element among the stressors within the environment that elicits aggression, he concludes a common trait is that they all produce a negative effect.

The third major feature concerns with the conditions that sustain aggressive behavior. Bandura (1973) proposed that behavior is controlled by its consequences. Therefore, aggression can be induced, However, social learning theory distinguishes the three forms of reinforcement that must be considered. These include direct internal reinforcement, vicarious or observed reinforcement and self-reinforcement.

Anger and Hostility

The aforementioned studies have consistently shown that negative behaviors, such as anger and hostility, are learned behaviors which children imitate from their environments. These behaviors manifest themselves in hostile and destructive patterns of behavior, which frequently cannot be controlled by the schools, thus creating conflict and tension between children, parents, and the schools (Matsueda, 1987).

Expressing anger and hostility constructively requires a great deal of inner control. Internal awareness of anger must first be recognized. If one is not aware of anger, it cannot be controlled. When anger is repressed or ignored, it will surface later and add to one's frustration. Usually by this time, anger will be expressed in aggressive behaviors such as attempts to harm someone, destroy something, insults, and hostile statements and actions. Aggressive behaviors manifest themselves in ways which infringe upon the rights of others.

Controlling anger and managing feelings are essential in developing appropriate interpersonal skills. Disabled individuals should be taught how to control anger through application of the following:

1.   Recognizing and describing anger.
2.   Finding appropriate ways of expressing anger.
3.   Analyzing and understanding factors responsible for anger.
4.   Managing anger by looking at events differently or talking oneself out of anger.

5. Learning how to repress feelings.
6. Expressing anger constructively.
7. Experimenting with various and alternative ways of expressing anger.

Teachers may employ a variety of strategies to assist pupils in controlling or reducing anger. Role playing, creative dramatics, physical activities, time out, relaxation therapy, writing and talking out feelings, assertive behavioral techniques, managing provocations, and resolving interpersonal conflicts through cooperative approaches are, to name a few, strategies and techniques that teachers may employ.

SOCIAL SKILLS TEACHING STRATEGIES

Teaching Apology Strategies

Apologies can restore relationships, heal humiliations, and generate forgiveness, if taught appropriately. It is a powerful social skill which generally is not considered to be important by the school. It may be concluded that the school considers this skill to be a function of the home. As reflected throughout this book, the school must assume the leadership in teaching all social skills. This approach is especially true for a significant number of disabled individuals.

Like all social skills, appropriate ways to apologize must be taught, otherwise, they can strain relationships, create grudges and instill bitter vengeances. Apologies are a show of strength because not only restore the self-concepts of those offended, but make us more sensitive to the feelings and needs of others. Specific strategies have been outlined and developed to assist educators in teaching appropriate ways that disabled individuals can apologize without diminishing their "egos."

Specific strategies have been outlined for teaching most of the social skills to disabled individuals in Chapter 8. The examples of anger and hostility and the teaching of apology and other social skills strategies have been observed and associated with many of the poor social skills shown by some disabled individuals. These skills appear to interface, interact, and are associated with many poor social skills.

Teaching Self-Regulation Skills

Instructional programs must be developed and designed to enable disabled individuals to gain knowledge about appropriate interpersonal skills and to employ this newly acquired knowledge in solving their social problems. In order for this goal to be accomplished, they must be taught effective ways of internalizing their behaviors and assessing how their behaviors affect others. Helping disabled individuals develop self-regulation skills appears to be an excellent technique for bringing behaviors to the conscious level where they can be controlled. Some of the more commonly used self-regulation skills are summarized.

Be Aware Of One's Thinking Patterns

Provide "think-aloud" activities and model behaviors to reflect solving problems by working through tasks and asking questions such as: (1) What is needed to solve the problem? (2) Things are not working out, should I try another way? (3) What assistance do I need to solve the problem? As the teacher performs these think-aloud activities, he/she may ask for input from the student observance relevant to the type of self-regulation skills being demonstrated. Those skills may have to be modeled and demonstrated several times. Provide opportunities for the disabled individuals to demonstrate them individually and in cooperative groups, as well as evaluate the effectiveness of their actions.

Making A Plan

Have disabled individuals to identify specific examples where self-regulation is useful. Motivation may come from a story, file, tape, or creative dramatic activities. Instruct them to develop a plan to reduce, correct, or eliminate the undesired behaviors. As they demonstrate he behaviors, the teacher should reinforce and praise them.

Develop and Evaluate Long-Term Goals

Employ self-regulation strategies to assist disabled individuals in accomplishing long-term goals. Have them to identify social and behavioral goals. Record the goals and assist them in making a plan as outlined previously. Provide a scheduled time to meet with them to determine how well the goals are being achieved. In some instances, the goals will need to be modified or adapted in order to focus on specific behaviors. Self-regulation strategies make actions more controllable by making one aware of his/her own behavior. Once awareness is achieved, the plan outlined earlier may be taught to bring behaviors under control. These strategies frequently will need to be adapted and modified to meet the uniqueness of the class. A variety of techniques and strategies may be used to aid the teacher in developing the skills of self-regulation: (1) role playing activities; (2) classifying behaviors and identifying types of self-regulation strategies to employ; (3) working in cooperative groups; (4) positively reinforce the mental habits; (5) reading and developing stories; (6) being sensitive to feedback and criticism; (7) teaching self-monitoring skills; (8) seeking outside advice when needed; and (9) evaluating progress made.

Self-regulation strategies are one of several strategies which may be used to teach appropriate social skills to disabled individuals. Appropriate social skills are essential for developing personal relationships and accepting the roles of authority figures. Social behaviors are learned, therefore, they can be changed and modified with appropriate intervention. They require that an individual evaluate the situation, choose the appropriate social skills, and perform the social tasks appropriately (Katz, 1991). Unfortunately, many disabled individuals have not been exposed to appropriate social models or do not possess enough prerequisite skills, such as maturity and self-control, to successfully perform the social skills. Development of social skills requires that disabled individuals have appropriate models to copy and imitate, to recognize nonverbal clues and to adjust their behaviors accordingly.

Matsueda's (1987) research supports the findings of Katz (1991); they indicated that negative behaviors are learned behaviors which children imitate from their environments. The schools view these behaviors as hostile and destructive and respond to children in a negative fashion, thus creating conflict and tension between schools and children.

Several researchers, (Hilliard, 1989; Biklen, 1989; Taylor, 1992; Hatch, 1992; Forest, 1990; Collins, 1992; Kagan, 1989; Johnson,

1990) have directly or indirectly implied that social skills must be taught and integrated into the curriculum and assume a position of primacy along with the basic three R's.

Findings from other studies support the aforementioned research by concluding that many disabled individuals may have developed or adapted alternative ways and styles of coping with problems within their communities. These behavioral styles are frequently in conflict with the school and society in general and may be viewed as negative or destructive. Behavioral styles and models copied and imitated by many disabled individuals may serve them well in their environments but are frequently viewed as dysfunctional by the school (Taylor, 1992).

INTEGRATIVE ASPECTS OF SOCIAL SKILLS DEVELOPMENT

As indicated throughout this test, one of the major reasons that disabled individuals' behaviors are frequently rejected by the school and social institutions may be attributed to the failure of them to display appropriate social skills needed for different social inter-actions. The types of role models to which they have been exposed to, do not frequently provide them with the appropriate behaviors to copy or transfer to other social functions in our society.

Various types of social skills instruction must be developed and systematically taught to disabled individuals. The earlier the inter-vention, the sooner negative behaviors can be addressed, eradicated, or reduced. Both the home and the school should play dominant roles in developing pro-social skills for disabled individuals (Oswald, 1992; Walker, 1992).

The school may be the most appropriate agency along with parental input, to conduct the social skills training or intervention. Teaching students pro-social skills necessary to cope with the social demands of society creates a climate in which positive relationships can exist and empower students to direct their own successes. A safe, supportive environment tends to facilitate learning. Pro-social skills taught and practiced daily in a nurturing environment assist in reducing negative behavior and in promoting positive ones.

Social skills of individuals are developed through interactions with family, school and community. Social skills are shaped by reinforcement received as a result of interaction with the environment. Often, children do not learn effectively from past experiences. Frequently, they are enabled to transfer one social reaction to another socially acceptable situation; thus their behaviors are frequently interpreted as immature, inept or intrusive. This negative feedback prohibits future social interactions. This is especially true for disabled individuals.

Research findings suggest that a significant relationship exists between social skills intervention and academic achievement. Many social skill procedures, such as attending and positive interaction techniques, have been shown to increase academic performance. Oswald (1992) wrote that social skills interventions appear to work best when they correspond to actual social interactions in the naturalistic environment. Similar findings by Walker (1992) indicated that the probability of individuals failing and not adjusting to school and peer acceptance are significant. He further articulated that some individuals do not have sufficient social skills to be successful in school. Finally, he voiced that there is an urgent need for social skills training which should be integrated into the curriculum.

Disabled individuals are faced with double challenges; lack of appropriate social training may not permit many of them to engage productively in many social events. Special techniques and interventions related to remediating poor or inappropriate skills must be addressed early in their school experiences in order to bring their social skills up to acceptable school standards. According to Taylor (1992), early intervention is needed to expose disabled individuals to appropriate social models.

Many individual cultural experiences have not provided them with appropriate social skills to be successful in the larger community or cope with appropriate social behavior. The same principle applies to disabled individuals. Changing inappropriate social behavior involves infusing principles of social learning theories, such as modeling, imitation and behavioral techniques, with social skills instruction. Once social skills deficits have been identified, the aforementioned social learning principles may be used to reinforce or reward appropriate social behavior.

SOCIAL SKILLS MODELS OF DISABLED INDIVIDUALS

Research findings have clearly demonstrated that diverse groups of children, such as disabled individuals, are at risk for developing appropriate interpersonal skills (Achenback & Zigler, 1968; Coleman, 1986; Cummings & Rodda, 1989: Kauffman, 1993). Social skills deficiencies are commonly observed in this population. Several factors may attribute to these deficiencies such as child-rearing practices, deprived cultural environments, and lack of understanding the social expectations or rules. These deficiencies may lead to demonstrating inappropriate or inadequate social behaviors.

Social skills are learned throughout a lifetime from imitating or modeling both negative and positive behaviors. Consequently, many disabled individuals lack basic interpersonal skills. These individuals are frequently at a disadvantage in society. Some disabled individuals tend to feel inadequate and use unproductive, inadequate and socially unacceptable ways of relating and communicating with others.

Many disabled individuals may have developed or adapted alternative ways and styles of coping with problems. These behavioral styles are frequently in conflict with the school and society in general and may be viewed as negative or destructive. Behavioral styles and models copied and imitated by disabled individuals may serve them well in their environments, but are frequently viewed as dysfunctional by the school and society (Carrol, 1993; Damon, 1977).

The ability of many disabled individuals to function satisfactorily in social groups and to maintain dispositions, habits, and attitudes customarily associated with character and personality, is usually below expected levels set by the school. They are more likely than other children to be rejected by their peers; have fewer, less rigid controls over their impulses; have learned hostile and destructive patterns of behavior, and often seem unable to respond to traditional classroom instruction. As with all children, disabled individuals imitate behavioral techniques from their environments (Taylor, 1992; Ashton & Webb, 1989).

The importance and values of interpersonal skills instruction has been minimized in the schools. Mastering of these skills requires training and practice in order for children to interact appropriately with others. Interpersonal skills allow children to take appropriate social behaviors, understand individuals' responses to the behaviors, and respond appropriately to them. Lack of this development may lead to feelings of rejection and isolation in a classroom setting. There is also ample evidence to suggest that children's social difficulties may emanate from vastly different deficit areas. These deficit areas must be identified and remediated during the early years. Schools must design direct and immediate intervention programs that will permit disabled individuals to experience success (Brody & Stoneman, 1977; Oswald, 1992; Ayers, 1989).

SUMMARY

Social learning theories offer the school a common context through which environment, developmental sequence, and early experiences of disabled individuals' development can be understood and researched. These theories enable educators to better understand how disabled individuals think, how they feel about themselves, and how to become aware of factors in the environment precipitating cognitive and affective problems which may have some bearing on academic performance. The relationship between social learning theories and the academic performance of disabled individuals are not well-established. Most research reported today simply indicate that there is a causal relationship. There is a dire need to conduct empirical studies to determine to what degree social learning theories impact on the academic performance of these children.

Social learning theories appear to be an appropriate approach for integration skills for disabled individuals. These theories provide teachers with a common language by which they can communicate about the effects of social learning theories on academic performance.

The study of social learning theories enables the school to better understand both how disabled individuals think about school-related processes and how they are likely to be feeling about themselves in relation to these processes. The school's understanding of both the cognitive and the affective characteristics of disabled individuals may be termed as "empathic." One way of showing empathy to children is through designing effective classroom environments that considers the cognitive and affect levels of the children.

Social development is a major area in which many disabled individuals need assistance. They frequently have developed inappropriate interpersonal skills which are not accepted by the school. Inability to conform to expected social standards may result in unacceptable social skills which are essential for developing personal relationships and accepting the role of authority figures (Taylor, 1992). Research findings by Hilliard (1989), Butler (1989), and Johnson (1990) support the notion that the culture plays a dominant role in shaping behavior. Children model and imitate behaviors from their environments. Innovative ways must be found by the schools to provide appropriate role models for disabled individuals to imitate and copy.

REFERENCES

Achenback, T. & Zigler, E. (1968). Cue-learning and problem learning strategies in normal and retarded children. *Child Development, 39,* 827-848.

Ashton, P.T. & Webb, R.B. (1986). Making a difference: Teachers' sense of efficacy and student achievement. White Plains, NY: Longman.

Ayers, William (1989). Childhood at risk. *Educational Leadership, 46,* 70-72.

Bandura, A. (1995). *Self-Efficacy in Changing Societies.* Cambridge: University Press.

Bandura, A. (1989). Human agency in social cognitive theory. *American Psychologist, 44,* 1175-1184.

Bandura, A. (1976). Social learning analysis of aggression. In E. Ribes-Inesta & A. Bandura (Eds.), *Analysis of Delinquency and Aggression.* Hillsdale, NJ: Halsted Press.

Bandura, A. (1971). Psychotherapy based upon modeling principles. In A.E. Bergin & S.L. Garfield (Eds.). *Handbook of Psychotherapy and Behavior Change.* Englewood Cliffs, NJ: Prentice Hall.

Bandura, A. (1970). *A Social Learning Theory.* Englewood Cliffs, NJ: Prentice Hall.

Bandura, A., Ross, D., & Ross, S.A. (1961). Transmission of aggression through imitation of aggressive models. *Journal of Abnormal and Social Psychology, 63,* 575-582.

Bilken, D. (1989). Making Differences Ordinary. In W. Stainback, & M. Forest (Eds.). *Educating All Children in the Mainstream of Regular Education.* Baltimore: Paul H. Brookes.

Brody, G., & Stoneman, Z. (1977). Social Competencies in the Developmental Disabled: Some suggestions for research and training. *Mental Retardation, 15,* 41-43.

Carrol, J. (1993). Self-efficacy related to transfer of learning and theory-based instructional design. *Journal of Adult Education, 22,* 37-43.

Charles, C.M. (1985). *Building Classroom Discipline.* New York: Longman.

Coleman, M. (1986). *Behavior Disorders: Theory and Practice.* Englewood Cliffs: Prentice Hall.

Collins, T.W. & Hatch, J.A. (1992). Supporting the Social-Emotional Growth of Young Children. *Dimensions of Early Childhood, 21,* 17-21.

Cummings, C., & Rodda, A. (1989). Advocacy, prejudice, and role modeling in the deaf community. *Journal of Social Psychology, 129,* 5-12.

Damon, W. (1977). The Social World of the Child. San Francisco: Jossey Bass.

Eron, L. (1987). The development of aggressive behavior from the perspective of a developing behaviorism. *American Psychologist, 42,* 435-442.

Evans, R. (1989). Albert Bandura: *The Man and His Ideas–A Dialogue.* New York: Praeger.

Forest, M. (1990). Maps and Cities. Presentation at Peak Parent Center Workshop. Colorado Springs.

Hatch, T., & Gardner, H. (1988). How kids learn: What scientists say: New research on intelligence. *Learning, 37.*

Hilliard, Asa G. (1989). Teachers and cultural styles in a pluralistic society. *NEA Today, 7,* 65-69.

Johnson, W,. & Johnson, R. (1990). Social skills for successful group work. *Educational Leadership, 47,* 29-33.

Kagan, S.L. (1989). Early care and education: Beyond the school house doors. *Phi Delta Kappan,* 107-112.

Katz, L.G. (1991). The teacher's role in social development of young children. ED Clearinghouse on Elementary and Early Childhood Education. ERIC 331642.

Kauffman, J. (1993). Characteristics of emotional and behavioral disorders of children and youth. New York: Merrill.

Kazdin, A. (1980). Behavior modification in applied settings. Homewood, IL: Dorsey.

Matsueda, R.L. & Heimer, K. (Dec.1987). Race, family structure, and delinquency: A test differential association and social control theories. *American Sociological Review, 52,* 826-840.

Moll, I. (1991). The material and the social in Vzygotsky's *Theory of Cognitive Development.* Clearinghouse on Teacher Education. ED 352186.

Oswald, D. P., & Sinah-Nirbay, N. (1992). Current Research on Social Behavior Modification, 16, 443-447.

Stuart, R. B. (1989). Social Learning Theory: A vanishing or expanding presence? *Psychology: A Journal of Human Behavior, 26,* 35-50.

Taylor, G. (1992). Impact of Social Learning Theory on Educating Deprived Minority Children. Clearinghouse on Teacher Education, ERIC. 349260.

Walker, H.; Irvin, M, Larry, K., Noell, J., & George, H.S. (1992). A construct score approach to the assessment of social competence. *Behavior Modification, 16,* 449-452.

Zaragoza, N., Vaughn, S. & McIntosh, R. (1991). Social skill intervention and children with behavior problems: a review. *Behavioral Disorders, 16,* 260-275.

Chapter 6

PRACTICAL APPLICATION OF SOCIAL LEARNING THEORIES TO EDUCATING DISABLED INDIVIDUALS

GEORGE R. TAYLOR & THADDAUS PHILLIPS

INTRODUCTION

S ocial learning theories offer the school a common context through which environment, development sequence, and early experiences of disabled individuals' development can be understood and researched (Brody, 1977). These theories enable educators to better understand how these individuals think and feel about themselves, and to become aware of factors in the environment precipitating social affective problems.

A perusal of research, relevant to the application of learning theories to teaching disabled individuals appears to be in agreement. The importance of teaching social skills to disabled individuals has been well-documented (Goldstein & Wickstrom, 1986; Gresham, 1993). Storey, (1992) conducted a follow-up study of pre-schoolers with developmental delays and low levels of social interaction. The students were followed up for one year. A peer-mediated social skills program was developed. Pupils showed positive interaction skills with peers after a year of intervention. Anita (1993) stressed the importance of improving social interaction of disabled individuals with their nondisabled peers. Social interaction is a prime element in promoting appropriate social skills (McEvoy, 1992).

TYPES OF SOCIAL SKILL DEFICITS

There are four major types of social skills deficits. They are as follows: (1) Skill deficits, (2) Inadequate skill performance, (3) Performance deficits and (4) Self-control deficits:

1.   Skill deficits occur when individuals simply do not know how to perform the social skill in question.

2.   Inadequate skill performance implies that the individual has partly performed the social skill but due to lack of understanding, does not complete the skill. An example may be when an individual is blamed for an act he/she did not commit. Initially, the individual would say he/she did not commit the act. However, when that other individual keeps insisting that he/she committed the act, the accused individual may resort to aggressive behavior, rather than using negotiation strategies.

3.   Performance deficits indicate that the individual knows how to perform the task, but due to physical or other problems does not complete the task.

4.   Self-control deficits include a variety of behaviors in which the individual cannot control his/her behavior. A multitude of problems may be associated with this deficit. Frequently, individuals have to be taught how to control their behaviors. Specific techniques have been summarized in Chapter 4.

EFFECTS OF SOCIAL SKILLS DEFICITS

An increasing number of disabled individuals are failing to succeed in school because of their inadequate social skills as well as their low rating of social acceptance by peers. It has been suggested that not only do social skills deficits interfere with success to the peer group and educational mainstream, they also are predictive of long term maladaptive behavior patterns including delinquency, dropping out of school, job instability, social rejection and mental health problems (Vaugh, Hogan, Kouzekanani and Shapiro, 1990). Social skills deficits place students at risk for failure in the educational and cultural mainstream. The acquisition of social communication skills is extremely important for disabled individuals, primarily because social communication skills are the foundation of interpersonal competence. The inclusion of social skills training in curriculum and specific lesson plan design, provides the classroom teacher with the opportunity to effectively address social skills deficits.

Social skills training should be an important place in curricula for disabled individuals. Research has indicated that social skills training promote acquisition of socially appropriate behaviors (McIntosh, Vaugh, Zaragoza, & Hogan, 1990). However, there is little evidence that suggests instruction directed at improving students' social competence works over time and across settings (Vaugh, McIntosh & Hogan, 1990). Several reasons for this generalization are presented. First, social interaction is reciprocal; it involves social exchange among individuals, training that involves interaction among disabled individuals in the absence of socially competent nondisabled peers as models. Training must take place in settings where disabled individuals interact with their normal peers in order for newly acquired skills to be generalized and maintained. Second, exposure to adequate peer models are insufficient, due to the organizational structure of many special classes. Inclusion could provide an opportunity for many disabled individuals to be exposed to appropriate social models from their disabled peers. Social training and reinforcement must occur in settings in which these individuals interact naturally with their peers. Third, disabled individuals must be taught to exhibit behaviors that will be reinforced naturally by peers. It is important to select target behaviors that are adaptive and desirable, contribute to the development of social competence, and prompt peer responses that are likely to be reinforcing.

McIntosh, Vaugh & Bennerson (1995) outlined two innovative strategies for social skill training.[1] The first strategy discussed was the "Fast Strategy." This is a four-part mnemonic strategy designed to aid in interpersonal problem-solving. The strategy is interpreted as:

F = Freeze and Think
A = Alternatives
S = Solution
T = Try It

---

[1]   Refer to McIntosh, Ruth, Vaugh, Sharon, & Bennerson (1995). Fast Social Skills with a Slam and a Rap: Providing Social Skills Training for Students with Learning Disabilities.

The strategy assists students in developing questioning and monitoring skills, generates realistic and functional solutions, selects a plan to solve the problem, and implements the plan. Students are exposed to a variety of skills training activities, such as modeling, role playing, group and individual activities designed to improve social and interpersonal skills. Opportunity is provided for children to practice the skill. Proficiency students may become "social skill trainers" and teach the strategy to the class under the supervision of the teacher.

Many disabled individuals have not learned to accept negative remarks without acting aggressively. Vaugh, McIntosh & Spencer-Rowe (1991) developed a new strategy "SLAM" to assist students in accepting negative criticisms and remarks.

Two strategies were combined. Activities are similar to those advocated in the fast strategy. The "SLAM strategy" is translated to the following:

S = Stop
L = Look
A = Ask
M = Make

Specific activities have been developed for children to demonstrate and model the strategy. Children practice in small groups and present the strategy to the class.

The lack of necessary social skills training, inappropriate behavioral activity, and poor interpersonal relationship problems are combined to reflect deficits in social skills for many disabled individuals.

Research has also shown a positive relationship between certain social skills and school achievement of disabled individuals. Acts of social communication such as initiating contact about work assignments, asking and answering questions, and engaging in academic-related discussions are experiences needed (Taylor, 1992). Teachers tend to place less value on these social communication skills, thus few opportunities for development of social communication are likely to be provided in classrooms for disabled individuals (Katz, 1991). These findings suggest that social communication problems are not being adequately taught to these individuals in the schools. Systematic assessment procedures are needed to aid the teacher in employing appropriate intervention strategies (Brody, 1977; Brookes & Collins, 1992).

ASSESSING SOCIAL SKILLS DEFICITS

Several tests are available for assessing social skills of disabled individuals. These tests measure all aspects of social behaviors and may be classified as formal or informal. Many of the tests are designed for different populations and will have to be modified for use with disabled individuals.

There are several types of instruments which may be used to assess social skills. Teacher-made tests are commonly used. There are several testing formats for teacher-made tests. They include checklists, observation schedules, rating scales, interviews, direct observations, role play assessment, tests of social competence, and a variety of assessment inventories (Pike & Salend, 1995). These tests cover the gamut of social behaviors and may be teacher or commercially made. Examples of assessment inventories appear in Appendices B and C.

McClelland (1992) stresses the importance of assessing children's social skills during the early years using both formal and informal techniques. With some modifications, these techniques may be adapted for disabled individuals. One of the techniques discussed is the "Social Attributes Checklist." Areas covered in the checklist include 8 individual, 14 social skills, and 2 peer relationship attributes. Results from the checklist will pinpoint areas of social development in the above attributes which should be addressed.

Anecdotal records may be used in obtaining data about disabled individuals. These records provide an opportunity to study a pupil's behavior over a period of time as well as providing information that is essential in planning instructional programs. Additionally, anecdotal records provide a means of understanding the dynamics of the learner over a period of time (Rhodes & Nathenson-Mejia, 1992; Alberto & Troutman, 1990).

Self-Evaluations

Self-evaluations may take several forms. Students may evaluate themselves, teachers may interview the students, students may complete questionnaires or checklists. Many disabled individuals might not have the necessary skills to complete a self-evaluation. Teachers may have to assist them in completing the instrument. In some instances, opportunities should be provided for individuals to practice the technique. Self-evaluations can yield valuable information concerning strengths and weaknesses of children in several areas, including social skills and interpersonal development. Results should be discussed with disabled individuals and a plan developed by both teacher and pupil to reduce, emanate or correct the social skill deficit. Periodical evaluations should be made and progress recorded.

Portfolio Assessment

Portfolio assessment is used to document work in several areas as well as to judge the effectiveness of learning. While portfolios assessment can be used with all subject areas for disabled individuals, they appear to be very useful for summarizing and documenting social skills development. Social skill development may not be adequately measured by traditional testing methods. Portfolio assessment permits the teacher to collect social behaviors on a regular basis and to compare the achievement of children on a regular basis. Salinger (1991) suggested that teachers review with pupils on a regular basis information which should be included in portfolios and assist them in selecting work to be included.

The Pediatric Evaluation of Disabilities Inventory

The Pediatric Evaluation of Disabilities Inventory is a measure of functional skills in the social function domain. It is a checklist type larger sample of parents of young children. A major component of the study was to interview these parents, to determine the amount of assistance they provided their children for each skill on the checklist. Analysis of the checklist showed that disabled individuals who were successful, received at least, minimal assistance or supervision from their parents. Results of this study clearly showed the value and importance of involving parent in the education of their children. Chapter 7 explores parental involvement in greater detail.

The Preschool Checklist

The preschool checklist[2] is designed to improve the social growth of disabled and nondisabled individuals. It has been successfully used with disabled individuals. It assesses information in four areas; scheduling and instructional arrangements, socialization and communication, alternative communication, and appearance of children. All of the four areas have significant relevancy for assisting teachers in planning for full inclusion of disabled individuals (Vandercook & York, 1990; Drinkwater & Demchak, 1995; Campbell, 1991; Strain, 1990).

All of the strategies under the four areas can promote social growth and acceptance of disabled children in the mainstream. The checklist is easily administered, no formal training is needed. The teacher simply checks yes or no for each of the items in the checklist. Responses for each of the four areas may be totaled individually to determine areas in need of improvement. A total score may also be computed. Results may be used to assist teachers in programming for successful integration of disabled children into the regular class.

There are few tests designed to assess social skills of disabled individuals. As indicated, most tests will have to be modified to assess social traits of this unique group. The reader is referred to the latest issue of Buros' Mental Measurements Year Book for additional tests and The Social Prevocation Information Battery (SPIB).

Social skills are difficult to assess due chiefly to validity, reliability and interpretability of the tests. Many social skills are directly associated with one's culture and when assessed outside of that culture, results can be misleading. Assessment instruments for measuring social skills have their advantages and disadvantages, and should be interpreted with the uniqueness of the disabled individual in mind, and the type of intervention which is being attempted to change the negative behavior.

---

2   Refer to "A Team Approach to Program Development and Support" by T. Vandercook and J. York, 1990, in Stainback & Stainback (Eds.) *Support Networks for Inclusive Schooling: Interdependent Integrated Education,* pp. 95-122 for additional details and the checklist.

APPLICATION OF BEHAVIORAL
INTERVENTION STRATEGIES

Learning depends upon the following factors: drive, response, cue and reward. The principle theoretical concepts drawn from this assumption are reinforcement values and expectations. The primary assumption is the tendency for behavior to occur in any given situation, is a function of the individual's expectations of reinforcement in that situation and of the value of the reinforcements.

Reinforcement values and expectations of some disabled individuals are different than those values expected from the school. What has been successful for them at home may be a source of conflict in the school. In essence, these disabled individuals have frequently been reinforced at home by what the school may term "negative behaviors." Historically, they have responded to behaviors which have brought them success at home. The goal-driven behaviors, responses to events, and the cues which they have developed, are frequently not challenged by the home. These behaviors work well for them, until they attend school. At school, the copying and imitative tendencies learned at home are generally not tolerated or accepted by the school, causing frustration, poor self-image, and sometimes aggressive behavior.

Most disabled individuals can learn from rewards and punishments, and then they can make a judgement in a new social situation as a result of previous experiences. Social referencing involves using information from other people to guide behavior and affect ambiguous situations. Unfortunately, many disabled individuals cannot learn effective social skills without direction intervention. Several studies have been conducted with nondisabled individuals relevant to social skills development. Results from the following studies may have implications for reducing aggressive behaviors among disabled individuals.

Frequently, behavior problems arise in class because successful intervention techniques have not been tried. Most traditional methods simply do not work for many disabled learners. A learning environment is needed which foster the reduction of negative behaviors, and recognizes the uniqueness of the individual. One intervention strategy which appeared to be used to reduce aggressive behavior was conducted by Hudley (1993).

A sample (101) of aggressive and nonaggressive elementary school boys were randomly assigned to an attributional intervention, and a nontreatment control group. The study was designed to determine the effects of an attribution intervention program on reducing aggressive males' tendency toward ambiguous negative peer interactions. Findings revealed that the experimental group of boys (attributional intervention) showed a significant reduction in hostile intent and disciplinary action as rated by their teachers (Hudley, 1992, 1993).

Research findings by Jewett (1992) focused on the role of aggression and cooperation in helping young children with appropriate strategies for coping with them. He asserted that aggression and cooperation have one common element which emerges from children's strong development push to initiate, control, and maintain relationships with their peers. Aggression was defined as any intentional act that resulted in physical or mental injury. Aggressive actions can be accidental, instrumental, or hostile acts of behavior. It was further voiced that aggression should not be confused with assertion. Assertion was defined as a process or behavior through which children maintain and defend their rights.

Cooperation was defined as any activity that involves willing interdependence of two or more students. Cooperation was distinguished from compliance in that compliance denoted obedience to authority rather than intentional cooperation. Aggressive behavior may be reduced by employing strategies which will permit students to verbalize their feelings, develop appropriate problem-solving techniques to conflict, and internalize and be cognizant of the effects of their aggressive behaviors upon others.

Collins (1992) and Katz (1991) summed effective strategies for supporting social and emotional growth of young children by recommending the following strategies: (1) Model social behavior; (2) Establish environments that encourage positive social exchange; (3) Encourage children to become aware of the consequences of their behaviors; (4) Help children produce acceptable behavior; and (5) Encourage the development of children's self-esteem. These behavioral techniques are also designed to make individuals aware of their impact on reacting and interacting with others.

SUMMARY

One of the valuable roles that a teacher conducts is that of an observer. Observing behavior in the classroom provides valuable information for intervention (Alberto & Troutman, 1990). Frequently, on the basis of the information supplied, appropriate action can be taken to change negative behaviors. The same rationale may be advanced for other recommended interventions discussed. Equally important will be the interpretation of the information from assessment for disabled learners. It is recommended that resource individuals be consulted before intervention is attempted.

REFERENCES

Alberto, P.A. & Troutman, A.C. (1990). *Applied Behavior Analysis for Teacher* (3rd Ed.), Columbus, OH: Merrill.

Anita, Shirin, Kreimeyer, & Eldredge (1993). Promoting Social Interaction Between Young Children with Hearing Impairments and Their Peers. *Exceptional Children, 60,* 262-275.

Brody, G., & Stoneman, Z. (1977). Social Competencies in the Development of the Disabled: Some Suggestions for Research and Training. *Mental Retardation, 15,* 41-43.

Brookes, P., Collins, T.W., & Hatch, J.A. (1992). Supporting the Social-Emotional Growth of Young Children. *Dimensions of Early Childhood, 21,* 17-21.

Campbell, P.H. (1991). An Essay on Preschool Integration in L.H. Meyer, C.A. Deck & L. Brown (Eds.). Critical Issues in the Lives of Peoples with Severe Disabilities. Baltimore, MD: Paul H. Brookes.

Collins, T.W. & Hatch, J.A. (1992). Supporting the Social-Emotional Growth of Young Children. *Dimensions of Early Childhood, 21,* 17-21.

Drinkwater, S., & Demchak, M. (1995). The Preschool Checklist: Integration of Children with Severe Disabilities. *Teaching Exceptional Children, 23,* 4-8.

Goldstein, H., & Wickstrom, S. (1986). Peer Intervention Effects on Communicative Interaction Among Handicapped and Nonhandicapped Preschoolers. *Journal of Applied Behavior Analysis, 19,* 209-214.

Gresham, F. M. (1993). Social Skills and Learning Disabilities as a Type III Error: Rejoinder to Conte and Andrews. *Journal of Learning Disabilities, 26,* 154-158.

Haltiwanger, J., (1992). A Normative Study of Development in Context: Growth Towards Independence in Social Function Skills of Young Children. *Clearinghouse for Teacher Education.* ERIC. ED 342504.

Hudley, C.A., (1993). An Attributional Intervention to Reduce Peer-Directed

Aggression Among African-American Boys. *Child Development, 64,* 124-138.

Jewett, J. (1992). Aggression and Cooperation: Helping Young Children Develop Constructive Strategies. *Clearinghouse for Teacher Education.* ERIC. ED 351147.

Katz, L.G. (1991). The Teacher's Role in Social Development of Young Children. *Clearinghouse for Elementary and Early Childhood Education.* ERIC. ED 331642.

McClelland, D. (1992). Assessing the Social Development of Young Children. *Clearinghouse for Teacher Education* ERIC. ED 346988.

McEvoy M., Odom, S.L., & McConnell, S.R. (1992). Peer Social Competence Intervention for Young Children with Disabilities, in S. Odom, S. McConnell &

M. McEvoy (Eds.). Social Competence of Young Children with Disabilities: Issues and Strategies for Intervention. Baltimore, MD: Paul H. Brookes.

McIntosh, R., Vaugh, S., & Zaragoza, M. (1991). Social Interventions for Students with Learning Disabilities: *An Examination of the Research Journal of Learning Disabilities, 24,* 451-458.

McIntosh, R., Vaugh, S., & Bennerson, D. (1995). Fast Social Skills with a Slam and a Rap: Providing Social Skills Training for Students with Learning Disabilities. *Teaching Exceptional Children, 28,* 37-41.

Pike, K., & Salend, S. J. (1995). Authentic Assessment Strategies: Alternatives to Normal Reference Testing. *Teaching Exceptional Children, 28,* 15-20.

Rhodes, L.K., & Nathenson-Mejia, S. (1992). Anecdotal Records: A Powerful Tool for Ongoing Literacy Assessment. *The Reading Teacher, 4,* 502-509.

Salinger, T. (1991). *Getting Started with Alternative Assessment Methods.* Workshop presented at the New York Reading Association Conference. Lake Kiamesha, New York.

Storey, K. et al. (1992). A follow-up of social skills instruction for preschoolers with developmental delays. *Education and Treatment of Children, 15,* 125-139.

Strain, P.S. (1990). LRE for Preschool Children with Handicaps: What We Know, What We Should Be Doing. *Journal of Early Intervention, 14,* 291-296.

Taylor, G. (1992). Impact of Social Learning Theory on Educating Deprived/Minority Children. *Clearinghouse for Teacher Education.* ERIC. ED 349260.

Vandercook, T., & York, J. (1990). A Team Approach to Program Development and Support. In W. Stainback & S. Stainback (Eds.). Support Networks for Inclusive Schooling: *Interdependent Integrated Education.* Baltimore, MD: Paul H. Brookes.

Vaugh, S.R., Hogan, A., Kouzekanani, K, & Shapiro, S. (1990). Peer Acceptance, Self-Perceptions, and Social Skills of LD Students Prior to Identification. *Journal of Educational Psychology, 32,* 101-106.

Vaugh, S.R., McIntosh, R.M., & Spencer-Rowe, J. (1991). Peer Rejection Is a Stubborn Thing: Increasing Peer Acceptance of Rejected Students with Learning Disabilities. *Learning Disabilities Research and Practice, 6,* 83-88.

Chapter 7

DIRECT INTERVENTION TECHNIQUES FOR TEACHING SOCIAL SKILLS TO DISABLED INDIVIDUALS

SHIRLEY EDWARDS & LOIS NIXON

INTRODUCTION

Intervention should reflect the assessed social needs of disabled individuals. Teacher-made checklists, outlining social skills development, may be used as outlined in Chapter 5. There are several approaches which may be used to promote pro-social skills of disabled individuals.

Direct Instruction

Goldstein and McGinnis (1984) supported the concept of direct instruction of social skills. These authors indicate that modeling, role playing, practice, and feedback are principal procedures and techniques used to teach social skills. Additional instruction using the following techniques can facilitate the teaching of social skills through direct instruction.

Direct instruction implies that the teacher is directly intervening to bring about a desired change, by providing basic information for children to master the task, which is a prerequisite. Direct instruction may be used with any subject area to assist children in learning basic skills, as well as employing the concept of task analysis (step-by-step sequence of learning a task).

Bandura (1970) provided us with the conceptual framework for using direct instruction. Bandura advanced the concept of "Social Learning Theory" and "Behavioral Modeling." He advocated that much of what the student learns is through modeling from observing others. Carefully and systematically conducted information gained through modeling may be transferred to other academic, social and nonacademic functions. Specific techniques for using effective modeling strategies have been delineated later in this chapter.

Skillstreaming

Skillstreaming is a comprehensive social skills program developed by Goldstein (1984).[1] In this program, social skills are clustered in several categories with specific skills to be demonstrated. Clear directions are provided for forming the skillstreaming groups, group meetings and rules. Activities include modeling, role playing, feedback, and transfer of training. The program is designed to foster human interaction skills needed to perform appropriate social acts. Feedback is received in the form of praise, encouragement, and constructive criticism. The feedback is designed to reinforce correct performance of the skills.

Cognitive Behavior Modification

These techniques focus on having disabled individuals to think and internalize their feelings and behaviors before reacting. The process involves learning responses from the environment by listening, observing and imitating others in their environments. Both cognition and language processes are mediated in solving problems and developing patterns of behaviors (Gresham, 1985).

Cognitive behavioral strategies are designed to increase self-control of behavior through self-monitoring, self-evaluation and self-reinforcement. These strategies are designed to assist children in internalizing their behaviors, to compare their behaviors against predetermined standards, and for children to provide positive and negative feedback to themselves. Research findings indicate that there is a positive relationship between what individuals think about themselves, and the types of behaviors they display (Rizzo, 1988). Matching the cognitive and affective processes in designing learning experiences for disabled individuals appears to be realistic and achievable within the school.

---

[1] Specific directions for conducting a skillstreaming program may be found in Goldstein (1984) Skillstreaming the Elementary Child. IL: Research Press Company.

Behavior Modification Techniques

Behavioral modification techniques may provide the teacher with strategies for assisting disabled individuals in performing desirable and appropriate behaviors, as well as promoting socially acceptable behaviors. The technique is designed to provide teachers, educators, and parents with a method to modify disabled individuals' behaviors to the extent that when they are emitted in a variety of situations, it is consistently more appropriate than inappropriate (Aksamit, 1990; Shores, Gunter & Jack, 1993).

There are some cautions for teachers using behavioral strategies in the classroom. The chief purpose of the teacher using this technique is to change or modify behaviors. The teacher is not generally concerned with the cause of the behaviors, rather with observing and recording overt behaviors. These behavioral responses may be measured and quantified in any attempt to explain behaviors. Motivation and the dynamic causes of the behaviors are primary concerns for the teacher.

In spite of the cautions involving using behavioral modification techniques, most of the research supports its use (Salend, 1983; Lane, 1992; Rizzo, 1988; Katz, 1991; Taylor, 1992). The major concerns voiced were that the technique must by systematically employed, the environmental constraints must be considered, and teachers, educators, and parents are well-versed in using the technique.

There are many effective ways in which behavior can be modified. Contingency contracting, the task center approach, peer mediation and proximity control are four of the most promising techniques to employ.

CONTINGENCY CONTRACTING. This technique involves pupils in planning and executing contracts. Gradually, pupils take over record keeping, analyze their own behavior, and even suggest the timing for cessation of contracts. Micro contracts are made with the pupil in which he/she agrees to execute some amount of low probability behavior after which he/she may engage immediately in some high probability behavior (Pre-mack Principle) for a specified time.

TASK-CENTERED APPROACH. The task centered approach to learning is another approach for modifying behaviors of disabled individuals. This system provides disabled individuals a highly structured learning environment. Individuals may be experiencing difficulty because they cannot grasp certain social skill concepts.

Behavioral problems may stem from the frustration of repeated failure, such as poor attention or the inability to work with independently or in groups. Elements in the task-centered approach may include activities to promote:

1. Attention level tasks designed to gain and hold disabled individuals' attention;
2   Development of visual and auditory discrimination activities as needed;
3. Interpretation and reaction to social level tasks emphasizing skills related to social interaction;
4. Imitation of social exchanges, the development of verbal and social courtesies, and group participation activities.

PEER MEDIATION STRATEGIES. Peer mediation strategies have been successfully employed to manage behavior. The model is student-driven and enables students to make decisions about issues and conflicts which have impact upon their lives. The model requires that students exercise self-regulation strategies which involves generating socially appropriate behavior in the absence of external control imposed by teachers or other authorities. To be effective, the concept must be practiced by disabled individuals and frequently reinforced by the teachers through role models, and demonstrations of pro-social skills.

Several investigations have shown that negative behaviors and discipline problems decrease when using this strategy. There is an increase in cooperative relationships and academic achievement. Findings also show an increase in task behaviors (Salend, 1982; Lane, 1992). Implications for using this strategy with disabled individuals may assist them in internalizing appropriate behaviors and significantly influence developing appropriate social skills (Storey, 1992; Odom, 1984).

Several studies have investigated the importance of using microcomputers to improve interpersonal skills of disabled individuals. Students tended to make less errors in subject areas when they worked in groups. Disabled individuals' behaviors also improved. They tended to imitate the behaviors of their nondisabled peers by increasing their personal and social awareness skills and competencies. Nonhandicapped peers tended to accept disabled individuals more readily with the use of computers (Hines, 1990; Cosden, 1990; Hedley, 1987; Thorkildsen, 1985).

Proximity Control

Studies have shown that teacher movement in the class may provide effective control of student behaviors by bringing the teacher and student into closer proximity. It is believed that this close proximity will improve interaction between student and teacher (Shores, Gunter, and Jack, 1993; Aksamit, 1990; Banbury & Herbert, 1992; Denny, Erstein & Rose, 1992).

The technique is easily implemented. The teacher stands close to pupils or arranges desks close to their desk. It is believed that this close proximity provides an external type of control for the pupil. Findings by Denny, Epstein, and Rose (1992) found that teachers generally are not taking advantage of this technique. It was recommended that teachers move freely throughout the room and monitor activities.

Coaching

Appropriate coaching techniques may be employed by teachers to develop social skills for disabled individuals. Some of the commonly known techniques include: (1) participation; (2) paying attention; (3) cooperation; (4) taking turns; (5) sharing; (6) communication; and (7) offering assistance and encouragement. These techniques are designed to make individuals cognizant of using alternative methods to solving problems; anticipating the consequences of their behaviors; and to develop plans for successfully coping with problems.

Cuing

Cuing is a technique employed to remind students to act appropriately just before the correct action is expected rather than after it is performed incorrectly. This technique is an excellent way of reminding students about prior standards and instruction. A major advantage of this technique is that it can be employed anywhere, using a variety of techniques such as glances, hand signals, painting, nodding or shaking the head and holding up the hand, are to name but a few.

Cuing can be utilized without interrupting the instructional program or planned activities for disabled individuals. The technique assists in reducing negative practices and prevents students from performing inappropriate behaviors.

Successful implementation of this technique requires that students thoroughly understand the requirement, as well as recognizing the specific cue. Failure to employ the above may result in confused students, especially when they are held accountable for not responding appropriate to the intended cue.

Modeling

Modeling assumes that an individual will imitate the behaviors displayed by others. The process is considered important because disabled, as well as all individuals, acquire social skills through replicating behaviors demonstrated by others. Educators and adults may employ modeling techniques to change and influence behaviors of children by demonstrating appropriate skills to model. The impact and importance of this valuable technique is frequently overlooked by teachers. Teachers frequently do not assess the impact of their behaviors on children.

Modeling, if used appropriately, may influence or change behaviors more effectively than positive behavior. This is promised upon the fact that once a behavior pattern is learned through imitation, it is maintained without employing positive reinforcement techniques. Teachers should be apprised and cognizant of the importance of modeling or promoting appropriate social skills of disabled individuals. Additionally, they should be trained and exposed to various techniques to facilitate the process. Children do not automatically imitate models they see. Several factors are involved; (1) Rapport established between teachers and children; and (2) The reinforcing consequences for demonstrating or not demonstrating the modeled behavior; and (3) Determining the appropriate setting for modeling certain behaviors.

Disabled individuals should be taught how to show or demonstrate positive behaviors in structured situations. The technique provides for the structured learning of appropriate behaviors through examples and demonstration of others. Internal or incidental modeling may occur at any time, however, a regular structured time or period of day is recommended in order to develop structure in a variety of social conditions. Teaching behavioral skills through modeling is best accomplished by beginning with impersonal situations which most students encounter, such as the correct way to show respect to others. As disabled individuals master the modeling process, additional behavioral problems may be emphasized.

Modeling activities may be infused throughout the curriculum at random, however; a specific time is recommended for modeling instruction. Activities should be planned based upon the assessed needs of the class and be flexible enough to allow for changes when situations dictate.

Role Playing

Role playing is an excellent technique for allowing disabled individuals to act out both appropriate and inappropriate behaviors without embarrassment, or experiencing the consequences of their actions. It permits disabled individuals to experience hypothetical conditions which may cause some anxiety or emotional responses in ways which may enable them to better understand themselves. Once entrenched, these activities may be transferred to real life experiences. Role playing may assist disabled individuals in learning appropriate social skills through developing appropriate models by observing and discussing alternative behavioral approaches. Role playing may be conducted in any type of classroom structure, level or group size. It may be individually or grouped induced. Through appropriate observations and assessment procedures, areas of intervention may be identified for role playing activities.

Role playing assists individuals in identifying and solving problems within a group context. It is also beneficial to shy students. It encourages their interactions with classmates without aversive consequences. As with most group activities, role playing must be structured by the teacher. Activities should be designed to reduce, minimize, correct, or eliminate identified areas of deficits through the assessment process. Gills (1991) listed the following advantages of role playing:

1. Allows the student to express hidden feelings.
2. Is student-centered and addresses itself to the needs and concerns of the student.

3.   Permits the group to control the content and pace.
4.   Enables the student to empathize with others and understand their problems.
5.   Portrays generalized social problems and dynamics of group interaction, formal and informal.
6.   Gives more reality and immediacy to academic descriptive material (history, geography, social skills, English).
7.   Enables the student to discuss private issues and problems.
8.   Provides an opportunity for nonarticulate students and emphasizes the importance of nonverbal and emotional responses.
9.   Gives practice in various types of behavior.

Disadvantages listed include:

1.   The teacher can lose control over what is learned and the order in which it is learned.
2.   Simplifications can mislead.
3.   It may dominate the learning experiences to the exclusion of solid theory and facts.
4.   It is dependent upon the personality, quality and mix of the teacher and students.
5.   It may be seen as too entertaining and frivolous.

Gills (1991) investigated the effects of role playing, modeling, and videotape playback on the self-concept of elementary school children. The Piers-Harris children's self-concept scale was employed on a pre-post test basis. Intervention was for a six month period. Data showed that the combination of role playing, modeling, and videotape playback had some effect upon various dimensions of self-concept.

Videotape Modeling

Videotape modeling is an effective measure to improve self-concept of disabled individuals. They may be encouraged to analyze classroom behavior and patterns of interaction through reviewing videotapes. This technique can show disabled individuals the behaviors expected before they are exposed to them in various settings. Videotape modeling affords the teachers the opportunity to reproduce the natural conditions of any behavior in the classroom setting. Videotape modeling may provide realistic training which can be transferred to real experiences inside and outside of the classroom (Banbury & Herbert, 1992; Shores, Gunter & Jack, 1993).

For disabled learners, educators may employ this technique to bridge the gap between transferring modeling skills to real life situations. It has been proven as an effective tool to teach pro-social skills to this group.

Cooperative Learning

A basic definition of cooperative learning is a method of learning through the use of groups. Five basic elements of cooperative learning are:

1. Positive interdependence.
2. Individual accountability.
3. Group processing.
4. Small group/social skills.
5. Face-to-face primitive interaction.

A cooperative learning group is one in which two or more students are working together toward a common goal in which every member of the group is included. Cooperative learning seems ideal for mainstreaming. Learning together in small groups has proven to provide a sense of responsibility and an understanding the importance of cooperation among youngsters. Disabled individuals socialize and interact with each other (Adams, 1990; Slavin, 1984; Johnson, 1983; Gemma, 1989).

Cooperative learning strategies have the power to transform classrooms by encouraging communities of caring, supportive students whose achievements improve and whose social skills grow. Harnessing and directing the power of cooperative learning strategies present a challenge to the classroom teacher. Decisions about the contend appropriateness of the structures, the necessary management routines, and the current social skill development of disabled individuals call for special teacher preparation (Johnson, 1988). For successful outcomes with students, teachers also need the follow-up of peer coaches, administrative support, parent understanding, and time to adapt to the strategies (Slavin, 1991).

While cooperative models replace individual seat work, they continue to require individual accountability. Teachers who use cooperative structures recognize that it is important for students to both cooperate and compete.

Cooperative learning organizes students to work together in structured groups toward a common goal. Among the best known cooperative structures are Jigsaw, Student Teams Achievement Divisions (STAD), Think-Pair-Share, Group Investigation, Circle of Learning, and Simple Structures. To use a cooperative structure effectively, teachers need to make some preliminary decisions. According to Kagan (1990) the following questions should be asked:

1.   What kind of cognitive and academic development does it foster?
2.   What kind of social development does it foster?
3.   Where in the lesson plan (content) does it best fit?

Teachers also need to examine what conditions increase the effect of cooperative strategies. Positive interdependence, face-to-face (primitive) interaction, individual accountability, and group processing affects cooperative learning outcomes.

The benefits of cooperative learning appear to be reflected in the following:

1.   Academic gains, especially among disabled and low-achieving students.
2.   Improved race relations among students in integrated classrooms.
3.   Improved social and affective development among all students (Kagan, 1990; Johnson, 1988; Slavin, 1991).

Cooperative learning practices vary tremendously. The models can be complex or simple. Whatever their design, cooperative strategies include:

1.   A common goal.
2.   A structured task.
3.   A structured team.
4.   Clear roles.
5.   Designated time frame.
6.   Individual accountability.
7.   A structured process.

We need cooperative learning structures in our classrooms because many traditional socialization practices are absent. Not all students come to school with a social orientation, and students appear to master content more efficiently with these structures (Kagan, 1990; Cosden, 1985). The preponderance of research indicates that cooperative learning strategies motivate students to care about each other and to share responsibility in completing tasks. (Refer to Appendix D for some Cooperative Learning Strategies to use in the classroom).

Cooperative Learning vs. Peer Tutoring

It is frequently assumed by some parents that cooperative learning is another concept of peer tutoring, but there are many significant differences between cooperative learning and peer tutoring. In cooperative learning, everyone is responsible for learning and nobody is acting as a teacher or as a tutor. On the other hand, in peer tutoring, one child has the role of teacher and another of student or tutor. The tutor already knows that subject and material and teaches it to a peer who needs individualized remedial help to master a specific skill. In cooperative learning, the initial teaching comes not from a student but from the teacher, because all students grasp concepts quickly and some slowly. These students reinforce what they have just learned by explaining concepts and skills to teammates who need help (Slavin, 1991). Cooperative work puts a heterogenous group of students together to share ideas and knowledge.

SPECIAL GROUP ACTIVITIES

In a paper presented at the annual meeting of the American Education Research Association, Dorr (1992) advanced some unique techniques for improving social identity in kindergarten and first grade. Students sat in groups and planned daily activities; these activities were videotaped. Analysis of the videotapes revealed several dimensions of social identity to be important, such as academic capability; maturity; talkativeness; independence; aggressiveness; ability to follow through; and leadership ability. The teacher responded to students individually and as circle participants, depending upon how the behavior was viewed. Findings indicated that social identity was the combined responsibility of everyone in the classroom interacting to bring about the most positive social behavior. Interactions between individual students and the teacher were minimized.

Group Play Activities

The values and benefits of group play therapy cannot be over-emphasized when employed with many disabled individuals. These activities may assist disabled individuals in developing appropriate interpersonal skills and relationships. Many disabled individuals tend to settle differences with peers by physical means. This trend may be attributed to poor impulse control, poor modeling and imitation strategies and inability to internalize their behaviors (Coker & Thyer, 1990; Istre, 1993; Goldstein, 1990; Brattons, 1994).

In order for disabled individuals to internalize their behaviors, activities must be designed to bring behaviors to the conscience level. Disabled individuals frequently have problems in self-control which may be manifested in behavioral problems. Group play activities should be designed to enable disabled individuals to cope with problems which may cause loss of control. Properly employed, these activities will assist disabled individuals in understanding the consequences of their behaviors. Once disabled individuals under-stand the consequences of their behavior, they are moving toward self-management.

Social-Cognitive Approaches

These techniques are designed to instruct disabled individuals to deal more effectively with social matters through self-correction and problem solving. Self-monitoring or instruction involves verbal prompting by the student concerning his/her social behavior. Verbal prompting may be overt or covert. The approach is designed to help students maintain better control over their behaviors.

Making Better Choices

This social-cognitive approach is designed to assist disabled individuals in making better choices. Group lessons are developed around improving social skills. Lessons are designed to promote forethought before engaging in a behavior and to examine the consequences of the behavior. The major components of this program include the following cognitive sequence:

1. Stop (inhibit response);
2. Plan (behaviors leading to positive behaviors);
3. Do (follow plan and monitor behavior);
4. Check (evaluate the success of the plan)

The aforementioned steps should be practiced by disabled individuals and reinforced by the teacher. Various social skills are identified by the teacher for the student to practice. Progress reports should be kept and assessed periodically by both teachers and students.

ROLE OF THE SCHOOL IN A BEHAVIOR SETTING

A meaningful course of action for dealing with negative behavior would be to isolate the behavior and then to quantify, record and observe the number of acts involved. When this determination has been made, the teacher is equipped to undertake a course of action to change the negative behaviors. Social skills training is the technique advocate. Analysis of the behavior, using the checklist outlined in Appendix C, may lead the teacher to pursue a course of action.

Disabled individuals, as well as all children, enter school with a wide range of learning abilities, interests, motivation, personality, attitudes, cultural orientations and social economic status. These traits and abilities must be recognized and incorporated into the instructional program. Promoting positive behavior may take several forms such as using praise frequently, eye contact, special signals and having individual conferences with pupils.

Disabled individuals enter school with set behavioral styles. Frequently, these styles are inappropriate for the school. Several techniques are recommended to change inappropriate behaviors in the classroom:

1. Have teachers to raise their tolerance levels. Teachers generally expect disabled individuals to perform up to acceptable standards. Additionally, it is assumed that they have been taught appropriate social skills at home. Whereas,

the above premise may be true for most pupils, frequently, it is not true for pupils with disabilities. By the teacher recognizing causal factors, such as environment, culture, and value, tolerance levels may be raised.

2.   Change teacher expectations for pupils. Pupils generally live up to expectations of teachers. Teachers should expect positive behaviors from children. To accomplish this goal, behaviors will sometimes have to be modeled. It is also recommended that individual time be allowed for certain pupils, through interviews and individual conferences where the teacher honestly relates how the child's behavior is objectional.

3.   A teacher's behavior toward a pupil. Pupils use the teacher's overt behavior as a mirror for a picture of his strength in the classroom. When a positive reflection is projected, this increases the achievement level. When the message is overtly or covertly negative, the pupil has nothing to support his/her efforts. If there is little positive interaction between pupil and the teacher, the pupil may conclude that his/her behavior is not approved by the teacher. Because the pupil depends so heavily on the teacher's behavior for clues, it is crucial that the teacher objectively analyze his/her interaction with disabled individuals.

SUMMARY

Most learning is social and is mediated by other people. Consequently, pupils with disabilities, as well as all children, profit when working in groups. Individual and group activities have proven to be successful in teaching appropriate social skills. Behavioral intervention techniques have proven to be equally successful. There are many individual and group experiences designed to promote social growth among and between children. One of the most promising techniques is cooperative learning. It appears to be a promising technique for improving the social skills of disabled individuals. As the term implies, students work together in groups, to help each other attain the behavioral objective when engaged in cooperative learning. Students benefit both socially and academically when participating in group activities. Therefore, the disabled's social skills are being dually challenged and developed.

Although cooperative models call for group activities, they require individual accountability. And teachers who use such structures of cooperative learning recognize the need for each and every student to cooperate and compete while working toward the group goal (Lyman, 1993). The most widely used cooperative learning programs are Jigsaw, Student Teams Achievement Divisions (STAD), Think-Pair-Share, Group Investigation and Circle of Learning.

With the movements of mainstreaming and inclusion, more and more disabled students will be interacting with their peers. Some of them may engage in offensive behaviors because of the inability to interact positively. Others have difficulties in communication, which may also result in integration failure (Kaplan, 1990). Teachers must recognize the importance and need for improved interpersonal relationships or increased interaction among all students.

Most disabled learners do not meet academic success due partly to their inability to implement the above social skills or techniques. These techniques are designed to reduce student isolation and increase students' abilities to react and work with other students toward the solution of common problems. Teachers should experiment with various forms of individual, group, and behavioral intervention strategies to improve social skills of disabled individuals (Taylor, 1992). Since most behaviors are learned, they can be changed through behavioral intervention strategies, once social skills are learned through the application of these techniques, they become automatic.

Lutfiyya's approach (1991) outlined three strategies needed for successful group facilitation: (1) facilitation, (2) interpretation, and (3) accommodation. He concluded that all three approaches depend upon cooperation within the group. Roles are shared by all involved. Although this approach is primarily used to diagnose and evaluate disabled individuals, implications for group planning are clear.

Social skills interventions are needed if disabled individuals are to be successfully integrated into the mainstream. Activities such as greeting, sharing, cooperation, assisting, complementing, and inviting should be developed and modeled. Social skills development assist disabled individuals in several ways:

1.   Social competence helps compensate for academic deficits.
2.   Social skills are needed for success in the mainstream and in

employment.

3. Social skills training helps derive maximum benefit from academic and/or vocational instruction.

4. Social competence is fundamental to good interpersonal relationships and fosters improved leisure and recreational activities.

With these in mind, it is incumbent upon our educational systems to focus on designing social skills curricula in all disabled students.

The teaching of social skills for the disabled student can be as subtle as the teacher incidentally modeling the correct social behavior in a classroom situation to overt direct instruction in the form of approaches or techniques such as skillstreaming, coaching cooperative learning, structured modeling, role playing or creative dramatics. The manner in which social skills are taught and the specific teacher characteristics can determine the quality of the entire educational experience for the disabled youngster.

Positive behavior is a prerequisite for attaining the other skills necessary for school success. For whatever reason, social skills are a major deficit area for the disabled student. Social skills include the ability to follow instruction, accept criticism, disagree appropriately, greet someone, make a request, reinforce and compliment others as well as using acceptable ways of getting attention. Thus, activities should be infused throughout the curriculum (Anita, 1992).

REFERENCES

Adams, D.N. (1990). Involving students in cooperative learning. *Teaching Pre-K, 8,* 51-52.

Aksamit, D.L. (1990). Practicing teachers' perceptions of their pre-service preparation for mainstreaming. *Teacher Education and Special Education, 13,* 21-29.

Anita, S.D., & Kreimeyer, K. (1992). Project interact: Intervention for social integration of young hearing-impaired children. *Office of Special Education and Rehabilitative Services.*

Banbury, M.M., & Herbert, C.R. (1992). Do You See What I Mean? *Teaching Exceptional Children, 24,* 34-48.

Bandura, A. (1970). *A Social Learning Theory.* Englewood Cliffs, NJ: Prentice Hall.

Bratton, S.C. (1994). Filial therapy with single parents. *Doctoral Dissertation.* University of North Texas: Dissertation Abstracts International. ERIC. ED 082890.

Coker, K.H., & Thyer, B.A. (1990). School and family-based treatment of children with Attention-Deficit Hyperactivity Disorder. Families in society. *The Journal of*

Contemporary Human Services. 276-281.

Cosden, M. (1985). The effects of cooperative and individual goal structure on learning disabled and nondisabled students. *Teaching Exceptional Children, 52,* 103-114.

Denny, R.K., Epstein, M.N., & Rose, E. (1992). Direct observation of adolescent with behavioral disorders and their nonhandicapped peers in mainstream. *Vocational Education Classrooms, Behavioral Disorders, 18,* 33-41.

Dorr-Bremme, D.W. (1992). Discourse and society identity in kindergarten-first grade classroom. *Clearinghouse for Teacher Education.* ERIC. ED 352111.

Gemma, A. (1989). Social skills instruction in mainstreamed preschool classroom. *Clearinghouse for Teacher Education.* ERIC. ED 326033.

Gills, W. (1991). Jewish Day Schools and African-American youth. *Journal of Negro Education, 60,* 566-580.

Goldstein, S., & Goldstein, M. (1990). *Managing Attention Disorders in Children: A Guide for Practitioners.* New York: Wiley.

Goldstein, A., & McGinnis, E. (1984). *Skillstreaming Elementary Children.* Chicago, IL: Research Press Company.

Gresham, F.M. (1985). Utility of Cognitive-Behavioral Procedures for social skills training with children: Critical review. *Journal of Abnormal Child Psychology, 13,* 491.

Hedley, C.N. (1987). What's new in software? Computer programs for social skills. *Journal of Reading, Writing, and Learning Disabilities International, 3,* 187-191.

Hines, M.S. (1990). Error monitoring by learning handicapped students engaged in collaborative microcomputer-based writing. *Journal of Special Education, 23,* 407-422.

Istre, S.M. (1993). Social skills of preadolescent boys with attention deficit hyperactivity disorder. *Doctoral Dissertation.* Oklahoma State University, 1992: Dissertation Abstracts International, *53.*

Johnson, R.T., & Johnson, D.W. (1983). Effects on Cooperative, Competitive, and Individualistic Learning Experiences on Social Development. *Exceptional Children, 49,* 323-329.

Johnson, D.W., Johnson, R., & Holubec, E. (1988). *Cooperation in the Classroom.* Edina, MN: Interaction Book Company.

Kagan, S. (1990). The Structural Approach to Cooperative Learning. *Educational Leadership, 47,* 12-15.

Katz, L.G. (1991). The Teacher's Role in Social Development of Young Children. *Clearinghouse on Elementary and Early Childhood Education.* ERIC. ED 331642.

Lane, P.S., & McWhirter (1992). A Peer Mediation Model: Conflict Resolution for Elementary and Middle School Children. *Elementary School Guidance and Counseling, 27,* 15-21.

Lutfiyya, Z. (1991). *Tony Sati and Bakery–The Roles of Facilitation, Accommodation, and Interpretation.* Syracuse, NY: Syracuse University, Center on Human Policy.

Odom, S.L. & Strain, P.S. (1984). Classroom-based social skills instruction for severely handicapped preschool children. *Topics in Early Childhood Special Education, 4,* 97-116.

Rizzo, J.V., & Zabel, R.H. (1988). *Educating Children and Adolescents with Behavioral Disorders: An Integrative Approach.* Boston: Allyn and Bacon, Inc.

Slavin, R.E., & Oickle, E. (1981). Effects of cooperative learning teams on student achievement and race relations: Treatment by race interactions. *Sociology of Education, 54,* 174-180.

Slavin, R.E. (1984). Team assisted individualization: Cooperative learning and individualized instruction in the mainstreamed classroom. *Remedial and Special Education, 5,* 33-42.

Slavin, R.E. (1984). Effects on team assisted individualization on the mathematics achievements of academically handicapped and nonhandicapped students. *Journal of Educational Psychology, 76,* 813-819.

Slavin, R.E. (1991). *Using Student Team Learning.* Baltimore, MD: The Center for Social Organization of Schools. Johns Hopkins University.

Storey, K. (1992). A follow-up of social skills instruction for preschoolers with developmental delays. *Education and Treatment of Children, 15,* 125-139.

Salend, S.J., & Whittaker, C.R. (1992). Group Evaluation: A Collaborative, Peer-mediated Behavior Management System. *Exceptional Children, 59,* 203-209.

Shores, R.E., Gunter, P.L., & Jack, S.L. (1993). Classroom management strategies: Are they settling for coercion? *Behavior Disorders, 18,* 92-102.

Taylor, G. (1992). Impact of social learning theory on educating deprived/minority children. *Clearinghouse for Teacher Education, 44,* 349-359.

Thorkildsen, R. (1985). Using an interactive videodisc program to teach social skills to handicapped children. *American Annals of the Deaf, 130,* 383-385.

Chapter 8

PARENTAL ROLES
IN SOCIAL SKILLS DEVELOPMENT

LAVANIA LEE RICE-FITZPATRICK & FRANCES HARRINGTON

INTRODUCTION

E ducators must think of an experiment with innovative ways of involving parents in the school over the last several decades, the school has had a difficult time in establishing effective partnerships with parents. Much of the fragment has occurred because of noninvolvement, hostility, or parental indifference toward the school. Many schools serving parents of disabled individuals consider them a nuisance, unproductive, uneducated, lacking social grace, and not well informed on education and social issues. The relationship is further strained when parents internalize the negative behaviors displayed by the school and view the school as an unaccepted place which has no interest in them as individuals. There must be a total shift in the paradigm. The school must accept these parents and provide training and assistance in desired areas.

Parents may stimulate social growth and development of their children in various ways. Some ways may include designing everyday situations for them to explore, providing activities to promote self-esteem and confidence, praising them frequently, providing support, and creating a healthy and safe environment, to name but a few positive activities needed for normal child development.

Armstrong (1991) informed us that parental involvement is essential in assisting the school in developing appropriate social skills for disabled individuals. He concluded that by involving parents in social skills homework makes transferring of social skills functional and realistic for disabled individuals. Parents may assist the schools in several ways. They may reinforce the social skills taught at home by providing practice and reinforcement for their disabled children. They may also provide the school with valuable information concerning developmental issues, safety concerns, community resources, and demonstrations. Additionally, they may serve as resource individuals and accommodate the class on field trips.

Social changes are constantly occurring in early childhood. During this rapid expanding period, children gain self-awareness and learn how to respond appropriately in different social situations. Making sure that appropriate social models are provided is a responsibility of parents. Children who are products of a stimulating and positive environment bring a sense of social maturity and independence to the learning environment. Research findings by Lareau, 1987; Delgado-Gaitan, 1991; and Salli, 1991, support the above premise.

A recent Reader's Digest poll revealed that strong families give children an edge in school. Children who socially participate with family functions scored higher on tests than those who did not. The survey also revealed that strong family ties improved self-image and confidence in children. The family is the cornerstone for success in later life. Parent education appears to play a role in how well the student performs in school.

The quality of family life appears to be significant factors in all of the groups. Disabled individuals from intact families performed better than those who lived only with their mothers. Strong family ties appear to reduce some of the anxiety faced by disabled individuals. Disabled individuals from families who attended houses of worship also scored higher on tests.

Creative and innovative ways relevant to family involvement must be experimented with to improve parental involvement, especially for parents of disabled individuals (Mansbach, 1993). Factors such as (1) diverse school experiences, (2) diverse economic and time constraints, and (3) diverse linguistic and cultural practices all combine to inhibit parental involvements. Diversity should be recognized as a strength rather than a weakness. Parents need to feel that their cultural styles and language are valued knowledge, and that this knowledge is needed and welcomed in the school.

P.L. 94-142 and other federal legislation has mandated that parents be involved in planning education experiences of their disabled children. I.E.P. (Individualized Education Plan), which is part of P.L.

94-142 mandates parental involvement, from initial identification to placement of disabled individuals into educational settings. Additional mandates and ways of involving parents have been highlighted in Chapter 1. One recommended approach is to dialogue with parents in order to understand what they think can be done to improve involvement (Finders, 1994).

Unless the aforementioned strategies are adhered to, academic and social development of children will be impeded. The combined cooperation of both school and home are needed if social skills training is to be effective. There is an urgent need to involve parents by making them aware of, as well as training them in the use of social skills techniques to implement at home.

Parental Guidelines for Promoting Social Growth

Individuals with disabilities, as well as all children, follow developmental milestones in social skills. This sequence permits parents to work with their children where they are developmentally and to pattern the learning of social skills in a more predictable manner. Several guidelines are offered to aid parents:

GUIDELINE I. Initially, all learning comes through the five senses. Early experiences should be provided with as many concrete examples as possible, using the five senses. Children's self-awareness, discovery, and interests in their environments are enhanced.

GUIDELINE II. Children should be permitted and encouraged to use the "discovery process" as much as possible by experimenting with appropriate social behaviors. The child explores his/her social world by trying out new behaviors. The effects that these behaviors have on others—how you respond—will help shape the direction children will take. Children usually increase social behaviors that are rewarded by positive attention.

GUIDELINE III. Behaviors are learned by imitating others in the environment. The child observes the actions of others and imitates those actions thus acquiring new skills. Repeating those actions eventually leads to using them in functional situations. As the child develops, he/she is usually eager to imitate the "big kid" ways of older brothers and sisters or other children. This is especially true when applied to parents.

GUIDELINE IV. Play provides an opportunity for children to learn many social skills. The chief business of childhood is "play." Children gradually learn the give-and- take of group play. Enjoying playing near other children comes before the ability to play cooperatively with others. As play skills progress, the child can practice many social roles and act out many social situations within the security of make-believe play.

GUIDELINE V. Having friends is an important part of childhood development. Many social skills are learned such as sharing, taking turns, being a leader and follower, and respecting the rights of others. As children develop, they need the companionship of other people. Follow the child's preference in selecting friends and provide opportunities for frequent play experiences at home and in the neighborhood. Being accepted and liked by other children becomes increasingly important as children develop. Learning to survive squabbles, hurt feelings, and changing affections is part of the normal but sometimes painful process of making friends.

GUIDELINE VI. Praise your child frequently for successful completion of tasks. Provide social activities which will ensure success. Set up the social situation for the child to be successful and show your pleasure through hugs, smiles, and perhaps, special treats. Step in to help if your child is frustrated and on the brink of failure. Reward him/her with plenty of praise for accomplishing what he/she could and having the courage to attempt the rest.

GUIDELINE VII. Provide activities to promote social decision making. Support the child in his/her decision making. Demonstrate alternative ways of arriving at appropriate decisions. As your child begins to signal definite opinions about his/her world, you can help him/her to practice making appropriate decisions. Whenever possible, offer two acceptable choices and let your child make the decision, e.g., "Do you want to play inside or outside today?" "Do you want to wear your baseball shirt or your PTA shirt to school?" or "How could you have done this another way?"

GUIDELINE VIII. Teach your child to respect ownership by recognizing the rights of others' possessions and property. Gaining a sense of "mine" marks a developmental step in self-awareness. As your child shows a preference for certain objects, make sure that he/she has ready access to these favorites. Talk about things and people in terms of what is the child's and what belongs to others (e.g., his/her shoes, his/her brother's shoes). Your child may also appreciate a special place within the home to use as his/her quiet play area and a secure space for treasured possessions.

GUIDELINE IX. Demonstrate appropriate social behaviors in a variety of situations. Have children to copy and model appropriate behaviors. Knowing "how to act" in different social situations is not easy for young children. By giving your child clear guidelines for good behavior, rewarding his/her efforts, and giving him/her opportunities to practice, he/she will learn patterns of acceptable social skills. For example, practicing a quiet voice or whisper in make-believe play will prepare your child for appropriate quiet manners in the library. Acting out the giving of presents can be a rehearsal for a first time away from home birthday party. Model and teach good manners. Your child will learn from a wide variety of ordinary social experiences; going shopping, eating at restaurants, playing in the parks, visiting friends and relatives. Don't expect your child's social behavior to be 100% perfect. All children have lapses into less mature behavior, especially when they are tired, frustrated, or in strange situations. Don't let the occasional embarrassment of a loud temper tantrum in a crowded shopping mall discourage you. Try to evaluate your child's behavior objectively, noting the successes as well as the problems.

GUIDELINE X. Employ a variety of community resources to promote social experiences, through direct participation by the child. Participating in community activities is one way of your child having fun while gaining social experiences with peers. Many communities offer a variety of activities designed to build social skills such as:

a. Preschool story hour at the library
b. Water play and swimming lessons
c. Children's films
d. Holiday parades
e. Holiday parties
f. Supervised play at "tot lots"
g. Dance classes
h. Children's exhibits at museums
i. Special events at shopping malls
j. Community outreach centers
k. Community fairs at neighborhood schools

Some suggested strategies for facilitating the social learning process of disabled learners are listed below:

1. RELATE TASKS TO THE DEVELOPMENTAL LEVEL OF THE CHILD. Some children are eager for new tasks and experiences. Others need to be coaxed and encouraged. Regardless of how your child approaches challenges, success will be important for the development of self-concept. Direct your child toward challenges that he is developmentally ready for. Break down big tasks into smaller parts; e.g., if your child wants to make a garden, breakdown the project into easy steps-digging, making holes, dropping seeds, covering them, watering. Show him each step, but let your child do it for himself.

2. BUILD A SENSE OF SECURITY AND TRUST. Given a loving and responsive home environment, your child will be able to establish a sense of self apart from the people and things about him. Patience, consistency and loving discipline are acts of caring which support your child as he strives toward independence.

3. BE SENSITIVE TO YOUR CHILD'S SIGNALS. As an individual, your child shows unique ways of responding to new people and new experiences. Although he amy not be able to put his feelings into words, he may need your reassurance when entering into unknown territory. Sometimes fearfulness and negative behaviors are signs that your child is not quite ready for the challenge at hand.

4. MAKE YOUR CHILD AN EQUAL IN THE FAMILY. Membership in a family involves learning to share: sharing time, sharing material resources, sharing one another's love. As your child grows more capable, he/she should be given the opportunity to perform tasks which contribute to the functioning of the family. Your child also needs to be shown ways to express how much he cares about the people that he loves.

5. BE AWARE OF YOUR CHILD'S LIMITATIONS. Realize that your child's present social capabilities are largely determined by his overall developmental level. Your expectations of his social behavior should be based on developmental age, not chronological age.

6. GO FROM THE KNOWN TO THE UNKNOWN. Prepare your child for new experiences by linking the familiar to the unknown. If your child has met the librarian and visited the children's room in the neighborhood library many times, participating in preschool story hour is not so scary a prospect.

SUMMARY

From the very beginning, your disabled child has an important place within your family. By being responsive to your child's needs for comfort, play and love, you build a foundation for interactive social relationships. The drive for independence emerges as developmental skills grow. As your child tries to do more and more for himself, he continues to depend on you for guidance and support. Parental delight in the small accomplishments of a child can set expectations for larger successes.

Parents of disabled individuals, as well as all parents, have a tremendous influence and impact on setting appropriate models for developing social skills. As well as all skills, the developmental level of the child as well as developmental sequence must be considered in social skills training. Parents can contribute significantly to their disabled children's self-concept and control through appropriate modeling strategies.

In order for parents of disabled individuals to be effective change agents in promoting appropriate social skills development, early intervention in health care, counseling, housing, nutrition, education, and child rearing practices, etc., must be improved. Early intervention and parental involvements are essential for preparing children to master social skill tasks successfully.

There has been strong support from the federal government to include the family in the early educational process of their children. Parental involvement permits children to successfully manipulate their environments. The federal government created guidelines for the educational community in developing and implementing a comprehensive, coordinate, multidisciplinary, interagency program of early intervention services for infants, toddlers and their families (Gallager, 1989).

The role of parental participation in educating their disabled children, according to much of the research in the field, has shown limited participation between them and the school. This view has been interpreted to imply that parents simply had no interest in the education of their children (Lynch & Stein, 1987; Marion, 1981). Several factors may contribute to lack of parental participation and involvement. Many parents do not feel welcome in the schools. They believe that they have little to offer in educating their children.

Cassidy (1988) reported that problems with scheduling, transportation, and the lack of knowledge of instructional programs and I.E.P. procedures, are partly responsible for poor parental participation.

The role of parents of disabled individuals in the school must supersede the mandates of P.L. 94-142. Parents must feel that they are welcome in the school and be given responsibilities concerned with planning, collaborating with teachers, and involved in policymaking. Parents should have an active role in planning and instructing their children and function as advocates for them if children are to profit significantly from their school experiences. Schools should experiment with various ways of improving parental participation, since they are the foremost educators of their children.

REFERENCES

Armstrong, S.W., & McPherson, A. (1991). Homework as a critical component in social skills instruction. *Teaching Exceptional Children,* 24, 45-47.

Cassidy, E. (1988). Reaching and involving Black parents of handicapped children in their child's education program. ED Document Reproduction Service. ERIC 302582.

Delgado-Gaitan, C. (1991). Involving parents in the schools: A process of empowerment. *American Journal of Education,* 100, 20-46.

Finders, M., & Lewis, C. (1994). Why some parents don't come to school. *Educational Leadership,* 51, 50-54.

Gallager, J.J. (1989). The impact of policies for handicapped children on future education policy. *Phi Delta Kappan,* 121-124.

Lareau, A. (1987). Social class differences in family-school relationships: The importance of cultural capital. *Sociology of Education,* 60, 73-85.

Lynch, E.W., & Stein, R. (1987). Parental participation by ethnicity: A comparison of Hispanic, Black and Anglo families. *Exceptional Children,* 54, 105-111.

Mansbach, S.C. (1993). We must put family literacy on the national agenda. *Reading Today,* 37.

Salli, C. (1991). *Scripts for Children's Lives: What Do Parents and Early Childhood Teachers Contribute to Children's Understanding of Events in Their Lives.* ERIC. ED 344664.

Chapter 9

SOCIAL/INTERPERSONAL SKILLS CURRICULUM FOR DISABLED INDIVIDUALS

GEORGE R. TAYLOR, BERNADETTE FRANCISCO & LORETTA MACKENNEY

CURRICULUM DEVELOPMENT-AN OVERVIEW

Curriculum development is designed to reflect the course of study in schools. It is intended to present information to students in an organized manner through various methods and instructional strategies. Teachers must be cognizant of creative and innovative ways to individualize and maximize learning for pupils by providing practical learning activities.

Designing curriculum involves two major methodologies. The first methodology is experimental instruction. Experimental instruction is designed to intrinsically motivate student interests inside and outside of the classroom. The second approach is systematic instruction. Teacher-student interaction underline this methodology. The major purpose of systematic instruction is to develop a skill on concept and develop materials and activities which will enable students to achieve selected objectives.

Curriculum development in most school districts are concerned with developing academics in order to equip pupils to master the complex tasks in our society. This point of view is endorsed for most pupils. However, due to poor social and interpersonal skills development of many individuals with disabilities, social skill development may be necessary before academic skills can be mastered.

It is generally agreed by most professionals in the field of special education that schools should be involved in teaching social and interpersonal skills to disabled individuals. Social skill education and interpersonal skill development are an ideal way to teach responsibility for self and others, for exploring the meaning of human interaction and relationships. The subject is too important for the home to assume this awesome responsibility alone.

A social skills curriculum can also assist disabled students to understand: (1) How to develop self-esteem and control their emotions, and how their emotions affect others; (2) How to develop positive social relationships; (3) Respect for others; (4) Respect for rules and regulations; (5) Ways for developing moral and character traits; (6) Ways to examine one's values; (7) Ways for making responsible choices; (8) Their potentials and worthiness as human beings; (9) Developing a sense of responsibility toward others; (10) Ways of behaving appropriately in public places; (11) The roles and duties of responsible citizens; (12) Developing effective communication skills; and (13) How appropriate social skills can promote safety. Curriculum strategies outlined in the text are designed to address the aforementioned social skills, and others, as they relate specifically to disabled individuals. Experimental, direct, and systematic curriculum methodologies will be employed to provide appropriate social skills training necessary for successful social interaction (Clees, 1994).

The phenomenon of educating disabled school-aged individuals has been studied and investigated extensively, with numerous special educators advocating that these individuals demonstrate appropriate social skills/behaviors inside as well as outside the classroom, due chiefly to them not being taught appropriate social skills, or mental or physical disabilities impeding their learning social skills (Francisco, 1993). It is a well-established fact that developing the appropriate social skills for successful interaction with one's peers and significant adults (teachers, parents) can be considered as one of the most important accomplishments of childhood (Gresham, 1985). Social skills deficits during the childhood and early adolescence periods of disabled individuals should be addressed as soon as possible (Furnham, 1986). This is particularly true in the establishment and maintenance of relations with peers and authority figures. These deficits not only have a negative impact on future interpersonal functioning in adulthood but may also affect current functioning, reducing the quality and quantity of the learning experiences to which disabled students are exposed in their educational settings.

Social skills have been defined as goal-oriented, rule-governed, situation-specific learned behaviors that vary according to social context, involving both observable and nonobservable cognitive and affective elements that help elicit positive or neutral responses and avoid negative responses from others. As such, social behavior constitutes an intricate interfactional process herein the behavior of school-aged disabled children influences and is influenced by that of their partners (e.g., teachers, mentors, tutors, and peers) within the interaction. As a result, society expects that when children reach various development stages, they will demonstrate greater foresight and controlled behaviors and be capable not only of meeting increased demands within the learning tasks but also of facing more complex, subtle social situations. Disabled individuals' failure to meet these expectations may increase their sense of social alienation and helplessness. Early exposure to appropriate social skills development for disabled individuals will significantly reduce these social failures. As much as possible, social skills intervention should be conducted with nondisabled individuals.

Integrating disabled individuals into regular classes has generated much debate in the professional literature. It appears that the greater the disability, the more resistant to integration. Odom's (1984) investigation demonstrated that integration of disabled individuals can be successfully achieved by:

1. Appropriate scheduling integrated classes at conducive times;
2. Considering ecological factors in the educational setting;
3. Alternating the instructional program, including those factors in which disabled individuals can successfully participate; and
4. Select appropriate materials and resources.

It is recommended that students participate as much **as possible in the preparation, planning and execution of the integrated program**.

Social and interpersonal skills involve teaching disabled individuals those skills needed to be successful in our society. Strategies have been developed to assist educators in providing appropriate social skills training for these students to operate successfully in the schools and society (Goldstein, 1984). Intervention techniques have been selected based upon research techniques, to assist disabled individuals in controlling aggression, assuming responsibility, and becoming a productive member of the group. A proactive approach is highly endorsed by the author.

A Proactive Approach

A proactive approach should be employed when teaching social skills to individuals with disabilities. Proactive instruction provide children with social intervention before negative behaviors occur. This approach is preferable to reactive teaching. Proactive instruction is designed to teach social skills before social rejection is experienced. Reactive instruction waits for the individual to fail and then apply intervention strategies. Many disabled individuals have problems developing appropriate social skills due to problems outlined through the test. Proactive instruction will prevent many of the negative consequences of inappropriate social skills occurring, as well as improving the self-image of disabled individuals. Some recommended strategies for proactive instruction may be to assist disabled and nondisabled individuals in:

1. Dealing positively with accusations;
2. Accepting feelings of others in a nonthreatening manner;
3. Respecting the feelings of others;
4. Avoiding fights and conflicts;
5. Dealing effectively with teasing;
6. Volunteering for class projects;
7. Giving praise or compliments to others;
8. Contributing to class projects;
9. Accepting compliments from others;
10. Cooperating with the class;
11. Apologizing for inappropriate behavior;
12. Expressing anger in a positive way;
13. Being well-groomed;
14. Showing affection and appreciation toward others;
15. Asking permission to borrow or use others properties.
16. Practicing self-control;
17. Practicing good hygiene.

As indicated throughout this book, disabled individuals must be taught appropriate social skills if they are going to be contributing members of society. The social skills outlined, should be infused throughout the curriculum and integrated as needed by the teacher. These strategies are seen as immediate, useful resources for teaching pro-social skills to these individuals. It is a how-to-do guide, providing specific examples and strategies for teachers and other professionals to immediately institute. Additionally, the construction of the curriculum has been based upon indepth research, and years of teaching and observing the social skill development of disabled individuals.

A Functional Approach

A functional approach to teaching social skills to disabled individuals can easily be infused throughout the curriculum. A functional approach involves exposing the learner with real-life situations and activities such as, self-identity, acquiring self-concepts, achieving socially acceptable behaviors, bonding, respecting the rights of others, maintaining good interpersonal skills, achieving independence, employing problem-solving skills, taking turns, and communicating appropriately with others.

Several group activities, such as role playing, modeling, cooperative groups and other group activities may be used to teach social skills to disabled individuals from a functional and holistic viewpoint within the context of real-life experiences. In essence, disabled children should be taught to model, imitate and demonstrate appropriate social skills in the reality in which they exist.

CURRICULUM DEVELOPMENT

A social skills curriculum should be based upon these social skills needed in order for disabled individuals to function successfully in one's society. Much of the research reviewed indicate that a significant number of disabled individuals have not mastered the necessary social skills needed to function successfully in our society.

The initial step in developing a curriculum in social skills is to identify those general social behaviors that are critical to successful social functioning. These general social behaviors were rewritten as general objectives. These general objectives provide the framework for constructing other components of the curriculum.

The second stage is sequence-specific objectives as they relate to the general objectives. All specific objectives will be designed to achieve the general objectives. Specific objectives should be stated in behavioral and measurable terms

The third step is to identify activities and resources that will achieve the objectives. (Refer to Appendix F for selected resources). The activities should be functional and reflect real-life experiences that disabled individuals are exposed to. As much as possible, parents should be involved in reinforcing the social skills taught. They may be used as resource individuals, and offering suggestions relative to material and activities. See Chapter 6 for specific strategies for involving parents.

The fourth step involves structuring each activity to follow a set sequence: (1) The teacher models the behavior; (2) The student attempts to repeat the demonstrated behavior; (3) Other students critique the behavior, and (4) The student practices the skill independent of the group. These steps assisted disabled individuals in internalizing their behaviors and assessing how their behaviors impact upon others.

A structured social skills learning program should follow the listed format for each behavior taught:

1. Behaviors should be written in behavioral terms.
2. The application of task analysis should be followed until each skill is mastered before moving to the next skill.
3. Some classroom arrangements will be necessary to accomplish some of the skills.
4. No specific time of the day should be devoted to skill training, rather, the training should be infused into the regular curriculum whenever possible.

Assessment of Social Skills

Assessment is continuous and should always be preceded by evaluation. This process is designed to monitor how effective a strategy is achieving a desired goal. Both self-monitoring by students, and teacher-monitoring are recommended. Most disabled individuals welcome the opportunity to be involved in monitoring their progress toward attaining a skill. Chapter 4 overviews selected social assessment techniques.

Social Skills Unit

General Objective of the Unit:
1. Disabled individuals will achieve socially acceptable behaviors in social and interpersonal situations.

Specific Objectives:
A. Disabled individuals will respect members of the opposite sex.
B. Disabled individuals will demonstrate appropriate character traits needed for acceptance in the public.
C. Disabled individuals will demonstrate proper behavior in public places.
D. Disabled and nondisabled individuals will show respect for the rights and properties of others.
E. Disabled and nondisabled individuals will recognize authority and follow instructions of school, home and the community.
F. Disabled individuals will recognize personal roles in public places.
G. Disabled individuals will use terms such as "please," "thank you" and "excuse me" at the appropriate times and places.
H. Disabled individuals will practice sportsmanship by sharing toys and information.
I. Disabled individuals will stand in line without bothering others.
J. Given a description of behavior on the bus, disabled individuals will show appropriate behavior.
K. Disabled individuals will know how and when to give and accept apologies.

Recommended Activities (Individualize and expand as needed):
A. Disabled and nondisabled individuals will respect members

of the opposite sex.

1. Role play a variety of situations showing disabled and nondisabled individuals how to show respect to others.

2. During everyday activities and conversations, require disabled individuals to say "please," "thank you" and "excuse me."

3. If the disabled individual curses at or calls the individual derogatory names, try to distract them. Intervene by defining the word(s), and indicate that these are words which hurt people.

4. Show disabled individuals pictures of children working and playing together. Indicate that both boys and girls are playing and working together and that both sexes are respecting each other.

5. Reward disabled individuals when they show appropriate behavior toward others.

6. Assign disabled and nondisabled individuals to group activities. Assign equal responsibilities to disabled individuals.

B. Disabled individuals will demonstrate appropriate character traits and behaviors needed for acceptance in public.

1. Provide activities where disabled individuals will be required to assist in structured activities with nondisabled individuals.

2. Demonstrate to disabled individuals how to move in crowds by saying, "excuse me," "pardon me" when people are blocking the way.

3. Model appropriate behavior and all activities when meeting new people or where disabled individuals come in contact with the public.

4. Explain and demonstrate to disabled individuals how to observe safety rules and how to be considerate of others when using public transportation.

5. Role play a variety of situations that might occur when disabled individuals are using public transportation. Demonstrate socially acceptable behaviors in these situations.

6. Demonstrate, show films, and model appropriate behaviors

for disabled individuals to demonstrate when receiving services from the barber shop, banks, stores, or any other public places.

7. Role play a variety of situations where disabled individuals demonstrate appropriate behavior when receiving public services.

8. Show disabled individuals how to greet people in a socially acceptable language in public.

C. Disabled individuals will show respect for the rights and properties of others.

1. Provide activities where disabled individuals will have to protect and share others' properties with nondisabled individuals.

2. Role play activities where disabled individuals will be required to cooperate with nondisabled individuals in order for the success of the group.

3. Initiate a variety of games and activities that require disabled individuals to share or take turns with each other and nondisabled individuals.

4. Provide activities for disabled individuals to share games, discuss the importance of protecting others' properties.

5. Allow time for disabled individuals to bring their games to school to share with the class. Emphasize the importance of safeguarding personal property.

6. Discuss vandalism. Draw from the experiences of disabled individuals. Discuss the legal aspects of vandalism in terms that they can understand by disabled individuals.

7. Provide activities where disabled individuals will verbally compliment their classmates.

D. Disabled individuals will recognize authority and follow instructions at school, home, and the community.

1. Through films, videotapes, and demonstrations, show disabled individuals how to respond appropriately to authority and establish rules, supervised and unsupervised. Have disabled individuals to narrate or draw appropriate ways of responding to authority.

2. Provide time for disabled individuals to share with nondisabled individuals appropriate ways of responding to authorities.

3. Discuss the importance of rules and laws. Summarize the importance of classroom rules. What purpose do they serve and why it is important to obey them?

4. Plan an activity where a rule is broken. Have disabled individuals to discuss the consequences of breaking the rule, how it affects others and planning the consequences of the behavior.

5. When the disabled individual breaks a rule, explain the consequences and demonstrate alternative ways of solving or addressing the problem.

6. Invite a law enforcement officer to speak to the class. Encourage interaction between the children and the officers.

7. Encourage parents to establish rules at home for disabled individuals to follow and discuss the consequences of breaking rules.

8. Role play, show films where individuals break laws and are held responsible for their actions. Discuss alternative ways of responding to the behaviors.

E. Disabled individuals will recognize personal roles in public places.

1. Read disabled individuals stories of high interest in which the characters accept responsibility for their behaviors.

2. Role play a variety of conditions in which disabled individuals are required to make a decision, some appropriate or inappropriate. Evaluate and discuss both types of behaviors.

3. When a situation arises where disabled individuals have broken a rule, discuss the consequences of such behavior. When possible, involve both disabled and nondisabled individuals in the selection of the consequences.

4. Develop activities stressing that when individuals act inappropriately, they must accept the consequences of the behaviors.

5. Encourage disabled individuals to think about the outcomes

of their behaviors by providing situations in which they must make choices.

F. Disabled individuals will use terms such as "please," "thank you" and "excuse me" at appropriate times.

1. During everyday activities, infuse within the curriculum, conversations where disabled individuals will use terms such as "excuse me," "thank you," etc., at appropriate times. Reward them for positive responses.

2. Role play a variety of situations requiring courteous responses from disabled and nondisabled individuals.

3. Encourage disabled individuals to use good manners as a consumer, through demonstrations and dramatic day activities.

4. Provide activities where disabled individuals are required to model behaviors. Praise successful attempts and discuss why others are not successful.

5. Demonstrate to disabled individuals how to move through crowds by saying, "excuse me," "may I please pass," etc.

G. Disabled individuals will practice sportsmanship by sharing toys and information with each other and nondisabled individuals.

1. As disabled individuals play and work together, provide activities where they must take turns and share materials with the class. Praise them when their attempts are successful.

2. Discuss the concept of a "good sport." Encourage the disabled individual to accept successes and failures in sports and games. Praise them for being a "good sport" and a "good loser," as well as a "good winner."

3. In the school, infuse activities within the curriculum that requires that disabled individuals take turns such as dramatic play activities that can only be successfully completed through team work and cooperation with the class.

4. When disabled individuals lose, encourage them to try again. Discuss the idea that losing is a part of winning. Provide activities which will allow them to win sometimes.

H. Disabled individuals will stand in line without annoying others.

1. Model and demonstrate appropriate behavior while in line. Praise and reward them for appropriate behavior.
2. Role play situations where they show appropriate behavior in line.
3. Discuss the importance of following rules. Relate how appropriately standing in line is a part of obeying rules.
4. Demonstrate to disabled individuals how standing in line without bothering others is respecting the rights of others.
5. Relate showing appropriate behavior in line to "good citizenship."

I. Given a description of behavior on the bus, disabled individuals will show appropriate behaviors.

1. Provide appropriate models for disabled individuals to follow when riding on buses.
2. Demonstrate how to handle situations such as pushing, stepping on toes, loud language, etc., while riding on buses.
3. Role play a variety of situations, appropriate and inappropriate, while riding on the bus.
4. Review films and filmstrips showing appropriate and inappropriate behaviors, have disabled individuals evaluate both situations and provide alternative solutions.

J. Disabled individuals will know how and when to use rational processes to check their emotions.

1. After a fight or a disturbance, form a circle and play a game before discussing the incident.
2. Sing a favorite song with disabled individuals before trying to settle an issue.

General Objective of the Unit:

2. Disabled individuals will show positive self-concepts when dealing with others.

Specific Objectives:

A. The disabled individuals will know how and when to use

rational processes to evaluate their emotions.

B. The disabled individuals will emphasize their special uniqueness by recognizing their potentials.

C. The disabled individuals will recognize the impact of their behaviors on others.

D. Provide activities for the disabled to personally and positively interact with each other and nondisabled individuals.

E. Provide activities showing special traits of disabled individuals.

F. Demonstrate and model behaviors which will enhance the self-image and concepts of disabled individuals.

G. Demonstrate and discuss ways that disabled individuals can effectively deal with their fears.

Recommended Activities (Individualize and expand as needed:)

A. Disabled individuals will know how and when to use rational processes to evaluate their emotions.

   1. Have disabled individuals choose an attitude they would like to make into an attitude mask: angry, happy, sad, tired, bored, scared, sick, encourage a large variety of feelings. Provide materials for them to make the masks. While they are making the masks, ask them to be thinking about how their mask will "act." After completion, have them share with each other.

   2. Choose both positive and negative feelings masks to role play each situation.

   3. Have disabled individuals to identify the major emotions felt most of the time: happy, sad, angry, scared, tired. Have them associate a color with each of the emotions. Use the mobiles when identifying emotions.

   4. Have disabled individuals identify people being angry from pictures. Discuss the following:

     a. Why is this person angry?

     b. Have you ever been angry?

     c. What makes you really, really, really, angry?

     d. What do you do when you get angry? Make a list and discuss.

   5. Discuss some ways to handle anger. Categorize and list on

chart paper. Praise disabled individuals for controlling anger in the classroom.

6. Assign disabled individuals the task of interviewing a nondisabled classmate about a problem he had and how it was solved. Films that focus on a central character with a problem to solve serve as good models for them and are catalysts for class discussion. Disabled individuals first discuss their problems in small groups. Teammates can then contribute ideas for resolution as well as just being supportive.

7. Teaching the following problem-solving steps to disabled individuals:
   a. What is the problem?
   b. Think of solutions.
   c. Select the two or three preferred solutions.
   d. What might happen if they were chosen?
   e. Choose the best solution after reviewing the consequences.
   f. Make a plan.
   g. Do it!
   h. Write down messages that can be disruptive to a class environment. This exercise will assist disabled individuals to recognize how deadly put-downs are to others' feelings. It also helps them find ways to change negative responses to more positive ones. Have disabled individuals make a set of 10 index cards for each team. Instruct them to write a different negative statement on each card. Each team elects a disabled individual to be the dealer who passes out the cards. Each team member reads one put-down message to the group. After each reading, the team gives suggestions that could be said instead. Some disabled individuals will need teacher assistance to complete the task. The team chooses the best answer to each put-down statement and records them on chart paper.

9. Provide activities for group discussion by showing a picture of emotions taking control. Have disabled individuals to give alternative ways to solve the problem.

B. Disabled individuals will emphasize their special uniqueness by recognizing their potentials.

1. Tell them that they are going to be learning about a very special person. Who is the most special person in the whole world? When a disabled individual comes up with the answer that he/she is the most special person in the world, praise him/her.

2. Show disabled individuals a stuffed animal with a price tag. "How much is this animal worth?" "How much are you worth?" Indicate that they are **PRICELESS.** The teacher should remark, "You are worth more than all the stuffed animals in the world."

3. The teacher provides a jingle for disabled individuals to recite. A circle is formed and an object is passed around. Each disabled individual is instructed to say something positive about the disabled or nondisabled individual passing the object to him.

4. Have disabled individuals to draw pictures about things that they can do successfully. Emphasize the point that all of us have potentials for being successful.

5. Instruct disabled individuals to keep records of their achievements, as they accomplish each of their achievements, they are written down or drawn. The teacher periodically inspects and evaluates the record, making appropriate positive remarks.

6. Encourage disabled individuals to think about things they like about themselves and those they wish they could change. Remind them that there are some things we can change and other things we cannot change. Discuss with them things they can and cannot change.

7. Construct mobiles that have silhouettes of disabled individuals as the center. Have hanging from the silhouettes, words, magazine cut-outs or drawings that illustrate the various "specialties" of them. Disabled individuals' names will appear in big letters on the silhouette.

C. Disabled individuals will recognize the impact of their behaviors on others.

1. Use a hand puppet to demonstrate how negative behaviors, such as saying unkind words to others, can have a negative impact on them.

2. Discuss with disabled individuals how they can choose to treat disabled and nondisabled individuals in a positive way. Pictures or puppets may be used.

3. Group disabled individuals in a circle and have them relate how other people's behaviors have had a negative impact upon them. Solicit solutions from them as to how these behaviors can be changed to positive ones.

4. Use creative dramatics and role playing strategies showing how the negative impact of behaviors displayed by others can have an impact on them.

5. Provide activities and examples to assist disabled individuals in internalizing their behaviors, such as thinking out loud before acting, and examining the consequences of their behaviors on others.

6. Role play activities showing fair and unfair treatment of disabled and nondisabled individuals. Outline how unfair treatment may become fair.

D. Provide activities for disabled individuals to personally and positively interact with each other.

1. For each hour of the clock, have disabled individuals fill in a different classmate's name. Encourage them to initiate the meeting with the classmate by introducing themselves. Model to them how to make appropriate introductions.

2. Write each disabled individual's name on a slip of paper and put all slips into a small container. As the container is passed, each individual draws the name of another child and says what is special about that person. No negative comments are allowed. This activity requires a great deal of time to complete.

3. Choose a disabled individual to be the recipient of the greeting for the day. Each disabled individual writes a compliment to the chosen person. At the end of the day, the recipient collects all the messages from the class.

4. Encourage disabled individuals to write messages on special

occasions to a peer.

5. Have each disabled individual find a special character in a magazine. Give the character a special name, place and date of birth, family, friends, and occupation. Have the disabled individual describe how this special person feels.

E. Demonstrate ways that disabled individuals can reduce negative repercussions in the classroom.

1. Provide scenarios for the disabled individual to discuss and role play negative behaviors such as:
   a. Suppose that by telling your friend that you are angry with him. He becomes angry with you? Stress frequently the feelings inside to avoid conflicts.
   b. If someone called you ugly, stupid, or dumb, how would you react? How would you control your feelings?
   c. Suppose some says: "I don't like you?"; "I hate you, get out of my way!"
   d. Suppose someone calls you stupid?

2. Provide opportunities for disabled individuals to be involved in the construction of classroom rules, as well as the consequences for violating the rules.

3. Demonstrate to disabled individuals that all of us at times have many different feelings; some we can control and others that get out of control. Today we are going to discuss ways we can reduce negative feelings inside of us.

4. Use a hand puppet. Make the puppet look sad, shy, scared, and happy. The puppet should elicit empathy from the children as they identify with some of his feelings. Have disabled individuals discuss how they would handle the feelings.

F. Provide activities showing special traits of disabled individuals.

1. Give each disabled individual a piece of paper. Have them draw and paste pictures, photographs and souvenirs about who he/she is. When all the squares are completed, they can be taped together and displayed as a scrapbook.

2. Instruct disabled individuals to complete a promotional piece (poem, story, picture, etc.) about themselves.

3. Have promotional information shared with the class in order to affirm themselves in front of others.

4. Provide opportunities for disabled individuals to share information about themselves. Use the shared information to determine things which disabled individuals have in common with other nondisabled individuals. Have the information shared with the class. This activity may assist in developing the self-concept of shy disabled individuals.

5. Videotape disabled individuals performing positive behaviors. Show to the class and accent the positive behaviors.

6. Develop a citizen of the week award. Award certificates to disabled individuals who meet the established criteria.

G. Demonstrate, plan, and model behaviors which will enhance the self-images and concepts of disabled individuals.

1. Help disabled individuals develop an accurate self-description by modeling acceptable behaviors.

2. Model behaviors showing disabled individuals how not to be over-sensitive to criticism.

3. Plan activities that will assist disabled individuals to clarify or think more about themselves, such as showing photographs and telling stories about themselves.

4. Give examples of how disabled individuals can make positive statements toward self and others.

5. Provide opportunities for disabled individuals to discover major sources of influences upon self.

6. Make tokens that the teacher will give out for disabled individuals who have been "caught doing something good."

7. Construct a mobile and hang from it, words and phrases that are used in your classroom to promote positive behaviors such as:

I'm sorry	Thank you	Excuse me
Can I help	Good morning	I forgive you
I like you	May I help	Pardon me

H. Demonstrate and discuss ways that disabled individuals can effectively deal with their fears.

1. Structure group activities where disabled individuals can dis-

cuss their fears. Emphasize the fact that all of us have fears at one time or another.

2. Using chart paper, make a list of some of the fears stated by disabled individuals. Discuss ways of minimizing fears.

3. Have disabled individuals to use pictures to discuss the types of fears shown and what can be done to reduce the levels of fears.

4. Develop activities and dramatic activities showing how fears may be reduced in the following areas:
   a. Being ashamed of looks;
   b. Making fun of disabilities;
   c. Being left out of an important activity or an event;
   d. Looking different;
   e. Divorcing parents;
   f. Having disabilities;
   g. Presenting before a group or the class;
   h. Playing games;
   i. Making a mistake;
   j. Being chosen by a team;
   k. Being criticized;
   l. Having a few friends;
   m. Moving to another community;
   n. Playing alone.

5. Write and develop stories about fears, indicating a solution for controlling them.

6. Have disabled individuals share some of their past fears with the class and indicate how they overcome them.

General Objective of the Unit:

3. Disabled individuals will identify and evaluate their feelings and the feelings of others.

Specific Objectives:

A. Assist disabled individuals in realizing that other people have feelings and what can be done to help them and others feel better about themselves.

B. Make disabled individuals aware of how their anger can affect the feelings and well-being of others.

C. Provide activities showing the impact of negative behaviors regarding self and others.

D. Develop strategies for effectively identifying and appropriately expressing emotions and attitudes.

E. Demonstrate to disabled individuals the values of accepting praise.

F. Emphasize to disabled individuals that it is important to discuss their fears with someone who can assist them.

G. Show pictures, films, and videotapes about disabled and nondisabled individuals expressing feelings. Provide opportunities for disabled individuals to assess and evaluate the various types of feelings.

H. Instruct disabled individuals that it is okay to show feelings, sympathy, and good will toward others.

Recommended Activities (Individualize and expand as needed):

A. Assist disabled individuals in realizing that other people have feelings and what can be done to help people feel better about themselves.

1. Show pictures of disabled and nondisabled individuals feeling sad and/or scared. Why is this person sad? What do you think happened to her/him? What could he/she do to change those scary sad feelings?

2. Through pictures, show and emphasize that not everyone is afraid of the same things. Individuals express different feelings toward different things.

3. Discuss with disabled individuals the fact that we have all had times when we have so many feelings inside us at one time that we feel like we cannot handle them. We can control some of our feelings.

4. Instruct disabled individuals that the use of negative phrases and words such as "shut up," "you're stupid," "you dummy," "go away," "get out of here," and "leave me alone," do not make people feel good about themselves.

5. Use puppets to show different feelings. Pose the following questions to disabled individuals: "How did the puppet

choose to act on his feelings the first time? Second time? Why?" Just like we choose our eating habits, we also choose our feelings. We can choose to feel good about ourselves, or we can choose to feel bad about ourselves. We can choose to treat people in positive ways when we express our feelings, or we can choose to handle situations in a negative manner and keep all our feelings inside. Which is easier? Letting our feelings out in a positive way or keeping them in? Which is healthier?

B. Make disabled individuals aware of how their anger can affect the feelings and well-being of others.

1. Have incidents of angry behaviors discussed in groups consisting of disabled and nondisabled individuals, highlighting how the angry behaviors affected others in the group.

2. Show pictures of angry expressions. Discuss how other means of expressing anger could be done.

3. Using pictures, films, stories, etc., have disabled individuals to discuss what might have caused the anger. How could the incident have been prevented?

4. Teach and instruct disabled individuals techniques that will enable them to control their anger, such as being sensitive to feedback and evaluating their behaviors.

5. Instruct disabled individuals on how anger is manifested. Highlight the physical and social aspects of it.

6. Using role playing and creative dramatics to demonstrate various stages of anger. Discuss alternative ways of expressing anger.

7. Develop short stories and plays showing how anger can be expressed in a positive fashion.

8. Have various stages of anger modeled for disabled individuals alone with techniques for controlling it.

C. Provide activities showing the impact of negative behaviors regarding self and others.

1. Discuss with disabled individuals how negative behaviors impact upon others.

2. Through the use of pictures, discuss how negative behaviors are influencing their character.

3. Have disabled individuals to role play negative behaviors, reflecting their impact on others.

4. With disabled individuals develop short skits portraying how negative behaviors influence others.

5. Using a variety of media, art, painting, etc., have disabled individuals to develop stories displaying the consequences of negative behaviors on self and others.

6. Use puppets to show the negative impact of behaviors on others. Ask disabled individuals "How do you feel about yourself when you are happy? Sad? Mad?" Use the puppets to demonstrate the behaviors they would like to show.

7. Say something unkind to the puppet. Have it sit up tall and shake his/her head "no" as if to refuse to accept the remark.

D. Demonstrate to disabled individuals the values of accepting praise.

1. Role play incidents showing disabled individuals how not to be uncomfortable with praise.

2. Discuss with disabled individuals how not to become embarrassed when accepting praise.

3. Review films and videotapes showing individuals accepting praise.

4. Model appropriate behaviors for accepting praise.

5. Have disabled individuals to share their experiences in accepting praise.

6. Model appropriate behavior showing disabled individuals how to apologize.

7. Praise disabled individuals when they have accomplished a positive task or have displayed positive behaviors.

E. Develop strategies for effectively identifying and appropriately expressing emotions and attitudes.

1. Discuss with disabled individuals how the way they feel affects the way they behave. Use the puppets to help illustrate this. Have them identify the puppets' feelings by demonstrating various emotional moods. Ask them to demonstrate when they are glad, angry or sad.

2. Make a booklet for disabled individuals. Make a special key

for each booklet. Have them write the secret feelings or feelings that are very special to them inside their booklets and lock them up to keep them safe.

3. Have disabled individuals look through magazines. Find pictures of people who have great smiles. Cut out the smiles and paste them on the cover of books. Now look at the cover. How does it make you feel?

4. Disabled individuals will articulate their feelings and listen to the feelings of others during story and sharing time. Elicit criticism from the class.

5. Create scenarios expressing emotions and attitudes. These scenarios should be both negative and positive. Have disabled individuals group and classify the scenarios based on how they would act.

6. Using the information from #5, have disabled individuals draw pictures. Have each picture discussed.

F. Emphasize to disabled individuals that it is important to discuss their fears with someone who can assist them.

1. List and categorize fears with disabled individuals. Stress the fact that fears are often a result of our perceptions of a situation, rather than the danger inherent in them. Instruct the disabled individual to discuss their fears with parents, pastor, counselor, relatives, and/or a close friend. Seek their opinions and advice.

2. Ask disabled individuals to discuss their fears. Encourage them to explain and identify what the fears are and provide suggestions for dealing with the fears.

3. Relate to disabled individuals that most fears are imaginary. Have them write their fears on a piece of paper. Place the fears in a paper bag and separate real fears from imaginary fears. Discuss both types of fears.

4. Use puppets to demonstrate various stages of imaginary fears.

5. From the list of fears in #1, discuss with disabled individuals how these fears may be minimized or corrected.

6. Role play how fears originate and how many of them are based upon uncertainties, doubts, rumors, and untruth.

7. Discuss with disabled individuals and demonstrate how some fears are needed and are useful.

G. Show pictures, films, videotapes and model behaviors about disabled and nondisabled individuals expressing feelings. Provide opportunities for disabled individuals to assess and evaluate the various types of feelings.

1. Collect magazine pictures of people's faces expressing different feelings: surprise, contentment, anxiety, anger, grief, etc. Have disabled individuals study the pictures and decide on the circumstances that led to the emotion shown. May be used individually or in groups.

2. Emphasize important feelings by stressing that feelings make our lives rich and exciting, but they can cause us problems depending on how we act on those feelings as well as how we deal with them.

3. Instruct disabled individuals to reflect about things they feel good about in others and compare to their feelings.

4. Develop cooperative groups of disabled and nondisabled individuals. Have disabled individuals to role play certain feelings such as sad, happy, upset, disagreeable and agreeable. Have other groups to critique the feelings and give alternative ways they would have dealt with the feelings.

5. Review films and videotapes where people are expressing different feelings. Have disabled individuals group and classify them.

6. Write stories expressing different feelings. Have disabled individuals to share with the class.

H. Instruct disabled individuals that it is okay to show feelings, sympathy and respect toward others.

1. These behaviors will need to be modeled for many disabled individuals. Many have learned to hide their deepest feelings. Role playing and creative dramatics will assist as well as ask the basic question, "Why?"

2. Provide activities where disabled individuals can give supported positive comments to each other without embarrassment.

3. Show films and videotapes about having respect and disre-

spect for others. List both types of activities on the board and discuss with disabled individuals how alternative approaches may be used to correct disrespectable acts.

4. Have disabled individuals to role play both respectful and disrespectful acts.

5. Provide pictures for disabled individuals showing both respectful and disrespectful acts. Discuss with them how they felt about each type of act.

6. Role play activities showing feelings and sympathy toward others.

7. Instruct disabled individuals to develop stories showing feelings and sympathy toward others.

8. Use puppets to demonstrate and show feelings and respect toward others.

General Objective of the Unit:

4. Disabled individuals will use appropriate communication skills to develop new friendships and rekindle old ones.

Specific Objectives:

A. Review the importance of communication skills in developing appropriate interpersonal skills.

B. Develop activities and games to better acquaint disabled individuals with each other as well as nondisabled individuals.

C. Discuss the meaning of friendship. Outline ways that friendships may be developed.

D. Identify and articulate the characteristics of a good friend.

E. Provide disabled individuals with the knowledge to distinguish between friendly and unfriendly actions.

F. Provide activities for other disabled individuals to address the group on several points of interest. Develop criteria to evaluate the topics.

G. Invite other classes to group activities, such as talks and games; elicit their input.

Recommended Activities (Individualize and expand as needed):

A. Review the importance of communication skills in

developing appropriate interpersonal skills. Communication is an important component in developing social skills. The following are suggestions for building a communicative environment for the classroom. When used at the beginning, these exercises can help disabled individuals rekindle old friendships and develop

1. Review with disabled individuals the relationship of communication skills to the development of appropriate interpersonal skills.
2. Teach disabled individuals how to properly express themselves in public places.
3. Provide activities to make disabled individuals aware of appropriate language to use at public and social functions.
4. Model techniques for teaching disabled individuals how to monitor their oral expression of social functions.
5. Have disabled individuals to critique each other's communication skills while demonstrating social and interpersonal skills.
6. Use high profile individuals to compare the relationship between communication and interpersonal skills of disabled individuals.
7. Provide many activities for disabled individuals to express themselves.

B. Develop activities and games to better acquaint disabled individuals with each other.

1. Instruct disabled individuals how to play "people hung." Have them move the classroom in order to learn more about their classmates. Tell the children to move about for five minutes to collect a different classmate's signature for each item on the list. The list could contain items such as the following:

   Has a bird for a pet.
   Has black hair.
   Has the shortest hair in the room
   Likes popcorn.
   Has two brothers.

Has one sister.

Is the oldest child in the family.

Has been on a fishing trip.

Likes science best of all school subjects.

Was born in June.

Has won a medal in a sports competition.

2. Group disabled individuals by special characteristics such as birthdays. Have them to indicate on what day of the month they were born.

3. Provide activities for the individuals to share their interests with the class.

4. Have individuals to write stories concerning their favorite friends. Have them to identify similar characteristics between them.

C. Discuss the meaning of friendship. Outline ways that friendship may be developed.

1. Divide students into teams of three or four disabled and nondisabled individuals. Provide each team with a form. Inform them that as a team they must decide on a list of characteristics they all agree are important in a friend. List these characteristics on the form.

2. Each team must work together to rank the characteristics in order of importance. Review with each team that the characteristic they have agreed to as most important should be listed at #1, and so on. Instruct them to complete the remainder of the form by themselves. Tell them to look over the form and decide which characteristic(s) can be best applied to themselves.

3. Explain to disabled individuals that sometimes when working in a group, positions or ideas have to be agreed upon so that the group can come to a decision. Have them tell what happened to them and whether they can come up with a group answer. If the children have different answers, have them describe them to the large group.

4. Have disabled individuals to share their forms with the class.

5. Discuss with the class what constitutes good friendship. What are the components of good friendship.

6. Summarize how friendship may be developed and maintained.

7. Develop the concept that it is "okay" to develop friendships with others.

D. Identify and articulate the characteristics of a good friend.

1. Discuss the characteristics of a good friend. Ask disabled individuals to list at least five important friendship attributes, such as humor, availability, kindness, loyalty, and common interests.

2. Write the descriptions that come up on the chalkboard to refer to again and to add to as the class thinks of new descriptions. Encourage disabled individuals to write their own "recipes" for how to make a friend.

3. Have disabled individuals to work in teams to develop a mutually agreed upon recipe. The team's final recipe can be written on an index card in a "recipe" format. A cookbook may be used as a guide.

4. Instruct the class to draw pictures relevant to characteristics or attributes of good friendship.

5. Using pictures and photographs, have the class identify attributes of a good friendship.

6. Have disabled and nondisabled individuals to write stories about how they met their best friends.

E. Provide the class with the knowledge to distinguish between friendly and unfriendly actions.

1. Make a circle and cut it out. Divide the circle into at least eight parts. Cut a dial hand/pointer using a piece of plastic. Attach the spinner to the center of the wheel with a paper fastener. Ask disabled and nondisabled individuals to think of ways to be friendly. Write down appropriate deeds in each section of the circle. Provide opportunities for each child to spin the wheel and discuss the deed where the pointer stopped.

2. Cut out and glue small photographs which the children have brought from home onto a piece of chart paper. Have them

to classify friendly and unfriendly behaviors from the photographs.

3. Make a chart categorizing behaviors by friendly and
unfriendly. Seek input from both disabled and nondisabled
individuals.

4. Identify friendly and unfriendly behaviors from stories and
pictures,

5. Assist the class in constructing stories about friendly and
unfriendly behaviors.

6. From the list of friendly and unfriendly behaviors listed in
#3, have the class give examples of the two types of behav-
iors.

F. Provide activities for disabled and nondisabled individuals to
address the group on several points of interest. Develop criteria
for evaluating the topics.

1. Discuss with disabled and nondisabled individuals
standards for evaluating reports. Include such factors as:
   a. Being polite to the speaker.
   b. Showing respect for the speaker.
   c. Do not interrupt the speaker.
   d. Save questions to the end of the presentation.
   e. Give a valid criticism for a disagreement.

2. For disabled and nondisabled individuals who have similar
interests, permit them to report in groups.

3. Overview a common format for giving oral presentations.
Instruct individuals that preparation is needed in giving a
report.

4. Invite the librarian to instruct the class on library techniques
and finding information on selected topics.

G. Invite other classes to group activities such as talks and games.
Elicit their input.

1. Expand the circle of friends by inviting other classes to participate.

2. Attempt to develop teams involving other disabled and
nondisabled individuals from different classes.

3. New developed teams may report to joint classes. The devel-

oped format for evaluating reports in #1 will be used.

4. A joint culminating activity, involving all of the classes, may be used and presented to the total school relevant to friendly and unfriendly actions.

5. Group art projects may be developed and posted throughout the school.

General Objective of the Unit:

5. Disabled individuals will acquire self-confidence and employ appropriate social skills at home, school, and community.

Specific Objectives:

A. Disabled individuals will demonstrate how to cope with their feelings and emotions arising from conflicts.

B. Disabled individuals will practice acceptable social behaviors at school, home, and in the community.

C. Disabled individuals will accept praise when given.

D. Disabled individuals will accept criticism when given and demonstrate how to use the information for self-improvement.

E. Disabled individuals will develop a sense of pride and self-confidence in themselves.

F. Disabled individuals will control anger when provoked.

G. Disabled individuals will understand the impact of their behavior upon others.

Recommended Activities (Individualize and expand as needed):

A. Disabled individuals will demonstrate how to cope with their feelings and emotions arising from conflict.

1. From newspapers, filmstrips, and tapes, show pictures of sad, happy, and angry faces. Have disabled individuals to explain how the people are feeling.

2. Have disabled individuals to draw faces showing a variety of facial expressions. Have them to discuss and interpret their pictures, relating how the expressions can be changed.

3. Role play conditions which may create anger among children. Model and demonstrate ways of controlling anger.

4. Practice behavior intervention strategies with disabled indi-

viduals to assist them in controlling anger. Praise them for successful attempts.

5. Provide activities when disabled individuals can talk out their anger. Demonstrate how unacceptable behaviors are not appropriate ways for expressing anger, model and demonstrate strategies.

B. Disabled individuals will practice acceptable behaviors at school, home, and the community.

1. Discuss rules and laws with disabled and nondisabled individuals. Explain that rules are made for our protection. Have them to discuss classroom, home and community rules.

2. When children break a rule, explain to them why obeying rules are important. Elicit responses from them about how rules protect us.

3. Role play situations showing appropriate and inappropriate behaviors at school, home, and community. Have both disabled and nondisabled individuals critique each situation.

4. Show filmstrips, videos of individuals displaying appropriate behavior.

5. Provide training for parents to use interpersonal skills to improve acceptable behaviors.

C. Disabled individuals will accept praise when given.

1. Develop activities, such as demonstrations, role playing, modeling, and using magazines showing individuals accepting praise.

2. Discuss with disabled individuals that by accepting praise which is not a sign of weakness but of strength, individuals are attempting to show appreciation of tasks well done.

3. Provide activities throughout the day where both disabled and nondisabled individuals are praised for successfully completing assigned tasks.

4. Role play activities where an authoritative individual is accepting praise. Have the class to discuss why? What made the authoritative individual change?

D. Disabled individuals will accept criticism and use the information for self-improvement.

1. Role play situations in which disabled and nondisabled individuals are criticized by each other. Demonstrate activities showing the class how to respond to criticisms by explaining that the criticisms are not true.

2. When situations arise in which individuals behave badly, explain to them how their behaviors have affected the class. Require them to state an appropriate way that the situation could have been handled.

3. Discuss and model for disabled individuals positive types of criticisms; compare with negative criticisms.

4. Show films and videotapes where criticisms are true and provide activities by which disabled individuals will show how to use negative criticisms for self-improvement.

E. Disabled individuals will develop confidence in self by actively participating in groups and individual activities.

1. Discuss the concept of a family, relate the concept of a family to the class. Provide activities where disabled and nondisabled individuals will have to work as a unit.

2. Assign the class to teams of four or five, where each team, both disabled and nondisabled, will have a task to complete. Encourage each individual to do his share as a member of the team.

3. Encourage parents to include children in family activities. Give praise when earned as a contributing member of the group.

4. Provide activities where disabled individuals must assume leadership. Their leadership will depend upon the success or the failure of the activity.

5. Provide disabled individuals with situations in which they must make a decision. Give support, guidance, and praise until an appropriate decision is made.

F. Disabled individuals will control their anger when provoked.

1. Use puppets and have puppets call each other names. Discuss with disabled individuals techniques for ignoring name calling.

2. Provide a system for rewarding and praising disabled individuals when they ignore name calling.

3. Role play situations in which puppets call each other names because of an accidental bump or some other unavoidable situation. Stress that name-calling is unpleasant, but frequently it is best to ignore it.

4. Discuss with disabled individuals that frequent name calling reflects insecurity and the best way of dealing with the problem is to ignore it.

G. Disabled individuals will understand the impact of their behaviors upon others.

1. Videotape inappropriate behaviors of disabled and nondisabled individuals. Discuss how these behaviors impacted upon others.

2. Have disabled individuals to discuss incidents where negative behaviors have affected them.

3. Role play situations where inappropriate or negative behaviors have caused others to be sad.

4. During activities in the classroom, encourage disabled individuals to ask if the activity is disturbing to others. Remind both disabled and nondisabled individuals to be considerate of others.

5. Develop signals to indicate to the class that their negative behaviors are affecting others.

6. On bulletin boards, have individuals draw pictures and narrate how positive behavior impacts upon others.

7. Encourage parents to implement and to follow up strategies at home.

General Objective of the Unit:

6. Disabled individuals will use social skills strategies to solve problems by communicating appropriately to others at home, community and school.

Specific Objectives:

A. Disabled individuals will practice the art of compromising.

B. Disabled individuals will demonstrate the need to anticipate consequences.

C. Disabled individuals will understand the need to set

appropriate goals.

D. Disabled individuals will develop the skill of looking at alternatives.

E. Disabled individuals will know where to find good advice.

F. Disabled individuals will recognize emergency situations.

G. Disabled individuals will demonstrate how to interrupt appropriately.

Recommended Activities (Individualize and expand as needed):

A. Disabled individuals will practice the art of compromising.

1. Create situations and opportunities that offer a chance for compromise. Encourage both disabled and nondisabled individuals to practice the art of compromising. Provide guidance when needed.

2. Demonstrate and model compromises with disabled individuals. Use different occasions and events to demonstrate compromising strategies.

3. Provide activities where disabled individuals will have to compromise with themselves and nondisabled individuals. Provide guidance and praise to the class forbeing cooperative and accepting the compromises.

4. Provide opportunities for disabled individuals to make choices when choices conflict. Discuss the role of compromising.

B. Disabled individuals will demonstrate the need to anticipate consequences.

1. Role play situations in which the consequences of behaviors are anticipated by disabled individuals.

2. As disabled individuals participate in instructional activities, encourage them to anticipate the consequences of their behaviors.

3. Read disabled individuals stories and show filmstrips and have them to anticipate the consequences of the characters' behavior.

4. Provide activities which will require disabled individuals to think through behaviors by considering the consequences before reacting.

C. Disabled individuals will understand the need to set appropriate goals.

1. Provide time to discuss with disabled and nondisabled individuals the importance of setting realistic goals.
2. Assign activities to the class which will aid them in achieving their goals.
3. Initiate and review a variety of techniques to enable disabled individuals to self-monitor their achievements toward accomplishing their goals.
4. Provide support and encouragement to disabled individual praise them frequently.
5. Review films, stories, and videotapes relevant to famous individuals. Have disabled individuals to discuss whether or not they thought that these individuals have well-defined goals.

D. Disabled individuals will develop the skill of looking at alternatives.

1. Plan activities where disabled individuals will be introduced to alternative ways of solving problems.
2. Encourage disabled individuals to "try another way" when their initial approaches do not appear to be working. Provide demonstrations and models for disabled and nondisabled individuals to imitate. Give praise frequently.
3. Role play several situations involving using alternative approaches to conflict resolutions.

E. Disabled individuals will know where to find good advice.

1. Visit community agencies, such as recreational centers, health clubs and public libraries. Discuss the purposes and roles of these organizations indicating specific services they provide.
2. Invite community individuals to talk with disabled individuals on selected topics. Develop a pool of volunteers to be available for them to consult.
3. Role play situations in which disabled individuals are seeking both good and bad advice. Include situations the disabled individual is likely to experience.
4. Place pictures of community helpers on a bulletin board with a description of their duties and review situations in which

disabled individuals may react with them.

F. Disabled individuals will recognize emergency situations.
    1. Discuss with disabled individuals how to avoid emerging situations, such as name calling, fighting, stealing and other aggressive acts. Model and role play several situations.
    2. During instructional activities, remind disabled and nondisabled individuals not to interrupt. Praise them for successful attempts.
    3. Develop strategies which will give the class clues concerning their time to talk, such as if someone asks a question or stops talking.
    4. Role play situations in which disabled and nondisabled individuals are introduced to each other. Encourage them to respond to each other appropriately; to take turns speaking, and not to interrupt each other. Praise the class for their efforts.

General Objective of the Unit:

7. Disabled individuals will demonstrate how to experience positive self-acceptance and awareness.

Specific Objectives:

A. Instruct disabled individuals that changing old habits are very difficult and requires a systematic plan.
B. Identify individuals who can assist disabled individuals in bringing about positive changes.
C. Provide a monitoring and follow-up plan to assist disabled individuals in making changes.
D. Accent the positive things that disabled and nondisabled individuals do in the class. Praise them frequently.
E. Discuss special traits and characteristics of the class. Provide opportunities for each individual to record his/her special traits.

Recommended Activities (Individualize and expand as needed):

A. Instruct disabled individuals that changing old habits are very difficult and require a systematic plan.

1. Assist disabled individuals in identifying the source of the problems. They should be able to briefly describe the problem and explain why they consider it to be a problem.

2. Instruct disabled individuals to brainstorm as many solutions to the problem as they can. A good practice is for the disabled individual to write all the possibilities down.

3. Have disabled individuals look through the possibilities and choose two or three "best" choices.

4. Have disabled individuals discuss how they might arrive at the best solution to the problem. Have each disabled individual to list the solutions.

5. Develop group activities with disabled and nondisabled individuals whereby the group will choose the solution which appears to be the best.

6. Guide the class in constructing a course of action for changing old negative habits.

7. Monitor the plan frequently with feedback to the class.

B. Identify individuals who can assist disabled individuals in bringing about positive changes.

1. Direct disabled individuals to list individuals who they trust. Have them to indicate why they trust these individuals.

2. Expand the discussions by having both disabled and nondisabled individuals indicate how selected individuals may help them change negative habits.

3. Review film and videotapes showing famous individuals. Ask the children questions such as:

   a. What do you like about the individual?

   b. How do you believe these individuals can contribute to bring about positive change?

   c. Do you know anything about the history of this individual?

4. Using the dialogue established in #3, choose two or three famous individuals and summarize their histories, indicating how they overcame aversive conditions as well as individuals who assisted them in bringing about positive changes.

5. Discuss with disabled individuals what might have happened

if these famous individuals had not changed some of their negative behaviors.

6. Role play some of the famous individuals, emphasizing how they brought about positive changes.

7. Have disabled individuals to develop stories about individuals who overcome aversive conditions.

C. Provide a monitoring and follow-up plan to assist disabled individuals in making changes.

1. Develop an evaluation sheet for disabled individuals. They will indicate daily on the chart, progress made toward making changes in their behaviors. (See Appendix E for an example of an evaluation sheet).

2. Teachers should check the evaluation sheet weekly and confer individually with each child highlighting "positives" and minimizing "negatives."

3. Develop an award system for disabled individuals. Reward them for keeping their evaluation sheet in order as well as those who have shown improvement.

4. Teach disabled individuals how to graph the progress for the week by showing the number for each category. Assist them in interpreting what the graphs show.

5. Use role models in the school and community to demonstrate how successful changes can be made.

6. Have talk shows where disabled individuals can relate to how they brought about change.

7. Discuss with disabled individuals factors which should be considered when planning change.

D. Accent the positive things that disabled and nondisabled individuals do in the class. Praise frequently.

1. Frequently use positive statements about good deeds performed.

2. Provide opportunities where disabled individuals may discover positive things about themselves through role playing and creative dramatics.

3. Develop a citizen of the week award. Stipulate standards for achieving the award as well as a reward for both disabled

and nondisabled individuals.

    4. Develop activities where disabled individuals can be successful and reward them for achieving success.

    5. Have something positive to say about each disabled individual daily.

    6. Use disabled and nondisabled individuals as models to assist in shaping positive behaviors

F. Discuss special traits and characteristics of disabled individ uals. Provide opportunities for each disabled individual to record his special traits.

    1. Through observations and interviews with disabled individuals and parents, determine special traits and abilities of each disabled individual.

    2. Use the required knowledge gained from #1 to develop specific activities for disabled individuals to complete. Motivation and success should be high because of the high interest rate.

    3. Catch disabled and nondisabled individuals being good and videotape behaviors. Show and discuss behaviors with the class.

    4. Associate videotapes of positive behaviors with class room rules and acts of courtesy.

    5. Photograph both negative and positive behaviors. Post photographs on the board under appropriate or in appropriate behaviors. Discuss ways in which inappropriate behaviors can be made appropriate.

    6. Using information from the bulletin board, have disabled individuals to role play both types of behaviors.

    7. Determine special abilities of disabled individuals as outlined in #1, and assign them special functions such as setting up and operating the film projector.

EVALUATION OF SOCIAL SKILLS

General evaluation techniques were outlined in Chapter 4. If evaluation results are to be effectively used to gage to what extent the stated objectives have been achieved, then the evaluation process must be properly planned prior to employing procedures for assessing social skills of disabled individuals. A decision must be made on what to evaluate. This approach will facilitate the selection of appropriate methods and techniques such as:

1. Evaluating the competence of a particular social skill;
2. Determining the baseline behavior for a particular social skill;
3. Using results to revise the unit;
4. Providing information to gage the progress of disabled individuals;
5. Appraising the effectiveness of selected social skills activities;
6. Making sure that disabled individuals have the necessary prerequisites for performing the social skills;
7. Having the necessary physical and human resources to conduct the unit;
8. Eliciting the cooperation of parents;
9. Providing training for parents to follow up social skills at home;
10. Determining the reactions of disabled individuals toward selected activities (Taylor, 1992).

Specific Evaluation Techniques

Specific evaluation techniques for evaluating social skills development of disabled individuals are many. There are both formal and informal techniques which may be applied. Chapter 4 outlined specific formal techniques. This section will address informal procedures to employ. These techniques appear to be readily accessible or can be easily developed by the classroom teacher. Some recommended strategies are outlined:

1. Develop a brief checklist to assess social skills in a variety of situations.

2. Simulate social activities requiring disabled individuals to portray different roles that can be used to assess the understanding of appropriate behaviors in various settings. Group and individual appraisal of the activity may be conducted by the class.

3. Group assignments can be used to evaluate the ability of disabled individuals to work cooperatively. Record specific incidents, appropriate and inappropriate incidents.

4. Model and provide illustrations of appropriate and inappropriate behaviors. Have disabled individuals to demonstrate both types of behaviors and discriminate between them.

5. Structure activities and situations which call for specific kinds of behaviors and observe the performance of disabled individuals. A rating scale may be used.

6. Assess the frequency of inappropriate behaviors, assist disabled individuals in monitoring their own behaviors.

7. Use a variety of audio-visual aids such as filmstrips depicting appropriate and inappropriate social skills. Have disabled individuals critique what is taking place and give alternative responses.

Demonstrated Social Skills Competence

General Objective	Specific Objectives	Pre Yes/No		Post Yes/No	
I. Disabled individuals will achieve socially acceptable behaviors in social and interpersonal situations.	A. They will respect members of the opposite sex.	X			X
	B. They will demonstrate appropriate character traits needed for acceptance in the public.		X	X	
II. Disabled individuals will acquire self-confidence and employ appropriate social skills at home, school, and community.	A. They will demonstrate how to cope with their feelings and emotions arising from conflicts.		X		X
	B. They will practice acceptable social behaviors at home, school, and in the community.	X		X	

(General/Specific Objectives Checklist Chart Example)

A SAMPLE EVALUATION CHECKLIST FOR EVALUATING SOCIAL SKILLS

Activities and creative games are designed to improve social greetings; developing good relationships; respecting the feelings of others; practicing common courtesy; ways to make friends; acceptable ways to show anger; alternatives to cursing; learning when an apology is needed, appropriate and inappropriate touching; being a good sport; and importance of being a good neighbor. Activities should be age-appropriate.

Specific objectives are stated for each area of social skills development, with specific directions and procedures for completing each activity followed by a list of specific questions for disabled individuals. Desired outcomes are listed for each activity. An assessment sheet is provided to evaluate social growth. Games and activities may be infused into the curriculum or common criteria may be developed by children and teachers specifying conditions for playing the games. Games and activities may be placed in a learning center or station.

Social skills outlined should not be taught in isolation, but infused throughout the curriculum as needed. Approach and strategies outlined are not meant to be exclusive. Adaptations and modifications are encouraged.

The strategies and interventions reported have been tested with disabled individuals and were found to be successful. Results have shown a decrease in negative behaviors and an increase in positive behaviors and achievement. Specific techniques for evaluating the impact of social skills in reducing inappropriate behaviors have been comprehensively outlined in Chapter 4.

It is recommended that this type of checklist be revised for all of the social skills taught. The checklist or other informal techniques should be administered on a pre-post test basis. This procedure will permit the teacher to objectively determine to what degree the stated objectives have been achieved and what modifications or adaptations are needed in the unit.

SUMMARY

Social skills instruction should involve teaching disabled individuals those skills they must master if they are to become contributing members of society. Emphasis has been placed on developing instructional activities that will assist them to function successfully at school, home, the community and in social situations. Activities have been developed that will assist individuals with controlling their tempers, initiating compromises, developing improved interpersonal relationships, strategies for recognizing and respecting authority, and strategies for employing social skills to improve personal safety.

An excellent resource book to promote social skills is listed below: *Social Skills: Learning to Get Along With Other People.*[1] This resource book contains a list of games and activities designed to promote creative, fun-to-play format. It encourages socialization, and positive behavior reactions from children. The resource book focuses on skills needed to assist children toward independence.

REFERENCES

Clees, T.J., & Gast, D.L. (1994). Social skills instruction for individuals with disabilities: A sequential model. *Education and Treatment of Children, 17*, 163-184.

Francisco, B. (1993). Classroom instruction modalities; new treatment therapies in use with autistic children. *Program for Autistic-Like Children*, Baltimore, Maryland, 1993.

Furnham, A. (1986). Social skills training with adolescents and young adults. In C.R. Hollins & P. Trower (Eds.), *Handbook of Social Skills Training, 1*, 33-57. Oxford: Pergamin.

Goldstein, A., & McGinnis, E. (1984). *Skill Streaming the Elementary Child.* Illinois: Research Press Company.

Gresham, F.M. (1985). Utility of cognitive-behavioral procedures for social skills training with children: Critical review. *Journal of Abnormal Child Psychology, 13*, 491.

Odom, S.L. (1984). Classroom-based social skills instruction for severely handicapped preschool children. *Topics in Early Childhood Education, 4*, 97-116.

Taylor, G. (1992). Integrating social learning theory in educating the deprived. ERIC Clearinghouse for Education. ED 349260.

---

[1] Jane Haugen, (1993). *Learning to Get Along With Other People.* San Antonio, Texas: PCI Publishing Company.

Chapter 10

SUMMARY

GEORGE R. TAYLOR

It is commonly thought that young children adhere to different types of social conflicts using different standards than adults. DiMartino's (1990) study refuted this myth. His study showed that young children are able to distinguish and solve different types of social conflicts using the same criteria of solution as adults. Areas of social conflicts used in this experiment included: (1) morality; (2) social convention; (3) safety; and (4) institutional rules. The same premise may be applied to disabled individuals since all children basically precede through the same social developmental stages, however, disabled individuals appear to be at the highest risk for social development. Studies have shown that disabled individuals attained the lowest average and academic achievement scores, were over-represented in categories such as retained students, school dropouts, suspended and expelled students. These categories confirm that disabled individuals are at risk during the early elementary grades.

Many nondisabled individuals experience social competence through incidental learning, unfortunately, this is not true for many disabled individuals due to deficits in the major areas of development. These delays significantly impede social development. Lack of social development increase rejection and isolation of disabled individuals. The schools have to fully recognize the importance of teaching social skills. Social skills instruction is frequently neglected.

Failure of the schools to adequately incorporate social skills instruction in the curriculum may result in social rejection, poor self-concept, and inappropriate social behaviors. Improving the social competence of disabled individuals should be a long term goal of the school. This should be considered as a right of all disabled children since their rights to full participation in society may be impeded.

Social skills are developed through interactions with family, school and community. Social skills are shaped by reinforcement received as

160

a result of interaction with the environment. Often, disabled children do not learn effectively from past experiences. Frequently, they are enabled to transfer one social reaction to another socially acceptable situation, thus their behaviors are frequently interpreted as immature, inept or intrusive. This negative feedback prohibits future social interactions.

Research tends to suggest a relationship between social skills behavior in the classroom and academic achievement of disabled individuals (Gresham, 1993). Many social skills procedures such as attending and positive interaction techniques, have been shown to increase academic performance. Oswald (1992) wrote that social skills interventions appear to work best when they correspond to actual social interactions in the naturalistic environment. Similar findings by Walker (1992) indicated that the likelihood of disabled individuals failing and not adjusting to school and peer acceptance are significant. He further articulated that most disabled individuals do not have sufficient social skills to be successful in school. Finally, he voiced that there is an urgent need for social skills training which is integrated into the curriculum.

All children should be exposed to appropriate models to copy and imitate, to recognize nonverbal clues and to adjust their behaviors accordingly. Many disabled individuals have not been exposed to the above techniques.

Research findings have clearly demonstrated that diverse groups of children, such as disabled individuals, are at risk for developing appropriate interpersonal skills. Lack of this development may lead to feelings of rejection and isolation in classroom settings. There is also ample evidence to suggest that individuals' social difficulties may emanate from vastly different deficit areas. These deficit areas must be identified and remediated during the early years. Schools must design direct and immediate plan intervention programs which will permit these disabled individuals to experience success.

It is abundantly clear from the research that schools are not attuned or designed to educate disabled learners. Radical intervention models are needed stressing social skills and interpersonal skills development. The schools cannot accomplish this awesome task alone. There are deep-seated societal problems which must be addressed concurrently with education and educational problems, such as early environmental and home intervention strategies.

EARLY ENVIRONMENTAL EXPERIENCES

Children born in poverty and neglect often suffer from debilitating deprivation that seriously impairs their abilities to learn. Early prevention programs for these at-risk children and their parents (starting with prenatal care and including health care, quality day care, and preschool education) help prevent learning that disrupts later educational efforts (Butler, 1989). A key reason that some deprived individuals have such a high rate of educational failure is that they often lag in physical and psychological development and may be unprepared to meet the demands of academic learning. There is evidence to support that the lack of early experiences can affect brain development. Some areas of the brain require adequate stimulation at the right time in order to take on their normal functions. From case studies of some deprived individuals, findings indicate that there may be critical periods for cognitive and language development (Hatch and Gardner, 1988).

Intervention in the early years appears to be the most effective way to improve the prospects for disabled individuals to receive maximum benefits from their educational experiences.

Impoverishment of a child's early environmental experiences, including any major restrictions on play activities or lack of feedback from older individuals, is suspected of retarding his/her social development and learning. Lack of adequate adult stimulation in the early years can lead to disabled individuals developing negative social behavior which may be irreversible. First, in the absence of adequate stimulation and activity, neurophysiological mechanisms involved in learning may fail to develop. Second, conditions, impoverished environments, such as the slums, generally do not provide variety of duration of exposure to perceptual-motor experiences compared to children from more affluent environments (Dalli, 1991; Dewitt, 1994).

Children learn violent behaviors early. By the time they are in high school, we have lost them. The article urged that we need to start with the three year olds and teach them more appropriate ways to handle frustration, such as thinking about the consequences of their behaviors and decisions.

Home Environment

Individuals in mismatched environments often leave the environment or become less productive in it. Individuals are influenced by the elements within their environments. An individual who lives in an environment that is a good match for his needs and abilities will likely be more productive and prone to stay and will achieve academically. Individuals in mismatched environments, such as disabled individuals often have trouble transferring values from one environment to another; therefore, many leave school when they reach the legal age. Disabled individuals, as well as all individuals, do a great deal of learning outside of the classroom. They have accomplished a vast amount of nonacademic learning before they enter school, and continue to learn nonacademic sources while they are enrolled. Historically, the schools have not tapped this great learning resource. Values, styles, and concepts that disabled individuals bring to the schools must be matched and integrated into their own social reality if school experiences are to be meaningful.

Research reported by Erikson as early as 1959 supported that environments characterized by mistrust, doubt, limitations, feelings of inferiority and powerlessness are factors that contribute to identify confusion and inhibit the development of the mature individual (Erikson, 1959). In support of Erikson's view, Ayers (1989) wrote that children need the home base of family life in order to grow up healthy and strong. They need to be listened to and understood, nurtured and challenged by caring, committed adults. Parents need to contribute to their childrens' self-esteem, self-activity or self-control through appropriate modeling strategies.

If a child's early development status and its early home environment are both low, there is an increased likelihood of poor developmental outcomes. The home environment should be where the child receives support, experiences, love, and acquires important skills in becoming a productive, happy, social, and emotional person. The home environment is the foundation for further development within the child. Experiences from the home should be integrated with the school curriculum for meaningful experiences to occur, which will necessitate, including the family and the community in the education process (Kagan, 1989; Bradley, 1989).

Studies have consistently shown that negative behaviors are learned behaviors which individuals imitate from their environments. These behaviors manifest themselves in hostile and destructive patterns of behavior, which frequently cannot be controlled by the schools, thus creating conflict and tension between children, parents, and school (Matseuda, 1987; Taylor, 1992).

The preponderance of studies in the area of social learning, have consistently shown that the learning styles of disabled children are significantly different than their peers. Society and the school have failed to capitalize on this salient point. The school has not changed its basic approach to teaching these individuals over the last several decades. In spite of the vast amount of research and literature on innovative teaching techniques and strategies, school experiences for many disabled individuals are usually unrelated to the experiences they bring to school. Their abilities to function satisfactorily in social groups are usually below expected levels set by the school. They have fewer and less rigid control over their impulses and have learned hostile and destructive patterns of behavior as viewed by society and the school. The majority of disabled individuals will never become fully integrated in society and the school, unless early intervention is attempted and social skills are infused and systematically taught throughout the curriculum. It is incumbent upon the school to recognize and accept this fact and to develop strategies to modify, adapt, and gradually promote what is considered to be "appropriate social behavior" through the use of behavior intervention techniques and other strategies.

The impact of personality temperament, cognitive styles, sociological influences, and ethnic background may all influence development and learning of disabled individuals. The study of social learning theories enables the school to both understand how these individuals' cultures can be modified to promote expected learning outcomes as well as how they feel about themselves in relationship to learning. Activities and strategies must be developed to promote the emotional well-being of disabled individuals.

Public Law 99-457 (Part H Infants and Toddlers Program) is designed in part, to offset some of the deprivations by assisting states in setting up early intervention programs for children from birth through age two who need special services. Early intervention services include the following skills: physical, mental, social and emotional, language and speech, and self-help skills. Special education services may be provided to children from birth through age twenty-one years who have special needs such as physical disability, partial or total loss of sight, severe emotional problems, hearing or speech impairment, mental handicap, or learning disabilities. The key is early intervention, which should be designed to treat, prevent and reduce environmental factors associated with disabling conditions and the impediment of social growth and development.

Public Law 99-457 was greatly needed due to the public dissatisfaction with earlier legislation created for the handicapped. There was also a need for early care and education for not just the handicapped child, but also for the normal child. Two factors also contributed to educators searching for early child care services: (1) the increase in the number of mothers who were working outside the home and (2) the realization that many of these children were disadvantaged or from culturally different families. These children were also not developmentally ready for school (Gallagher, 1989). Kagan (1989) further supported the issues addressed in P.L. 99-457, and argued the importance of having the early care and education of children going beyond the school doors. Again, emphasis was placed on including the family and the community in the educational process of children. Her arguments for including the family and community stems from the ideas that children are coming from more fragmented families, yet the technological advances of today's society require more complex environments. The child is building on one stage of development to another by accomplishing certain learning tasks and by proceeding from the simple task to the more complex.

Transforming the Environment

A major factor affecting how well an individual functions in his environment is self-esteem. Promoting self-esteem among children assists in reducing problems which will surface later in life. Additional research is needed in this area to evaluate the impact of strategies and programs designed to promote self-esteem.

Educational leaders need empirical data on the effectiveness of programs to raise self-esteem of disabled individuals. High self-esteem appears to promote confidence, security, citizenship, and academic success. Some recommended strategies or principles for improving self-concepts of disabled individuals are as follows:

1. Praise rather than criticize.
2. Teach children to set achievable goals.
3. Teach children to praise themselves and to capitalize on their strong points.
4. Teach children to praise others.
5. Set realistic expectation levels.
6. Teach children to have confidence in themselves.
7. Praise children for achieving or failing after attempting to achieve.
8. Praise children for successfully completing a test or project.
9. Praise children for positive criticism.
10. Accept pupils contribution without judgment.
11. Listen to children, they have important information to share.
12. Maintain a "you can do it" philosophy.
13. Present challenges for children.
14. Provide movement and freedom within the classroom for children to achieve objectives.
15. Show concern and warmth.
16. Set high classroom control strategies with input from children.
17. Demonstrate and show respect for children.
18. Provide an atmosphere for success.
19. Listen to how you talk to children.
20. Catch someone doing something right and tell him/her about it.
21. Attack the behavior, not the student, separate the behavior from the child.
22. Use modeling or other techniques to reduce maladaptive behavior.
23. Teach children to respect themselves and others.
24. Teach children to be proud of their heritage.
25. Provide activities which incorporate parental involvement.

These strategies are not inconclusive and should be expanded as assessed by the teachers.

ENHANCING SELF-ESTEEM OF DISABLED INDIVIDUALS

Due to various factors within society and the community, the schools' role in enhancing self-esteem is of prime importance. Intervention must be made early to break or prevent failure due to low self-esteem. There appears to be a positive relationship between self-concept and student's success or failure in school (Taylor, 1992).

There are many factors influencing children with disabilities development prior to going to school. When the school accepts the child, it should be committed to accepting and attempting to teach the "whole child," not just developing the three R's. A major factor in a child's development in the beginning school years in the child's view of himself/herself as he/she communicates with other students. Disabled individuals' as well as other students' self-concept influences their motivation to learn. If students do not feel good about themselves generally, and good about themselves specifically as learners, they will lack the motivation to improve their performance in many academic areas. Group and individual activities are needed in order to improve the self-concepts of disabled individuals. Specific activities have been developed to improve self-concept in Chapter 8.

The role of the teacher in promoting self-control among disabled individuals cannot be over-emphasized. The teacher exerts considerable influence on shaping a child's self-concept through the type of treatments, beliefs and expectations imposed upon the child. Children quickly react to and easily interpret negative traits projected by the teacher. The child's interpretation of the teacher's actions and their significance play an important role in how the child reacts.

Children sift, seek, reject, and avoid information from individuals they do not respect or trust. They do not accept information from adults who have rejected them as readily but they do from adults who they feel have accepted them and are trustworthy.

Teachers can exert significant influence on the forming of the child's self-concept by the constructive and positive learning environments as well as showing positive attitudes and developing rapport toward children.

PERSONALITY DEVELOPMENT

A child's personality is organized around various aspects of self-awareness and self-concept. The structure of the school and the teachers' behavior greatly impacts upon personality development. What a person believes about himself affects what he does, what he sees and hears, and his ability to cope in the environment. It may be concluded that self-concept is significantly influenced by life experiences due chiefly to the fact that it is learned-much of it through modeling. Disabled individuals imitate experiences to which they have been exposed. Personality is conceived as a product of social learning. Its development is largely a function of the social conditions under which one grows up. Some social learning are much more important than others for disabled individuals. There is frequently a conflict between the social values of these children and expectations of the school. This is chiefly due to the school not being tolerant of the cultural and behavioral styles of disabled individuals. Appropriate social skills should be taught and modeled for them before a meaningful academic program can be pursued. The school should be cognizant of the fact that many of the habits developed by them are well entrenched. Consequently, surface attention will not have a significant impact on changing negative habits. A planned coordinated and integrated program will be needed.

If successful academic progress is to be realized for disabled individuals, the school must develop interpersonal and social skills strategies to enable them to feel better about themselves. Social skills should be taught to those disabled individuals who need them, and in some instances, should supersede academic skills. Appropriate social skills must be taught and modeled for many of these children before a meaningful academic program can be pursued.

Parental Involvement

Not only are social skills important in academic areas, they are also related to socialization. Several behaviors are necessary in the socialization process, including the emergence of self-identity and self-concept. Social skills are developed through the interactions with family, school, and the community, but none as important as the role of the parents.

There has been strong support from the federal government to include the family in the early educational process of the handicapped child. The passage of the Education of the Handicapped Act amendments of 1986 (P.L. 99-457) established guidelines for the relationship among federal, state, and local education agencies to provide professional resources to disabled children and their families. The federal government created guidelines for the educational community in developing and implementing a comprehensive, coordinate, multidisciplinary, interagency program of early intervention services for infants, toddlers and their families (Gallagher, 1989).

The role of parental participation in education in general, and special education in particular, according to much of the research in the field, has shown limited participation. This view has been interpreted to imply that parents simply had no interest in the education of their children (Marion, 1981). Several factors may contribute to the lack of parental participation. Many parents do not feel welcome in the school. They believe that they have little to offer in educating their children. Cassidy (1988) reported that problems with scheduling, transportation, and knowledge of the Individualized Education Program (IEP) and special education procedures were partly responsible for poor parental participation. Other researchers implied that many parents, especially minority parents, disagreed with the present classification system. Many believed that their children were misplaced, or rejected the diagnosis and assessment process used to place their children (Harry, 1992; Smith, Osborne, Crim, and Rhu, 1987).

The role of parents in the school must supersede the mandates of P.L. 94-142. Parents must feel that they are welcome in the school, and be given responsibilities concerned with planning, collaborating with teachers, made aware of the IEP and legal processes associated with special education and involved in policy-making (Harry, 1992; Turnbull & Turnbull, 1990). Parents should have an active role in planning and instructing their children and function as advocates for them if children are to profit significantly from their school experiences. Schools should experiment with various ways of improving parental participation. Parents provide the model of self-acceptance and the feeling that life is worthwhile. Also, parents who demonstrate a positive self-concept and high self-esteem treat their children with respect and acceptance and provide them with support and encouragement. A child's social skills are shaped by the reinforcement he or she receives as a result of an action in the environment (Wood, 1984). Lack of social development diminishes the social status within the group (Anita, 1992; Peck & Cooke, 1983). Environmental conditions which nurture negative and aggressive behaviors must be transformed. Massive financial, social and psychological support must be provided early. A coordinated holistic community effort is needed to offset the present conditions in many urban communities in this country.

A HOLISTIC APPROACH

Some young disabled individuals are being educated in substandard schools in some urban school districts. We have not done a satisfactory job in providing quality education for these individuals. The schools have failed in educating the "whole child." According to a recent report by the National Association of State Boards of Education (1992), it was voiced that a holistic view that is attuned to the students' nonacademic needs must be included as part of his/her instructional program, which includes social, emotional, personal and citizenship training.

Instruction that minimizes the teaching of social and civic responsibility in the quest for academic excellence may not produce well informed citizens in our society. Findings by other researchers have voiced similar concerns (Biklen, 1989; Forest, 1990; Barth, 1990; Eisner, 1991; O'Brien & O'Brien, 1991). They also support a holistic integrated approach to educating children. It was recommended that to avoid fragmenting school experiences, students' social and emotional well-being must be integrated and infused into a total program emphasizing social and interpersonal needs, communication needs, and academic needs. The schools must begin to use the vast amount of research present to experiment with various ways of including social skills development into the curriculum if disabled individuals are to achieve up to their maximum potentials.

The concept of teaching the "whole child" has been advocated since the beginning of this century. Historically, the school has mainly focused on academics, not the emotional development of children.

Transforming the School Environment

The educational application of emotional research is still in its infancy. Some general principles to guide classroom applications are:

1. We should seek to develop forms of self-control among students and staff that encourages nonjudgemental, nondisruptive venting of emotions.
2. Schools should focus more on metacognitive activities that encourage students to talk about their emotions, listen to their classmates' feelings.
3. Activities that emphasize social interaction and that engage the entire body tend to provide the most emotional support.
4. School activities that draw out emotions-stimulations, role playing, and cooperative projects may provide important contextual memory prompts.
5. Emotionally stressful school environments are counterproductive because they can reduce a students' ability to learn.

Over time, individuals tend to develop habitual ways of responding to experiences. Individuals are a product of their environment. The importance of emotions in teaching children, attention, learning and memory, are all associated with one's emotions. This concept does not appear to be readily understood by educators; thus it is not adequately reflected in the curriculum. The school should conduct empirical studies showing the relationship between an emotionally positive classroom and the academic achievement, and the emotional health of pupils (Kandel, 1994; Vincent, 1990).

Our emotional system is a complex, widely distributed and error-prone system that defines our basic personality early in life, and is quite resistant to change. The clear implication of this research is that positive models and early interventions are needed if healthy emotions are to emerge. The emotional system is a complex process under the direction and supervision of the brain. It is frequently viewed as a more powerful determinant of our behavior than our rational processes. A detailed discussion of the emotional system is outside the scope of this text. Please refer to chapter endnotes for additional sources.

Cummins (1984) findings supported educating the "whole child." He assessed traditional instruction models currently used by the public schools to educate minority and disabled individuals. These models are mostly based upon cognitive theories and include: (1) analysis of academic tasks, (2) the establishment of sequential learning objectives based on each task analysis, and (3) direct instruction of individual task components. Most instruction and teaching in the public schools are based on the aforementioned models (Tharp, 1989; Poplin, 1988). Many disabled individuals have various learning styles and frequently cannot achieve success with these traditional models. Drastic reforms must be made in special education. Strategies and interventions must focus on the individual needs of disabled individuals in the primary grades. The approach must be integrated and coordinated with available community resources.

Many disabled individuals may have developed or adapted alternative ways and styles of coping with problems in their neighborhoods. These behavioral styles are frequently in conflict with the school and society in general and may be viewed as negative or destructive. Behavioral styles and models copied and imitated by many disabled individuals may serve them well in their environments, but are frequently viewed as dysfunctional by the school and society.

As indicated throughout this book, instructional programs must be developed and designed to enable individuals with disabilities to gain knowledge about appropriate interpersonal skills, and to employ this newly-acquired knowledge in solving their social problems. In order for this goal to be accomplished, disabled individuals must be taught effective ways of internalizing their behaviors, and assessing how their behaviors affects others. Teaching appropriate social skills to disabled individuals appears to be a promising technique for improving pro-social skills (Taylor, 1992). Appropriate social skills are essentials for developing personal relationships and accepting the roles of authority figures. Social behaviors are learned, therefore, they can be changed and modified. They require that an individual evaluate a situation, choose the appropriate social skills, and perform the social tasks appropriately (Katz, 1991). Unfortunately, disabled individuals have not been exposed to appropriate social models or do not possess enough prerequisite skills, such as maturity and self-control to successfully perform the social skills.

Some observations appear relevant to educating disabled individuals:

1. Seem generally unaware of the "ground rules" for success in school;
2. Are less able to learn from being told than are their counterparts;
3. Are often unable to make simple symbolic interpretations;
4. Tend to have shorter attention spans, consequently have problems in following directions;
5. Are unable to use language in a flexible way;
6. Tend to have little concept of relative size of objects outside of their environments;
7. Are less likely to perceive adults as people to whom they can turn to for help;
8. Seem to have a low level of curiosity about things;
9. Seem to project a low self-image;
10. Have experiences within a very narrow range.

The difficult part of teaching is not developing appropriate learning strategies for individuals with disabilities, but dealing with the great influx of individuals who come from emotionally, physically, socially and financially stressed homes. This is not a school problem alone. Society in general must assume the major responsibilities for these environmental atrocities. The school is responsible to the extent that it has not changed its approach to teaching disabled individuals over the last several decades, in spite of the vast amount of research and literature on innovated teaching techniques and strategies successfully employed. School experiences for these individuals have virtually remained unchanged; are usually unrelated to the experiences they bring to school; and do not adequately address the aforementioned observations outlined. Life in school is mostly teacher-centered, textbook-dominated, restrictive, impersonal, and rigid (Goodlad, 1984).

These issues and more must be addressed by the school if it is to become responsive to the educational needs of disabled individuals. Policies must be changed at the local, state, and national levels. The position advanced by the Committee for Economic Development (1987) stated that, "for imperative and more practical reasons, our commitment to the young must go beyond political rhetoric; it must produce a well-planned curriculum of programs for children from birth through adulthood." This statement appears to be appropriate for the school to promote in providing equal educational opportunities for all children, including disabled individuals.

ENDNOTES

1. Levinthal, C. (1988). Messengers of paradise: Opiates and the Brain. New York: DoubleDay.
2. Gazzaniga, M. (1989). Mind Matters: How Mind and Brain Interact to Create our Conscious Lives. Boston: Houghton Mifflin.
3. Moyer, B. (1992). Healing and the Mind. New York: Double-Day.
4. Vincent, J.P. (1990). The Biology of Emotions. Cambridge, MA: Basil Blackwell.

REFERENCES

Anita, S.D. and Kreimeyer, K. (1992). Project interact. Interventions for social integration of young hearing-impaired children. *Office of Special Education and Rehabilitative Services, 414*, 14-20.

Ayers, W. (1989). Childhood at risk. *Educational Leadership, 46*, 70-72.

Barth, R. (1990). *Improving Schools From Within.* SanFrancisco: Jossey-Bass, Inc.

Bilken, D. (1989). Making a difference ordinary. In W. Stainback, & M. Forest (Eds.). *Educating All Children in the Mainstream of Regular Education.* Baltimore, MD: Paul H. Brookes.

Bradley, R.H., Caldwell, et al. (1989). Home environment and cognitive development in the first three years of life: A collaborative study involving Sikhites and three ethnic groups in North America. *Developmental Psychology, 25*, 217-235.

Butler, O.B. (1989). Early help for kids at risk: Our nation's best investment. *NEA Today, 7*, 51-53.

Cassidy, E. (1988). Reaching and involving Black parents of handicapped children in their child's education program. *Cause, Inc.*, Lansing MI: ERIC 302982.

Committee for Economic Development (1987). *Children in need: Investment strategies for the educationally disadvantaged.* New York.

Cummins, J. (1984). *Bilingual and special education: Issues in assessment pedagogy.* San Diego: College-Hill Press.

Dalli, C. (1991). Scripts for children's lives: What do parents and early childhood teachers contribute to children's understanding of events in their lives. ERIC ED. 344664.

Dewitt, P. (1994). The crucial early years. *Time Magazine, 143,* 16, 68.

DiMartino, E.C. (1990). The remarkable social competence of young children. *International Journal of Early Childhood, 22,* 23-31.

Eisner, E. (1991). What really counts in school? *Educational Leadership, 10,* 17.

Erikson, E.H. (1959). Identity and the life cycle. *Psychological Issues Monograph,* 1. New York: International Universities Press.

Forest, M. (1990). Maps and cities. Presentation at Peak Parent Center Workshop. Colorado Springs.

Gallagher, J.J. (1989). The impact of policies for handicapped children on future early education policy. *Phi Delta Kappan,* 121-124.

Goodlad, J.L. (1984). A place called school. New York: McGraw-Hill.

Gresham, F.M. (1993). Social Skills and Learning Disabilities as a Type III Error: Rejoiner to Conte and Andrews. *Journal of Learning Disabilities, 26,* 154-158.

Harry, B. (1992). Cultural diversity, families, and the special education system: Communication and empowerment. New York Teachers College Press.

Hatch, T., & Gardner, H. (1988). How kids learn: What scientists say: New research on intelligence. *Learning, 37.*

Hilliard, A.G. (1989). Teachers and cultural styles in a pluralistic society. *NEA Today, 7,* 65-69.

Kagan, S.L. (1989). Early care and education: Beyond the school house doors. *Phi Delta Kappan, 107*-112.

Kandel, M., & Kandel, E. (1994). Flights of memory. *Discover Magazine,* 32-38.

Katz, L.G. (1991). The teacher's role in social development of young children. ERIC ED. 331642.

Marion, R. (1981). Educators, parents and exceptional children. Rockville, MD: Aspen.

Matsueda, R.L., & Heimer, K. (1987). Race, family structure and delinquency: A test differential association and social control theories. *American Sociological Review, 52,* 826-840.

O'Brien, J., & O'Brien, C. (1991). Members of each other: Perspectives of social support for people with severe disabilities. Lithuania, GA: Responsive Systems Associates.

Oswald, D.P. & Sinah-Nirbay, N. (1992). Current research on social behavior. *Behavior Modification, 16,* 443-447.

Peck, C.A., & Cooke, T.P. (1983). Benefits of mainstreaming at the early childhood level: How much can we expect? *Analysis and Intervention in Developmental Disabilities, 3,* 1-22.

Poplin, M.S. (1988). Holistic/constructivist principles of the teaching/learning process: Implications for the field of learning disabilities. *Journal of Learning Disabilities, 21,* 410-416.

Smith, R.W., Osborne, L.T., Crim, D., & Rhu, A.H. (1986). Labeling theory as applied to learning disabilities: Findings and policy suggestions. *Journal of Learning Disabilities, 19*, 195-202.

Taylor, G.R. (1992). Integrating social learning theory in educating the deprived. ED. *Clearinghouse for Education, ERIC* 349260.

Tharp, R.G. (1989). Psychocultural variables and constraints: Effects on teaching and learning in schools. *American Psychologist, 44*, 349-359.

The National Association of State Boards of Education. Alexandria, VA: P.13.

Turnbull, A.P., & Turnbull, H.R. (1990). Families, professional and exceptionality (2nd ed.).

Vincent, J.P. (1990). The biology of emotions. Cambridge, MA: Basil Blackwell.

Walker, H.M., Irvin, L.K., Noell, J., & Singer, G.H.S. (1992). A construct score approach to the assessment of social competence. *Behavior Modification, 16*, 449-452.

Wood, J.W. (1984). Adapting instruction for the mainstream.

APPENDIX A

LIST OF RECOMMENDED SOCIAL SKILLS
TO BE TAUGHT IN INCLUSION

I. Bonding

    A. Pledge (first thing in the morning)

    B. Acknowledgment of Unity

        1. Handshake; secret signal; cue; smile.

        2. Words "we are family."

    C. Buddy (Explain to students:)

        1. A buddy can be selected for each unit to work with in the completion of a long-range project.

        2. A buddy you can work with in cooperative learning groups.

        3. A buddy you can share a common interest with (give an interest survey).

        4. A buddy you may eat lunch with, telephone to check over homework with, share a book with, walk with in line.

II. Social Skills

    A. Basic Needs

        1. *Attention* - children to take turns being group leaders, readers, student of the day.

        2. *Belonging* - name for the class, special pledge, motto, colors, other symbol that represent belonging.

        3. *Importance* - need you today to help us with this task. Your team buddy needs you; your participation is valuable to the group; we are depending on your help. This is your assigned responsibility everyday. Without you, this doesn't operate smoothly. [Biography Board].

        4. *Confidence* - encouragement; present a task that seems to be complex but encourages the student toward mastery.

        5. *Sense of Freedom* - out to students: Even in disciplinary situations; you can either do it now or after school. The choice is yours.

        Fighting: how could you have handled him/her differently? What can I do to help with the problem? What do you feel you would like or need to do now?

    B. Goals (Instruction should be used to foster):

        - Confidence

        - Motivation

- Effort
- Responsibility
- Initiative
- Perseverance
- Caring
- Teamwork
- Common sense
- Problem-solving skills

III. Curriculum

A. Curriculum guide list uses alternative unit approach.

- Incorporate the "Buddy" system, skills, oral responses, values and writing, research organizational skills around units.
- Use alternative unit approach for social skills development

B. Suggested Other Units

- Animals
- Jobs
- Weather
- Mysterious phenomena
- Living things
- Food

E. Projects

- Drawings
- Posters

APPENDIX B

INFORMAL ASSESSMENT INVENTORY CHECKLIST

Directions: Check always, sometimes, or never for each statement. There are no correct or incorrect answers.

KEY: A=Always   S=Sometimes   N=Never

AGGRESSION	A	S	N
I get mad often.			
I find other children are friendly to me.			
I get angry when treated unfairly.			
I can control my anger.			
People are always trying to get me.			
I usually hit first.			
Other people usually hit first.			
I must always protect myself.			
I feel protected.			
I don't get upset if I see something torn or messed up.			
I like fixing broken things.			
People don't hear me unless I talk loud.			
I like to talk loud.			
ORGANIZATION			
I am no good at getting work done.			
I complete tasks easily.			
I remember my books and materials needed for that day.			
I have often lost my lunch ticket.			
I have never lost anything.			
I hang up my coat and put my books away when I arrive home.			
I copy my assignments down and turn them in on time.			
I have trouble finding things in my room.			
It takes time to find papers asked for in my notebook.			
I have trouble trying to memorize facts and things.			
I remember the words to songs easily.			
I am doing well in school.			

BEHAVIOR PROBLEMS	A	S	N
I get in trouble for many little things.			
Nobody pays any attention to me.			
I can be happy one minute and sad the next.			
When I see something I need, I ask for it.			
When I see something I need, I take it.			
Other people get me into trouble.			
I control my own actions.			
I need adults to tell me how to act.			
STRESS			
Sometimes, I feel like running away.			
I don't like to laugh.			
It's bad to make a mistake.			
It's better to keep your feelings to yourself.			
I like to take risks to grow and learn.			
It is important to me to be the first in everything.			
I like to win at everything.			
I don't like for people to touch me or to stand too close to me.			
I hate to wait for things.			
I get embarrassed easily.			

APPENDIX C

OBSERVATION CHECKLIST

Teacher _____ Observer _____

Lesson _____ Date _____ Time _____

KEY: A=Always   F=Frequently   N=Never

BEHAVIORS	A	F	N
Student deals positively with accusations.			
Student accepts feelings of others in a non-threatening manner.			
Student respects the feelings of others.			
Student knows how to avoid fights and conflicts and displays good humor.			
Student deals effectively with teasing.			
Student moves about room independently to perform routing tasks.			
Student stays away from troublesome situations and accepts culture values of pupils.			
Student verbally shows appreciation when assisted.			
Student gives praise or compliments to other students.			
Student accepts compliments from others.			
Student apologizes for inappropriate behavior.			
Student expresses anger in a positive way.			
Student attempts to understand another's anger without getting angry.			
Student shows affection and appreciation toward others.			
Student asks permission to borrow or use other's belongings.			
Student does not lose control when left out of group activities.			
Student practices self-control.			
Student disagrees in an acceptable manner.			
Student accepts losing without becoming upset.			

APPENDIX D

SOME COOPERATIVE LEARNING STRATEGIES

Circle Activities

Circle activities have been specifically designed to include many different groupings:

Full–The full circle implies that all students would participate in the circle topic and sit together in one circle.

Team–The approach is based on Slavin and Johnson's concepts of cooperative learning (Slavin, 1991; Johnson et al., 1988). Teams consist of five to six students representing different characteristics and abilities. Permanent team assignments are recommended in order to save time assigning teams for each activity.

Recommended strategies for forming cooperative teams include:

Select a name–Team members select a name, take a vote, and then introduce the name to the larger group.

Construct a logo–Members approve of the logo, which will be used to identify the team. The art teacher may be used as a resource if needed.

Develop a group profile–Provide each team with paper and supplies for designing a group profile on the paper showing each separate individual's interests/strengths/desires onto a team profile chart.

Partner–Provide activities for two students to work together. Students may choose their own partner. After a while, ask students to choose another student whom they do not know as well.

Cooperative Learning Tools

Many of the materials used in circle activities are already accessible in the classroom. Teachers are encouraged to be as creative and innovative as possible.

Puppets–Any puppet that is friendly-looking is sufficient. The puppet introduces the circle activities and facilitates the discussion. Students may choose a puppet name or use the name of one of their story characters.

Timer–This can greatly facilitate circle discussions because it lets students know when the circle time is up. Set the timer for the designated time and inform students that when the timer buzzes, the circle is over.

Suggestion box–A small box with a removable top will suffice. Cut a slit one half inch by five inches along the top of the box. Have the children decorate the box and write "Suggestions" on the side in big bold letters. Students should be instructed to place their suggestions inside the box. Their suggestions may provide additional circle topics to discuss.

Name cards–Make a set of name cards on three inch by five inch strips of paper. Color code the cards using two colors. Divide the class in half; give the boys alternate colors. Colors may be changed as special events and holidays occur.

Writing book–Make a writing book ditto. Provide space for each student's name in the group. Make several copies of the sheet and staple them between construction paper covers. Use the book during circle time to record students' comments. On selected circles, name the topic at the top of the form and then quickly jot down the main idea of each student's contribution. This is also an incentive for listening.

Recommendations for increasing participation within groups and circles include:

1. **Accent strengths and uniqueness throughout the day.** Students won't be able to verbalize their strengths unless they are made aware of them.

2. **Have students keep individual records of their positive self-statements.**

3. **Model positive self-statements.** If students hear the teacher saying positive comments periodically about themselves, they'll begin to feel it's safe to do so too.

4. **Praise and support students for their use of positive self-statements.** Attempt to create an environment that's secure for such growth.

5. **Be supportive of any student who cannot quickly verbalize a positive self-statement in the circle.** Use whatever statement is generated and make a positive remark about it; seek approval and endorsement from the student.

6. **Discuss real-life experiences of students in the beginning circles.** Students are often more comfortable about sharing things that they have experienced. Invite students to bring something from home of which they are proud or have an interest in.

7. **Invite students to draw a picture of what they will be saying for the circle.** This is particularly helpful for shy students. The picture will provide support for the student during discussions.

APPENDIX E

EVALUATION SHEET

(Sample Items Expand As Needed)

KEY: Y=Yes   N=No   S=Sometimes

SAMPLE ITEMS	Y	N	S
I followed classroom and school rules today.			
I showed respect for others today.			
I attempted to control my anger today.			
Did I contribute to my group's discussions today?			
Did I practice good citizenship habits today?			
Was I always on my best behavior today?			
Was I polite and courteous to my classmates today?			
Was I considerate of others today?			
Did I consider the feelings of others before I responded?			
Did I show appreciation for a kind deed today?			
I added to my circle of friends today.			
I praised classmates for successful tasks completed today.			
I recorded my behavior on my performance chart today.			

APPENDIX F

FILMS AND FILMSTRIPS

Beginning Responsibility: Learning to Follow Directions. One reel; color or black/white. Coronet. Some of David's toy animals magically come to life and teach him that he must pay attention.

Good Citizens. Encyclopedia Britannica Educational Corporation, 1961. The file discusses courtesy, cooperation, dependability, and fair play.

Good Manners. Series of six filmstrips (average 48 frames each). Encyclopedia Britannica Education Corporation. Good manners are presented as a means of getting along with people.

Little Citizen Series. Society for Visual Education, 1960. The film highlights students' responsibility toward others.

Practicing Good Citizenship. Six filmstrips; individual filmstrips also available. Troll Associates, 1972. Film titles: Growing Up to Be a Good Citizen; When to Be a Leader, When to Be a Follower; Recognizing Individual Differences; A Good Citizen in School; Be a Danger Fighter; and A Newcomer Comes to Town.

Tales of the Wise Old Owl. Filmstrips and records in three groups. Society for Visual Education. Group 1: Dr. Retriever's Surprise and Silly Excuses. Group 2: Bushy the Squirrel and Peggy the Pup. Group 3: The Feather That Was Lost and Pearl of Great Price.

Values. Six color filmstrips with three cassette Teach-A-Tapes or filmstrips with cassettes. Eye Gate House, 1972. Film titles: Telling the Truth, What Is Stealing?, Kindness, Politeness, Responsibility, and Citizenship. This film is designed to help the student develop a standard of values; both appropriate and inappropriate responses to a conflict situation are given without a judgment being made. By discussing or role playing each problem and response, students can develop their own answers and formulate their own set of values.

Ways to Settle Disputes. One reel; color or black/white. Collaborator: Carter Davidson. The film emphasizes that settlement of conflict must be desired to be effective and gives four ways of settling disputes.

What Happens Between People? Two filmstrips, one 12-inch LP record or cassette, and teacher's guide. Guidance Associates. The film assists children in becoming aware of types of human interactions between individuals and groups.

You Got Mad: Are You Glad? Two filmstrips, one 12-inch LP record or cassette, and teacher's guide. Guidance Associates. The film helps children discover the cause and effects of hostility, stressing behavioral choices such as mediation, third-party judgment, and compromise as ways to resolve conflicts.

Yours, Mine, and Ours. Color or black/white 16mm film. Encyclopedia Britannica Educational Corporation. Reflects classroom situations showing proper responsibility for ownership; teaches children to recognize group and individual responsibilities.

Guidance Stories, Series No. 8490. Six color filmstrips. Encyclopedia Britannica Education Corporation Titles: Sharing With Others, Playing Fair, Sticking to Your Job, New Friends -Good Friends, One Kind of Bravery, and Taking Care of Your Things.

The Lemonade Stand: What's Fair? Color or black/white 16mm film. Encyclopedia Britannica Educational Corporation. Focuses on the meaning of commitment, obligations, and responsibility to others.

Little Things That Count. Eight color filmstrips with four records or cassette Teach-A-Tapes and teacher's manual. Eye Gate House. Freedom's Foundation Awards Winner. The stories involve the joy of helping others, honesty, perseverance, responsibility, justice, reverence, and love.

Minorities and Majorities. Six color filmstrips with three cassette Teach-A-Tapes and teacher's manual. Eye Gate House. The film deals with child-to-child prejudice, being part of a group, being outside of the group, and being within a group. Ethnic, national, religious, and color distinctions are not discussed as issues.

The Report Card: How Does Ricardo Feel? Color or black/white 16mm film. Encyclopedia Britannica Educational Corporation. The film teaches that when individuals do not control their emotions, anger can be destructive.

Teaching Children Values Through Unfinished Stories. Two color filmstrips, one $33^{1/3}$ rpm record or cassette, and teacher's guide. Educational Activities, Inc. Open-ended stories enable the pupil to identify with the central character and to think about and devise solutions to problems offered.

That's Not Fair. Two filmstrips with record or cassette. Guidance Associates. Part 1; Is it fair to take another's place in a gift line? Part 2; Two boys return some lost spectacles and are undecided about how to share the reward, which is a watch.

What Do You Expect of Others? Three filmstrips, one 12-inch LP record or cassette, and teacher's guide. Guidance Associates. The film helps children learn that what you expect a person to be like has much to do with how he or she acts toward you.

The Picture Life of Thurgood Marshall. Young, Margaret B., Watts, 1971. A brief biography of the Black lawyer who fights for the rights of African-American citizens and eventually becomes the first Black man to become an Associate Justice of the Supreme Court.

Aesop's Fables. Nine color-captioned filmstrips. Educational Projections Corporation. Titles: The Mean Old Elephant, The Lion and the Goat, The Silly Rabbit, Wolf in Sheep's Clothing, The Loud-Mouthed Frog, The Greedy Dog, The Evil Spider, The Mouse Who Boasted, and The Foolish Donkey. (1-3)

Beginning Responsibility: Being a Good Sport. Color or black/white 16mm film. Coronet Films. Poor sportsmanship over a checkers game leads to a discussion of sportsmanship.

But It Isn't Yours. Two filmstrips, one 12-inch LP record or cassette, and teacher's guide. Guidance Associates. Two unfinished stories included are these: Part 1, Is it permissible for Bill to keep a dog which has escaped from the pound?, Part 2, Is Jeff responsible for returning stolen property that he unknowingly accepted? (K-4)

Fairness for Beginners. Color or black/white 16mm film. Coronet Films. The film presents the ways of being fair: sharing, taking turns, choosing fairly, and respecting the rights of others.

Getting to Know Me. Four color filmstrips with two records or cassettes and teacher's guide. Society for Visual Education. The film is designed to develop self-understanding and self-acceptance. Titles: People Are Like Rainbows, A Boat Named George, Listen! Jimmy!, and Strike Three! You're In.

Developing Basic Values. Four color filmstrips and records or cassettes and teacher's guides. Society for Visual Education, Incorporated. Titles: Respect for Property, Consideration of Others, Acceptance of Others, and Recognition of Responsibilities.

Late for Dinner: Was Dawn Right? Color or black/white 16mm film. Encyclopedia Britannica Education Corporation. An open-ended film shows that conflicting feelings are normal.

Animal Stories Series. Six color filmstrips. Educational Reading Service. These filmstrips are made up of photographs of children and their pets and teach responsibility and consideration of others.

The Ant and The Dove. Color or black/white 16mm film. Coronet Films. This film is Aesop's fable "one good turn deserves another."

Appreciating Our Parents. Color or black/white 16mm film. Coronet Films. This film stresses the importance of family cooperation.

The "Be Kind" Stories. Four color filmstrips with two cassette Teach-A-Tapes and teacher's manual; coloring books available. Eye Gate House. The emphasis is on expressing more kindness in everyday living.

Beginning Responsibility: Lunchroom Manners. Color or black/white 16mm film. Coronet Films. Through a puppet show, the children in a class realize that clumsiness and impoliteness are funny with Mr. Bungle, but are not desirable among themselves. (1-3).

Conduct and Behavior. Ten color-captioned filmstrips. Educational Projections Corporation. Titles: In School, On the Playground, On the Street, At Home, Visiting Friends, Traveling, Shopping, In Public Buildings, The Picnic, and Responsibility.

Records

Aesop's Fables. 12-inch LP record. Caedman (Alesco). Boris Karloff reads 42 classic moral and ethical tales. (1-6)

Living With Others - Citizenship I, II. Six records or tape cassettes. Society for Visual Education, Incorporated. Subjects include: bad example of others, cheating, breaking family rules, stealing, lost friendships, safety, etc.

American Poems of Patriotism. 12-inch LP record. Caedman (Alesco). Nineteen selections are read by Ed Begley, Julie Harris, and Frederick O'Neal.

Filmloops

Understanding Ourselves and Others. Five filmloops. Educational Reading Service. Titles: Understanding the Difference Between Alone and Lonely; Fear - Real and Imaginary; Why We Get Angry; People Are Different, Aren't They? and Learning When and Where.

APPENDIX G

FEDERAL LEGISLATION

Prologue

The Congress finds that:

1. There are more than eight million children with disabilities in the United States today;
2. The special education needs of such children are not being fully met;
3. More than half of the children with disabilities in the United States do not receive appropriate educational services which would enable them to have full equality of opportunity;
4. One million children with disabilities in the United States are excluded entirely from the public school system and will not go through the educational process with their peers;
5. There are many children with disabilities throughout the United States participating in regular school programs whose disabilities prevent them from having a successful educational experience because their disabilities are undetected;
6. Because of the lack of adequate services within the public school system, families are often forced to find services outside the public school system, often at great distances from their residences and at their own expense;
7. Developments in the training of teachers and in diagnostic and instructional procedures and methods have advanced to the point that, given appropriate funding, state and local educational agencies can and will provide effective special education and related services to meet the needs of children with disabilities;
8. State and local educational agencies have a responsibility to provide education for all children with disabilities, but present financial resources are inadequate to meet the special education needs of children with disabilities;
9. It is in the national interest that the Federal Government assist state and local efforts to provide programs to meet the educational needs of children with disabilities to secure equal protection of the law.

20 U.S.C. §1400 (b)

Educating children with special needs provides both challenges and opportunities.Today, American schools are meeting the special education service needs of 5.373 million children from birth to age 21-a figure that is expected to increase.

Seventeenth Annual Report to Congress on the Implementation of the Individuals with Disabilities Education Act, U.S. Department of Education, 1995.

THE DISABLED
AND THE EVOLUTION OF SPECIAL EDUCATION

Current mandates to provide equal access and an appropriate education to he disabled are principally the result of Federal Congressional actions, often taken in response to litigation, as well as the encouragement and persistence of parents, professionals, and advocacy groups.Prior to the 1970s, efforts to meet the needs of the disabled within the public schools varied widely in form and intent.The landmark decision in Brown v. Board of Education (1954) established the right of all children to an equal educational opportunity.The sentiment of the following language contained in the Supreme Court's opinion, is common to litigation and legislation of the past four decades seeking equal educational access and opportunity for the disabled:

> Today, education is perhaps the most important function of state and local govern-ments.Compulsory school attendance laws and the great expenditures for education.demonstrate our recognition of the importance of education to our democratic society.It is required in the performance of our most basic public responsibilities, even service in the armed forces.It is the very foundation of good citizenship.Today, it is a principal instrument in awakening the child to cultural values, in preparing him for later professional training, and in helping him to adjust normally to his environment.In these days, it is doubtful that any child may reasonable be expected to succeed in life if he is denied the opportunity of an education.Such an opportunity, where the state has undertaken to provide it, is a right which must be made available to all on equal terms.

347 U.S. 483, 493

Although Congress (through adoption of the Education of the Handicapped Act of 1970) attempted to overcome the historical inadequacy of educational services to the disabled, it was two court cases decided during 1971-72 that helped establish the right of access of the disabled to a free appropriate public education and out-lined the protection that such students could be afforded.

In *Pennsylvania Association for Retarded Children v. Commonwealth* (PARC), the court was asked to examine policies that permitted Pennsylvania to deny access and a free appropriate education to mentally retarded children.

343 F.Supp. 279 (E.D.Pa. 1972)

The consent decree, approved by the district court, enjoined the state from denying education to mentally retarded children and required that retarded children be provided a:

> Free, public program of education and training appropriate to the child's capacity, within the context of the general education policy that, among the alternative programs of education and training required by statute to be available, placement in a regular public school class is preferable to placement in a special public school class [i.e., a class for "handicapped" children] and placement in a special public school class is preferable to placement in any other type of program of education and training...

343 F.Supp. at 307

The consent decree further required that retarded children be provided procedural due process and periodic reevaluation.*Mills v. Board of Education of the District of Columbia*

348 F.Supp. 866 (D.D.C. 1972)

Also approved by consent decree, greatly expanded the PARC decision to include all disabled children and incorporated an extensive plan created by the District of Columbia Board of Education to provide: (1) a free appropriate education, (2) and Individualized Education Plan, and (3) due process procedures.The language of the final order provided significant guidance for litigants in cases in other states as well as for the development of appropriate state and federal legislative responses to provide equal educational access and opportunity for the disabled.

Federal legislation was introduced following the PARC and Mills decisions to eliminate discrimination against the disabled.Section 504 of the Vocational Rehabilitation Act of 1973 (P.L.93-112), considered the first major legislation protecting the civil rights of disabled persons, provides that:

> No otherwise qualified handicapped individual in the United States...shall, solely by reason of his handicap, be excluded from participation in, be denied benefits of, or be subjected to discrimination under any program or activity receiving federal financial assistance.

29 U.S.C. §794

A principal concern of Section 504 is discrimination in employment and the provision of health, welfare, and other social services.However, it does recognize the educational needs of disabled children and requires five issues be considered in meeting those needs: (1) location and notification; (2) free appropriate public education; (3) educational setting; (4) evaluation and placement; and (5) procedural safeguards.

45 C.F.R. §84.32-84.36

Failure to comply with these requirements could result in the withdrawal of federal funding.

In 1975, Congress amended the Education of the Handicapped Act (EHA) with the Education for All Handicapped Children Act (EAHCA [P.L.94-142]).The new law was intended to make certain that disabled children receive equal educational access, and provided extensive rules and regulations to guide state and local school actions in providing an appropriate education.The basic educational rights of the EAHCA (see 20 U.S.C. §1401 [16-91]) have been described by Turnbull (1993) in six primary principles as:

Turnbull, H.R., III: *Free Appropriate Public Education: The Law and Children with Disabilities* (4th ed.) Reston, Love, 1993

1. Zero reject—every disabled child (regardless of the severity of his/her disability) must be provided a free, appropriate, publicly supported educa tion-no child may be excluded;
2. Nondiscriminatory assessment—each child must be provided a multifac- tored evaluation (free of race, cultural, or native language bias) to deter- mine the presence of a disability and guide special education program development;
3. Appropriate education—an individualized education program (IEP) is to be developed and implemented to meet the child's unique needs and to ensure a meaningful educational experience;
4. Least restrictive environment (LRE)—each disabled child is to be educated with nondisabled peers to the maximum extent practicable—favoring inclu- sion as a means of supporting the child's right to normalization;
5. Due process—procedures to protect the rights of disabled children and their parents must be provided—safeguarding the right to protest program plan- ning and placement decisions or records confidentiality issues by providing an impartial hearing and appeals process to resolve disputes;
6. Parent participation—parents have the right to participate in planning their child's educational program—mutual benefits can be realized through col- laboration in program development.

The EHA was amended in 1990.Though the basic provisions established in P.L. 94-142 were retained, several modifications were made as follows:

1. Public Law 101-476 changed the title to the Individuals with Disabilities Education Act-better known today by its' acronym IDEA.The same title change was made applicable to all laws making reference to the original Education of the Handicapped Act as well as replacing the term handicap with the term disability (e.g. "handicapped children" became "children with disabilities").Such modifications also made the language consistent with the Americans with Disabilities Act (P.L. 101-336) enacted earlier in the year.
2. Autism and traumatic brain injury were added to the list of distinct disabilities.
3. Monies were made available to establish centers "...to organize, synthesize, and disseminate current knowledge relating to children with attention deficit disorder...";

---

20 U.S.C. §1401 (f) (1)

---

4. Student's IEP's are to include transition services as may be required by individual need. Transition services are defined as "...a coordinated set of activities for a student, designed within an outcome-oriented process, which promotes movement from school to post-school activities..."

---

20 U.S.C. §1401 (a) (19)

---

5. Included the support services of "assistive technology devices" and "assistive technology services" as they appeared in the Technology-Related Assistance for Individuals with Disabilities Act of 1988.
6. Added rehabilitation counseling to the definition of related services.

It is essential that teachers working with disabled children, whether in fully-included or self-contained classrooms, have a basic understanding of the key provisions of current law. Three such provisions, least restrictive environment, individualized education program, and appropriate education, can have a significant impact on the curriculum strategies that may be employed in the teaching of social skills to the disabled.

The Individuals with Disabilities Education Act requires: "...to the maximum extent appropriate, children with disabilities, including children in public or private institutions or other care facilities, are educated with children who are not disabled and that special classes, separate schooling, or other removal of children with disabilities from the regular educational environment occurs only when the nature or severity of the disability is such that education in regular classes with the use of supplementary aids and services cannot be achieved satisfactorily..."

---

20 U.S.C. §1412 (5) (B)

Unfortunately, neither the statutory law nor the following language of the regulations clearly prescribes how school districts are to determine what the least restrictive environment is.

a. Each public agency shall ensure that a continuum of alternative placements is available to meet the needs of children with disabilities for special education and related services.

b. The continuum required under paragraph (a) of this section must:

　　1. Include the alternative placements listed in the definition of special education under §300.17 (instruction in regular classes, special classes, special schools, home instruction, and instruction in hospitals and institutions).

　　2. Make provision for supplementary services (such as resource room for itinerant instruction) to be provided in conjunction with regular class placement.

---
34 C.F.R. §300.551

As greater efforts are made to provide instruction to disabled children in inclusive settings, the possibility exists to misinterpret or misapply the concept of "maximum extent possible."The United States Court of Appeals (Sixth Circuit) in *Ronker v. Walter* identified three exceptions to inclusive placement that may be helpful to remember.Such placements may be precluded if there exists: (1) no benefit to the child; (2) greater benefits in segregated settings even after the feasibility standard is applied; and (3) the potential for disruption to a nonsegregated setting.

Ronker v. Walter §700 F.2d 1058, 1063 (6th Cir. 1983)

These are important considerations when creating the child's individualized education program.

An essential element of free appropriate education is the development of an individualized education program.The IDEA defines individualized education program as:

"...a written statement for each child with a disability developed in any meeting by a representative of the local educational agency or an intermediate educational unit who shall be qualified to provide, or supervise the provision of, specially designed instruction to meet the unique needs of children with disabilities, the teacher, the parents or guardian of such child, and whenever appropriate, such child, which statement shall include:

    a.   A statement of the present levels of educational performance of such child;

    b.   A statement of annual goals, including short-term instructional objectives;

    c.   A statement of the specific educational services to be provided to such child, and the extent to which such child will be able to participate in regular educational programs;

    d.   A statement of the needed transition services for students beginning no later than age 16 and annually thereafter (and, when determined appropriate for the individual, beginning at age 14 or younger), including, when appropriate, a statement of the interagency responsibilities or linkages (or both) before the student leaves the school setting;

    e.   The projected date for initiation and anticipated duration of such services;

    f.   Appropriate objective criteria and evaluation procedures and schedules for determining, on at least an annual basis, whether instructional objectives are being achieved.

---
20 U.S.C. §1401 (a) (20)

For younger children, ages birth through two years of age, P.L. 99-457 (The Education of the Handicapped Amendments of 1986) provided that the multidisciplinary team develop an individualized family service plan (IFSP).The development of an individualized education program (or IFSP) and the provision of that program utilizing the continuum of services associated with the least restrictive environment are fundamental to providing an appropriate education.

As defined in the Individuals with Disabilities Education Act (P.L. 94-142):

> The term "free appropriate public education" means special education and related services that: (a) have been provided at public expense, under public supervision and direction, and without charge,(b) meet the standards of the state educational agency, (c) include an appropriate preschool, elementary, or secondary school education in the state, and (d) are provided in conformity with the individualized education program under §1414 (a)(5) of this title.

---

20 U.S.C. §1401 (a)(18)

Differences of interpretation of the language of the statutory law were common.The Supreme Court, in *Board of Education of Hendrick Hudson Central School District v. Rowley* attempted to minimize confusion by establishing a standard to determine compliance.The Court indicated that a child's education program would be appropriate if it met the following criteria:

> First, has the state complied with the procedures set forth in the Act?And second, is the individualized education program developed through the Act's procedures reasonably calculated to enable the child to receive educational benefits.

---

458 U.S.C. at 207

Further, the Court did not agree that an appropriate education was one that assisted a child in reaching his/her maximum potential but rather, "the intent of the Act was more to open the door of public education to children with disabilities on appropriate terms than to guarantee any particular level of education once inside."

---

458 U.S.C. at 192

Special education programs were to provide "a basic floor of educational opportunity."

An examination of the case law following Rowley seems to indicate that judges are unwilling to overturn the decisions of education professionals as to what constitutes an appropriate education as long as the procedures, services, and rights afforded by the Act are provided.However, the courts appear to be moving away from such procedural evaluations to substantive evaluations of proposed education programs as the movement toward full inclusion continues.One substantive issue impacting curriculum decisions or strategies employed could be the need to respond to the Act's "related services" requirement.

> Title 34 §300.16 describes related services: "...as used in this part, the term "related services" means transportation and such developmental, corrective, and other supportive services as are required to assist a child with a disability to benefit from special education, and includes speech pathology, and audiology, psychological services, physical and occupational therapy, recreation, including therapeutic recreation, early identification and assessment of disabilities in children, counseling services, including

rehabilitation counseling, and medical services for diagnostic or evaluation purposes. The term also includes school health services, social work services in the schools, and parent counseling and training.

Subsequent sections of the regulation, taken collectively, demonstrate a recognition of the importance of having diverse services available to support the development of appropriate social skills. "Counseling services" means services provided by qualified social workers, psychologists, guidance counselors, or other qualified personnel.

42 C.F.R. §300.16 (b)(2)

"Parent counseling and training" means assisting parents in understanding the special needs of their child and providing parents with information about child development.

42 C.F.R. §300.16 (b)(6)

"Psychological services" includes:
1.   Administering psychological and other assessment procedures;
2.   Interpreting assessment results;
3.   Obtaining, integrating, and interpreting information about child behavior and conditions relating to learning;
4.   Consulting with other staff members in planning school programs to meet the special needs of children as indicated by psychological tests, interviews, and behavioral evaluations; and
5.   Planning and managing a program of services, including psychological counseling for children and parents.

42 C.F.R. §300.16 (b)(8)

"Social work services in schools" include:
1.   Preparing a social or developmental history on a child with a disability;
2.   Group and individual counseling with child and family;
3.   Working with those problems in a child's living situation (home, school, community) that affect the child's adjustment in school;
4.   Mobilizing school and community resources to enable the child to learn as effectively as possible in his or her education program.

42 C.F.R. §300.16 (b)(12)

Underwood and Mead (1995) suggest three questions that must be considered to determine whether a child will be eligible for related services:
1.   Is the service necessary for the student to gain access to or remain in the special program?
2.   Is the service necessary to resolve other needs for the student before educational efforts will be successful?
3.   Is the service necessary for the student to make meaningful progress on the identified goals?

Underwood, J., and Mead, J.: *Legal Aspects of Special Education and Pupil Services.* Needham Heights, Allyn and Bacon, 1995.

Because educators may find themselves unable to respond in the affirmative to these queries, access to the services described above may be severely limited or entirely prohibited. Therefore, having access to innovative and successful curriculum strategies in the development of social skills to the disabled is imperative and is the focus of the remaining chapters of this text.

GLOSSARY

Aggression - An attempt to physically harm someone.

Anger - A defensive emotional reaction that occurs when one is frustrated, denied, or attached.

Assessment - A process of collecting formal and informal data about pupils for the purpose of making instructional decisions.

Anxiety - A feeling that exists when one is afraid but cannot recognize the cause.

Behavior contract - Agreement between a teacher (or other adult) and student that clearly specifies student's performances, time frame for meeting them, and specification of the rewards for meeting the expectations.

Behavioral deficit - A response that presents a problem because there have been few opportunities to practice the appropriate behavior.

Behavioral description - A statement that includes a description of specific behaviors being observed.

Behavioral objective - A form for writing an instructional objective that emphasizes expected student outcomes, type of evaluation, and performance standards.

Cognitive behavior management - Behavior management strategy in which students learn to internalize and change their behaviors.

Communication - A message sent by an individual with the planned intention of affecting another individual's behavior.

Compromising - Giving up ones' goal while the other student does the same in order to reach an agreement.

Conformity - Changes in behavior that result from group influences; yielding to group pressure when no direct request has been made.

Cooperative learning - Student-centered instructional approach in which students work in small mixed groups with a shared learning goal.

Effective communication - When a students' message is interpreted in the same way it was intended.

Fear - Real or imaginary feelings shown by students, resulting in physiological responses.

Identity - A consistent set of attitudes that describe, characterize, and define who one is.

Imaginary - Feelings or experiences that exist only in the imagination or fancy; not real experiences.

Integration - Combining several concepts, practices, approaches, methods, etc., into one idea or expression.

Intentions - Planned, deliberated, and conscious acts to satisfy immediate goals.

Internalized behavior - Intrinsic motivation that occurs when students behave appropriately because the behavior brings them personal satisfaction.

Interpersonal communication skills - Skills that promote honest communication and positive attitudes among individuals.

Modeling - A term used in social learning theory to describe how students learn as a result of observing and imitating others.

Negotiation - A process by which students who have opposite views and interests attempt to come to an agreement.

Observation - A procedure in which the observer watches and records behaviors of other individuals.

Positive reinforcement - Presenting a reward or some object that will increase positive or appropriate behaviors of pupils.

Praise - Positive verbal and nonverbal statements made by teachers to strengthen appropriate student behaviors.

Reinforcements - Rewards given for students demonstrating appropriate behaviors to increase the possibilities of those behaviors being repeated.

Rewards - Reinforcers, tangible and intangible objects, given to students to strengthen appropriate behaviors.

Self-acceptance - Pride in yourself, or a high regard for yourself.

Self-control training - A technique employed to enable students who lack self-control to redirect their actions by talking to themselves.

Self-evaluation - A students' estimation of how positively his/her behaviors, manners, and actions compare with those of peers.

Self-monitoring - A strategy in which students are instructed to determine whether they have performed targeted behaviors.

Social interaction - A common bond linking two or more students together.

Social reinforcer - A positive interpersonal interaction that causes a behavior to increase.

Social skills - Behaviors that assists students to interact successfully with their peers and adults and assists them in becoming socially accepted.

Social skills training program - A program designed to provide systematic instruction to assist students in acquiring appropriate social skills.

Task analysis - A process for breaking down complex tasks into small manageable steps so that they can be successfully completed one at a time.

AUTHOR INDEX

A

Achenback, T., 76
Adams, D.N., 99
Adler, A., 20
Agran, M., 30
Aksamit, D.L., 93, 95
Alberto, P.A., 84, 89
Algozzine, B., 30
Algozzine, R., 30, 33, 34, 35, 38, 39
Anastasiow, N., 46
Anita, S.D., 80, 106, 170
Antonello, S., 40
Appelle, S., 47
Archenback, 25
Armstrong, S.W., 109
Ashton, P.T., 27, 76
Ayers, W., 77, 163

B

Baarda, B., 22, 25
Baily, D.B., 6
Banbury, M.M., 95, 99
Bandura, A., 16, 17, 22–27, 66, 67, 68, 69, 70, 91
Bank, J.A., 55
Baron, C., 30
Barth, R., 190
Bauer, A.M., 14
Becker, M., 27
Bender, W., 42
Bennerson, D., 82
Bennett, C., 55, 64
Berdine, W.H., 32, 33, 39
Bernstein, 48
Bert, C.R., 63
Bert, M., 63
Bigge, J., 35
Bilken, D., 73, 170
Birns, 46
Blackhurst, A.E., 32, 33, 39
Borkowski, J., 38

Bouffard, 27
Bradley, R.H., 63
Brantley, H., 43
Bratton, S.C., 102
Brody, G., 77, 80, 84
Brookes, P., 84
Brown, S., 27
Bryan, R., 13
Butler, O.B., 16, 56, 78
Butler-Nalin, P., 30, 31, 33, 36, 40
Buysse, V., 6

C

Campbell, P.H., 86
Cangemi, 17, 18, 21, 22, 23
Carpignano, J., 32
Carr, S., 33, 34
Carrol, J., 26, 76
Cassidy, E., 115, 169
Charles, C.M., 22, 67, 68
Civelli, E., 46
Clark, 42
Clees, T.J., 118
Coker, K.H., 102
Cole, P.R., 36
Coleman, M., 16, 22, 43, 76
Collins, T.W., 73, 84, 88
Cooke, T.P., 9, 170
Corcoran, K., 17
Cosden, M., 95, 101
Crim, D., 169
Cullinan, D., 30
Cummings, C., 25, 76
Cummins, J., 172

D

Dalli, C., 162
Damberg, P., 38
Damon, W., 25, 76
Davidson, P.W., 47
Delgado-Gaitan, C., 110

Demchak, M., 86
Denny, R.K., 95
Dewitt, P.,162
DiMartino, E.C., 160
Dollard, E., 18, 19
Dorr, D.W., 101
Drew, C.J., 34, 36, 37, 38
Drinkwater, S., 86
Dunn, G., 47

E

Edmondson, R., 6
Edwards, 24, 25
Egan, M.W., 34, 36, 37, 38
Egel, A.L., 56, 58
Eisner, E., 190
Epstein, M., 30, 38, 95
Erikson, E.H., 163
Eron, L., 25, 69
Evans, R., 22, 26, 27, 69

F

Farmer, E., 30, 31
Farmer, T., 30, 31
Filips, 25
Finders, M., 111
Forest, M., 73, 190
Forness, S.R., 30
Foster, W., 30
Fowler, S.A., 53, 54, 63
Fox, L.C., 9
Francisco, B., 118
Frayne, C., 27
Furnham, A., 118

G

Gallagher, J.J., 115, 165, 169
Gallagher, K., 46
Gardner, H., 162
Geen, 70
Geers, A., 36
Gemma, A., 99
George, T., 27
Gesec, 25
Gills, W., 97, 98
Glassberg, L., 34
Goldman, D., 42

Goldstein, A., 91, 92, 119
Goldstein, H., 80
Goldstein, S., 102
Goodlad, J.L., 173
Gorrell, 27
Greenberg, M.T., 35, 36
Greene, L.J., 11
Gresham, F.M., 8, 10, 31, 80, 92, 118
Groenveld, M., 47
Grossman, H., 37
Grube, C., 47
Guild, P., 57, 60, 61, 62, 63
Gunter, 93, 95, 99

H

Haager, D., 41
Hall, 25
Hallahan, D.P., 41, 42
Hallowell, E.M., 11
Hanson, M.J., 7, 8
Hardman, M.L., 34, 36, 37, 38
Haring, L., 44, 48
Haring, N., 35, 36, 39, 48
Harris, M., 30, 31
Harry, B., 169
Hatch, T., 73, 162
Hedley, C.N., 95
Henley, M., 30, 33, 34, 38, 39
Herbert, C.R., 95, 99
Heyward, W., 34, 39
Higgins, D., 36
Hilliard, A.G., 16, 54, 61, 62, 63, 64, 73, 78
Hines, M.S., 95
Hogan, A., 81, 82
Hosseini, A., 30
Hudley, C.A., 87, 88
Hyun, K.K., 53, 54, 63

I

Istre, S.M., 102
Ittyerah, 46

J

Jack, 93, 95, 99
Jan, J.E., 47
Jewett, J., 88
Johnson, E., 31

Johnson, R., 73, 78, 99, 100
Johnson, W., 73, 78

K

Kagan, S.L., 73, 100, 101, 163 165
Kahn, 17, 18, 21, 22, 23
Kalechestein, A., 27
Kandel, M., 171
Kaplan, P., 42, 43, 105
Katz, L.G., 73, 83, 88, 93, 172
Kauffman, J., 17, 34, 42, 76
Kavale, K.A., 11, 30
Kazdin, A., 25, 68
Kekelis, L., 45
Kiehl, W.S., 11
Kirkcaldy, B.D., 34
Kouzekanani, K., 81
Kusche, C.A., 35, 36
Kuttschreuter, O., 22, 25

L

LaGreca, A.M., 12, 41, 43
Lane, P.S., 93, 94
Lareau, A., 110
Latham, G., 27
Lent, R., 27
Leone, P., 30
Leonhardt, M., 45
Levine, M.D., 11
Lloyd, J., 41
Loper, A.B., 41
Luebke, J., 30, 38
Lutfiyya, Z., 105
Lyman, 105
Lynch, E.W., 115

M

MacCuspie, A.P., 45
Mansbach, S.C., 110
Manz, 25
Marion, R., 115, 169
Mason, S., 56, 58
Matsueda, M., 46
Matsueda, R.L., 70, 73, 164
McAninch, C., 30, 31
McClelland, D., 84
McCormick, L., 35, 36, 39, 44, 45, 48
McEvoy, M., 9, 80
McGinnis, E., 91

McIntosh, R.M., 33, 34, 68, 82, 83
Melloy, K.J., 11
Menlow, 25
Mercer, A.R., 30, 31
Mercer, C.D., 25, 30, 31
Merrell, K., 31
Merz, J., 31
Meyen, E., 35, 39, 40
Meyers, I.B., 57
Milich, R., 30
Miller, N.E., 18, 19
Moll, I., 67
Moore, D.M., 35, 36
Moore, S., 24
Mooshage, B., 34
Moulton, K., 27

N

Nathenson-Mejia, S., 84
Nelson, C.M., 30, 31
Norby, 25
Norris, G., 44, 45
Nowicki, S., 27

O

O'Brien, C., 170
O'Brien, J., 170
O'Donnell, 35
Oakland, 43
Obiakor, F.E., 55
Odom, S.L., 8, 9, 94, 119
Olivia, A.H., 12
Orlansky, D., 34, 39
Osborne, L.T., 169
Oswald, D.P., 74, 75, 77, 161

P

Padilla, C., 30, 31, 33, 36, 40
Patton, J., 30, 38
Peck, C.A., 8, 9, 170
Peck, V., 38
Pike, K., 84
Polloway, E., 30
Poplin, M.S., 172
Pungo, R., 33, 34

R

Ramsey, R., 33, 34, 38, 39
Reardon, M., 45
Reeve, R.E., 41
Rhodes, L.K., 84
Rhu, A.H., 169
Ring, E., 31
Rizzo, J.V., 92, 93
Roberts, C., 30
Rodda, A., 25, 76
Rose, E., 95
Rosenstock, I., 17, 27
Ross, D., 25
Ross, S.A., 25
Rotter, J.B., 16, 17, 20–22

S

Sacks, S., 45
Salend, S.J., 84, 93, 94
Salinger, T., 85
Salli, C., 110
Salzberg, C., 30
Samarapungavan, 46
Sapona, R.H., 14
Sasso, G.M., 8, 11
Schiefelbush, R.L., 48
Schloss, C.N., 11
Schloss, P.J., 11
Schmid, K., 30
Schoss, 25
Schunk, D., 27
Schwartz, T., 45
Scott, 44
Sedlak, 25
Seligman, M.E., 42
Shade, B.J., 63
Shapiro, S., 81
Shermis, 43
Shores, 93, 95, 99
Silver, L.B., 11
Simpson, R.L., 11
Sims, 25
Sirvis, B.O., 32
Slavin, R.E., 99, 100, 101
Smith, R.W., 169
Smith, S., 11, 12
Smith, T.M., 6
Spencer-Rowe, J., 83

Stein, R., 115
Stephens, B., 47
Stile, S., 45
Stone, W.L., 41, 43
Stoneman, Z., 77
Storey, K., 80, 94
Stowitschek, J., 30
Strain, P.S., 86
Strecher, V., 27
Strickland, B., 21
Stuart, R.B., 66
Sullivan, C.A., 30
Summers, J.A., 7

T

Taylor, G., 8, 55, 64, 73, 74, 75, 76, 78, 83, 93, 105, 156, 164, 167, 172
Tharp, R.G., 172
Thorkildsen, R., 95
Thurlow, M., 30
Thyer, B.A., 102
Tiegerman, 48
Torgesen, J.K., 41
Travers, 25
Trickett, E., 30
Troutman, A.C., 84, 89
Tudge, R., 22, 25
Turnbull, A.P., 169
Turnbull, H.R., 169
Tuttle, D., 45

U

Ubiakor, F., 45

V

Vandercook, T., 86
Vasques, J.A., 63
Vaugh, S., 33, 34, 41, 43, 68, 81, 82, 83
Vincent, J.P., 171
Vitello, S., 30

W

Walker, H., 74, 75, 161
Walters, R.H., 22, 23, 25, 67, 68
Warren, D., 46
Webb, R.B., 76
Wickstrom, S., 80

Wiegman, O., 22
Wiles-Kettenmann, M., 47
Winterhoff, P., 22, 25
Woeppel, P., 12
Wolf, B., 34, 36, 37, 38
Wood, C.E., 11
Wood, J.W., 170

Y

York, J., 86
Ysseldyle, J., 30

Z

Zaragoza, N., 68, 82
Zargota, N., 33, 34
Zetlin, A., 30, 38
Ziggler, E., 25, 76
Zubrick, S., 30

SUBJECT INDEX

A

Aggressiveness, 9, 12, 25, 33, 41, 69–70, 88
  assertiveness, 88
  modeling, 69, 162
  television violence, 25
  theory of development, 69–70
Americans With Disabilities Act, 32
Anger and hostility, 70–71
  apology strategies, 71
  self-management techniques, 70–71
Appendix A, social skills identification, 17–78
Appendix B, informal assessment inventory checklist, 179–80
Appendix C, observation checklist, 181
Appendix D, cooperative learning strategies, 183–84
Appendix E, evaluation sheet 185
Appendix F, films and filmstrips, 187–90
Appendix G, Federal legislation, 191–99
Assessment, identification, placement, 7
Auditory learning style, 59
Autism, 5, 7

B

Bandura (*see also* Social cognitive theory)
  aggression theory, 69–70
  behaviorism and learning, 22–28
  modeling and imitation, 22–25, 68–69, 91
  social transmission of behavior, 22
  stimulus-response integration with cognition, 17
Bandura thought, behavior, and environment, 17–18
  triadic reciprocality, 17
Behavior disorders of disabled, 33–34
  academic characteristics, 34
  social-emotional characteristics, 33
    aggressiveness, 9, 12, 25, 33
    anger and frustration management, 34

asocial behavior, 34
defiance, 33
destructiveness, 34
distractibility, 34
impulsivity, 34
noncompliance, 33
withdrawal and isolation, 34
Behavioral, cultural learning styles of disabled, 53–64
  impact of cultural learning styles, 54–55, 61
  learning styles, dimensions, 56–60
    affective, 56
    cognitive, 56
    physiological, 56
    psychological, 57
  learning styles, assessment tools, 59–60
  learning styles, evaluation, 57–59
  school relationship with cultural styles, 54–55, 61
    assimilation of individualized learning styles, 55
Behavioral modeling, 19, 24–25, 68–69, 91, 96–97, 162
Behaviorism, 16, 17–18, 19, 22–28
  self-efficacy, 25–28, 69

C

Coaching, 95
Cognitive behavior modification, 92
  contingency contracting, 93
  peer mediation, 94–95
  task-centered approach, 93–94
Cooperation, 88
Cooperative learning structure, 99–101, 104–5
  benefits, 100
  elements, 99
  peer tutoring, 101
  programs, 105
  strategies, 100

Copying behavior, 19
Counseling for rehabilitation, 7
Cue, 18–22, 95
Cue and response stimulus
  imitation
    copying behavior, 19
    learning through modeling, 22
    matched-dependent behavior, 19
    observational learning, 22
    same behavior, 19
  psychological principles
    cue, 18–19
    drive, 18–19
    response, 18–19
    reward, 18–19
Cultural sensitivity, 7, 53–54
  awareness techniques, 53
Cultural systems and cognitive learning
    styles, 53–55, 61–62, 67
  instructional delivery and learning styles,
    61–64
  instructional delivery and cultural learn-
    ing styles, 61–62
    cautionary notes, 61–62, 64
  learning style and cultural value system,
    54–55, 67
Curriculum development, 121–22
  identification of activities and resources,
    122
  identification of critical social behaviors,
    121
  sequence-specific objectives, 122
  social skills learning program format, 122
  structuring activity to follow sequence,
    122

D

Deaf and hard-of-hearing
  academic characteristics, 36
    testing interpretation, 36
  social-emotional characteristics, 35–36
    deaf family or hearing family, 36
    impulsive social interactions, 35
    inability to interpret emotional states,
      36
    isolation, 36
    language development, 35
    peer rejection, 36
    severity of loss of hearing, 36

Disabled
  behavior disorders, 33–34
    academic characteristics, 34
    social-emotional characteristics, 33–34
      aggressiveness, 9, 12, 25, 33
      anger and frustration management,
        34
      asocial behavior, 34
      defiance, 33
      destructive, 34
      disruptive behavior tendencies, 30
      distractibility, 34
      impulsivity, 34
      noncompliance, 33
      withdrawal and isolation, 34
  characteristics of interpersonal difficul-
    ties, 11
  classification criteria, 3
  deaf and hard-of-hearing
    academic characteristics, 36
      testing interpretation, 36
    social-emotional characteristics, 35–36
      deaf family or hearing family, 36
      impulsive social interactions, 35
      inability to interpret emotional
        states, 36
      intact self-esteem, 36
      isolation, 36
      language development, 35
      peer rejection, 36
      severity of loss of hearing, 36
  determination of needs, 5
  discrimination, 32
  early intervention, 6
  general observations of social competen-
    cy, 173
  holistic approach to education, 170–74
  learning disabilities, 41–44
    academic characteristics, 43–44
      auditory or visual processing
        deficits, 43
      average and above average intell-
        ect, 43
      discrepancy between learning abili-
        ty and academic achievement,
        43–44
      extraordinary abilities, 42–44
      gifted and talented, 42–44

Disabled (cont.)
  memorization and generalization
    difficulties, 43–44
  poor reflective thinking, 43
  reading problem characteristics, 44
  social-emotional characteristics, 41–43
    aggressiveness, 41
    emotional intelligence require
      ments, 42
    feelings of rejection, 41
    isolation, 41
    learned helplessness, 42
    loneliness, 41
    low motivation, 43
    low self-esteem, 42
    social anxiety, 42
  learning styles, 63–64
  mental retardation, 37–39
    academic characteristics, 37–38
    classifications, 37
      custodial, 37
      educable, 37
      trainable, 37
    generic classification, 3–5
      mildly to moderately disabled, 4
      severely to profoundly disabled, 4
    identification, 5
    social-emotional characteristics, 38–39
      adaptive behavior, 38
      low self-esteem, 38
      normal emotions, 39, 171
      socially immature, 38
      susceptible to peer influence, 38
  orthopedic and health impairments, 39–
    40
    academic characteristics, 40
      learning limitations, 40
    social-emotional characteristics, 39–40
      classifications and inclusions, 39
      dependence on mobility devices,
        40
      diminished attention, 40
      hyperactivity, 40
      limited feelings of peer acceptance,
        40
      socially undesirable body charac-
        teristics, 40
  peer relationships, 30–31
  self-esteem improvement strategies, 166

  social competency, 31–33, 173
  social integration, 31–32
  social rejection, 9, 13, 30, 31, 76
  speech and language impaired, 47–48
    academic characteristics, 47–48
      functional and structural language
        usage, 48
      input problems, 47
      semantic deficits, 47
    social-emotional characteristics, 48
      conversational skill deficits, 48
  stigma of labels, 31
  visually impaired, 44–47
    academic characteristics, 46–47
      auditory acuity, 46
      cognitive development, 46
      left/right orientation, 46
      spatial relationships, 46
      word meaning deficit, 46
    social-emotional characteristics, 45–46
      behavior void of creativity, flexibil-
        ity, and elaboration, 45
      intact self-esteem, 45
      lack of self-confidence factors, 45
      lack of visual cues for communica-
        tion, 45
      lack of visual cues for modeling, 45
Disabled and integration of social skills, 68–
  78
  aggression, 69–70
  anger and hostility management, 70–71
  apology strategies, 71
  application of modeling techniques, 68–
    69
  self-efficacy, 25–28, 69
  self-regulation skills, 72
  social learning theories' commonalities,
    16, 18, 22–25, 67–68, 77
Disabled and self-regulation skills, 72–74
  awareness of thinking patterns, 72
  development of long-term goals, 72–73
  making a plan, 72
Discovery process, 111
Disinhibitory effect, 24
Drive, 18

E

Early child care services, 6–7
    developmental ability of disabled children, 7
    working mothers, 7
Early childhood environmental experiences, 10–11
    lack of adult stimulation, 10
    lack of feedback, 10
    play activity restrictions, 10
Early intervention services, 6–7
    contributing factors, 6–7
Education of the Handicapped Act, 6–7
    provisions, 6–7
Emotional intelligence, 42

F

FAST strategy for interpersonal problem-solving, 82
Federal aid requirements, 5, 7–8
    determination of special needs, 5, 7–8
    due process to protect rights, 5, 7–8
    identification, 5, 7–8
    inclusion of all disabled, 5, 7–8
    individualized education program (IEP), 5–8, 110–11, 169
    least restrictive environment, 5, 8
    social development instruction, 8

G

Glossary, 201–2

H

Handicapped relabeled disabled, 7
Haptic learning style, 60
Holistic approach to education, 170–74

I

IEP (see Individualized education program)
Imitation and modeling
    behaviors, 19, 24
        copying mode, 19
        matched-dependency mode, 19
        same mode, 19
    learning subprocesses, 23–25
        attention, 23

motoric reproduction, 24
        retention of observed behavior, 23
    modeling, 24–25
        identification
        imitation
        social facilitation
    modeling influences, 24
    social learning theories commonality, 16, 18, 22–25, 67, 77
Inappropriate behavior, 8–10
    aggressiveness, 9
    social skills, 8–14
    withdrawal, 9
Individualized education program (IEP), 5–8, 110–11, 169
    parental consent, 5–6, 110–11, 169
Individuals With Disabilities Act, 7
    provisions, 7–8
Individual With Disabilities Education Act, 40
Infants and Toddlers Program provisions, 6–7, 164–65

L

Learning
    cultural systems and cognitive styles, 53–64
    self-efficacy theory and academic achievement, 27, 69
Learning disabilities, 41–44
    academic characteristics, 43–44
        auditory or visual processing deficits, 43
        average and above average intellect, 43
        discrepancy between learning ability and academic achievement, 43–44
        extraordinary abilities, 42–44
        gifted and talented, 42–44
        memorization and generalization difficulties, 43–44
        poor reflective thinking, 43
        reading problem characteristics, 44
Learning styles
    behavioral, cultural learning styles of disabled, 53–64, 164
    dimensions, 56–60, 164
        affective, 56

Learning styles (cont.)
    personality traits' affect on learning, 56
    cognitive, 56
      mental perception and ordering of information, 56
    physiological, 56
      interaction of senses and environment, 56
    psychological, 57
      inner strengths and individuality, 57
      nature vs. nurture, 57
  instructional delivery and learning styles, 61–64
  instructional delivery and cultural learning styles, 61–62
    cautionary notes, 61–62, 64
  learning style and cultural value system, 54–55, 61
Learning styles, assessment, 59–60
  Learning Channel Preference Checklist, 59–60
    auditory, 59
    haptic, 60
    visual, 59–60
  Myers-Briggs Type Indicator, 60
  Swassing-Barbe Modality Index, 60
Learning styles, evaluation, 57–59
  characteristics of individual learning styles, 57–59
  input styles, 58
  instructional techniques, 57–59
  internodal transfer, 58
  organizational styles, 57–58
  output styles, 58
  school relationship with cultural styles, 54–55, 61
    assimilation of individualized learning styles, 55

M

Matched-dependent behavior, 19
Mental retardation, 37–39
  academic characteristics, 37–38
  classifications, 37
    custodial, 37
    educable, 37
    trainable, 37
  generic classification, 3–5
    mildly to moderately disabled, 4
    severely to profoundly disabled, 4
  identification, 5
  social-emotional characteristics, 38–39
    adaptive behavior, 38
    low self-esteem, 38
    normal emotions, 39
    socially immature, 38
    susceptible to peer influence, 38
Mildly to moderately disabled, impairments, 4
  deaf-blindness, 4
  emotionally disturbed, 4
  hearing, 4
  health, 4
  learning disabled, 4
  mental retardation, 4
  orthopedic, 4
  speech and language, 4
  visual, 4
Miller & Dollard (see also Cue and response)
  imitation
    copying behavior, 19
    learning through modeling, 22
    matched-dependent behavior, 19
    observational learning, 22
    same behavior, 19
  psychological principles
    cue, 18–19
    drive, 18–19
    response, 18–19
    reward, 18–19
Modeling and imitation
  attitude of child toward model, 25
  behaviors, 19, 24
    copying mode, 19
    matched-dependency mode, 19
    same mode, 19
  learning subprocesses, 23–25
    attention, 23
    motoric reproduction, 24
    retention of observed behavior, 23
  modeling constructs, 24–25
    identification
    imitation
    social facilitation

Miller & Dollard (cont.)
    modeling influences, 24–25
        adult modeling, 25
        external, vicarious modeling, 25
        peer modeling, 25
        personality attribution, 25
    parental interactions, 9–10
    social learning theories commonality, 16,
        18, 22–25, 67, 77
    social skills, 8–10
Modeling techniques for disabled, 68–69,
    96, 98
Myers-Briggs Type Indicator, 60

O

Orthopedic and health impairments, 39–40
    academic characteristics, 40
        learning limitations, 40
    social-emotional characteristics, 39–40
        classifications and inclusions, 39
        dependence on mobility devices, 40
        diminished attention, 40
        hyperactivity, 40
        limited feelings of peer acceptance, 40
        socially undesirable body characteris-
            tics, 40

P

Parent-professional relationships, 7
Parental involvement in social skill develop-
    ment, 5, 7, 109–16
    guidelines for promoting social growth,
        111–13
    strategies for social learning processes,
        114
Passivity, 12
Pediatric Evaluation of Disabilities
Inventory, 85
Peer rejection, 9, 13, 30, 76
Preschool Checklist, 86
Proximity control, 95
Public Law 42–142, 3, 5–6, 110–11, 116,
    169
Public Law 99–457, 6–7, 164–65
Public Law 101–476, 5, 7–8, 40

R

Rehabilitation counseling, 7
Reinforcement, 20–21
Response, 18
Response facilitation, 24
Reward, 18
Role-playing, 97–98
    disadvantages, 98
Rotter (*see also* Social interactionist theory)
    expectancy-reinforcement, 21–22
    principles of learning theory, 20–21

S

Same behavior, 19
School adaptation and learning styles, 53–64
    anger management techniques, 70–71
    apology strategies, 71
    behavioral intervention strategies, 87–88
    integration of social skills development,
        74–78
School application of social learning theo-
    ries, 80–89
    assessment tools, 84–86
        Pediatric Evaluation of Disabilities
            Inventory, 85
        portfolio assessment, 85
        Preschool Checklist, 86
        self-evaluations, 84–85
        Social Attributes Checklist, 84
        teacher-made tests, 84
    behavior modification techniques, 103–4
    social interactions, 80
    social skill deficits, 81–86
        inadequate skill performance, 81
        performance deficits, 81
        self-control deficits, 81
        skill deficits, 81
    social skill deficit remediation, 81–86
        FAST strategy, 82
        SLAM strategy, 83
        social communications, 83
        strategies, 88
School curriculum for social/interpersonal
    skills, 117–59
    assessment of social skills, 122
    basic goals, ix, 69–74, 111–13, 118
    classroom integration of disabled, 119
    curriculum development, 121–22

School curriculum for social/interpersonal skills (cont.)
  functional approach, 121
  proactive approach strategies, 120–21
  social skills unit, objectives, activities, 123–28, 128–36, 136–41, 141–46, 146–49, 149–52, 152–55
School intervention for social skill training, 91–106
  behavioral modeling, 19, 22, 24–25, 68–69, 91, 96–97
  choice making skills, 102–3
  coaching, 95
  cognitive behavior modification techniques, 92–95
  cooperative learning, 99–101, 104–5
  cuing, 95
  direct instruction, 91–92
  group play activities, 102
  peer tutoring, 101
  proximity control, 95
  role playing, 97–98
    disadvantages, 98
  skillstreaming, 92
  social-cognitive approaches, 102
  special group activities, 101
  videotape modeling, 98
Self-concept/esteem
  affective dimension of learning style, 56
  development, 8, 9, 12, 56, 167
Self-concept (cont.)
  impact on social skills, 8–14
  life experiences, 8
  low self-esteem, 31, 38, 34, 40, 42
  peer rejections, 9, 13, 30, 76
  personality organization around self-concept, 8, 165, 168
  strategies for improving, 166
Self-directed mastery, 25–28
Self-efficacy, 25–28, 69
  empowerment model, 26
    emotional arousal, 26
    mastery experiences, 26
    social persuasion, 26
    vicarious experiences, 26
  expectation distinctions, 26
    efficacy expectations, 26
    response outcome expectations, 26
  theory's application to cognition of interest and learning, 27
Severe to profoundly disabled, teaching strategies, 4–5
  structured and individualized programs, 4
Skillstreaming, 92
SLAM strategy to accept negative remarks, 83
Social cognitive theory (Bandura), 9, 17–18, 22–28
  behaviorism and learning, 22–28, 66
  modeling and imitation, 22–25, 66, 91
  self-efficacy, 25–28, 69
  stimulus-response integration with cognition, 17
  thought, behavior, and environment, 17–18
  triadic reciprocality, 17
Social cognitive theory (Miller & Dollard), 18–19
  response and cue stimulus
    cue, 18–19
    drive, 18–19
    response, 18–19
    reward, 18–19
Social cognitive theory (Vzgotsky), 66–67
  cultural determinants, 67
  cultural systems and cognitive learning styles, 66, 67
  interpersonal, social process of mediation, 67
  internalization of cultural means, 67
  social relational boundaries and proximal development, 67
Social competency, 11–14, 31, 76–78, 160–74
  behavioral disorders, 33–34
    social-emotional characteristics, 33–34
  cognitive skills development, 12
  conflict situations, 12
  conversational skills, 13
  development of goals and strategies, 12–13
  engagement differences with LD children, 13
  expectancy-reinforcement relationships, 21–22
  interrelationships, 11
    remediation of behaviors, 11–14
    selection of friends, 12

Social competency (cont.)
    persuasiveness, 13
    self-management of behavior, 30–33
    social conflict management, 160
    social skills instruction, 72–78, 81–86,
        91–106
    tact, 13
Social interactionist theory (Rotter), 20–22
    expectancy-reinforcement, 21–22
    principles of learning theory, 20–21
Social learning, theories, 16–28, 66–78
    application of theory to education situa-
        tions, 80–89
    application of theory to social situations,
        66–78
    Bandura, 9, 17–18, 22–28
    behaviorism, 16, 66
    cognitive and affective characteristics, 16,
        66
    commonalities, 16, 18, 22–25, 67–68, 77
    definition of overall theory, 17
    environmental learner interaction, 66
    expectancy-reinforcement relationships,
        21–22
    Miller & Dollard, 18–19
    observation and imitation, 16, 18, 22–25,
        67
    personality temperament, 66
    reinforcement through imitation, model-
        ing, copying, 16, 18, 22–25, 67
    response and cue stimulus, 18
    Rotter, 20–22
    stimulus-response integration with cogni-
        tion, 17
    thought, behavior, environment, 17–18
    Vzgotsky, 66–67
Social Prevocation Information Battery
    (SPIB), 86
Social rejection, 9, 13, 30, 76
Social skills curriculum unit, objectives,
    activities, 123–55
    communication skill usage to develop
        friendships, 141–46
    identification and evaluation of feelings,
        136–41
    positive self-acceptance, 152–55
    positive self-concepts, 128–36
    problem-solving, 149–52
    self-confidence, 146–49,

socially acceptable behaviors, 123–28
Social skills, deficit remediation, 72–78, 81–
    86
    assessment tools, 84–86
        Pediatric Evaluation of Disabilities
Inventory, 85
        portfolio assessment, 85
        Preschool Checklist, 86
        self-evaluations, 84–85
        Social Attributes Checklist, 84
        teacher-made tests, 84
    behavioral intervention strategies, 87–88
    deficit types, 81
    FAST strategy components, 82
    SLAM strategy components, 83
    strategies, 88
Social skills, development and deficits, 8–14,
    72–78, 81–86
    deficit types, 81
    dysfunctional adult behaviors, 11–12
    inappropriate demonstration, 8, 9
        inability to predict situations to orga-
            nize behavior, 9–10
        remediation of behaviors, 11–14
    interactions with normal peers, 9, 11
    interpersonal difficulties, characteristics,
        11
    learning by observation, 22–25
    low self-esteem, 12
    modeling
        imitation, 22–25, 67
        observation, 22–25
        parental, 9–10
        school and community, 9, 12
    priority before academic skills, 8–9
    self-regulation, 72–73

Social skills, direct intervention, 91–106
    direct instruction, 91
Social skills, early environmental experi-
    ences, 10–11, 162–66
    children born in poverty, 162
    home environment influences, 163–65
    lack of adult stimulation, 10, 162
    lack of feedback, 10
    modeling violent behaviors 9, 12, 25, 162
    play activity restrictions, 10
    social communication skill deficits, 9–10
Social skills, evaluation, 156–59

checklist, 158
evaluation techniques, 156–58
Social skills, goals, ix, 69–74, 111–13, 118
    anger management, ix, 69–71
    apology skills, ix, 71
    dealing with threats, ix
    lying alternatives, ix
    profanity alternatives, ix
    public actions, ix
    respect for rights of privacy of others, ix, 112
    responsibility for own actions, ix, 112
    self-control, ix, 69–74
    sportsmanship, ix
Social skills, parental role, 5, 7, 109–16, 168–70
    family involvement, 110
    guidelines for promoting social growth, 111–13
    strategies for social learning process, 114
Social skills, school intervention, 91–106
    behavioral modeling, 19, 22, 24–25, 68–69, 91, 96–97
    choice making skills, 102–3
Social skills, school (cont.)
    coaching, 95
    cognitive behavior modification techniques, 92–95
    cooperative learning, 99–101, 104–5
    cuing, 95
    direct instruction, 91–92
    group play activities, 102
    peer tutoring, 101
    proximity control, 95
    role playing, 97–98
        disadvantages, 98
    skillstreaming, 92
    social-cognitive approaches, 102
    special group activities, 101
    videotape modeling, 98
Social skills, integration, 10–12, 74–78
Social skills, strategies, 11–14
Social transmission of behavior, 22–25. (*see also* Bandura)
    observational learning, 22–25
    modeling, 22–25, 76–78
Special education definition, 7
Speech and language impaired, 47–48
    academic characteristics, 47–48

functional and structural language usage, 48
    input problems, 47
    semantic deficits, 47
    social-emotional characteristics, 48
        conversational skill deficits, 48
Swassing-Barbe Modality Index, 60

T

Television violence, 25
Traumatic brain injury, 7, 40
Triadic reciprocality, 17

V

Verbal and nonverbal social responses, 12
Violent behavior patterning, 9, 12, 25, 162
Visual learning style, 59–60
Visually impaired, 44–47
    academic characteristics, 46–47
        auditory acuity, 46
        cognitive development, 46
        left/right orientation, 46
        spatial relationships, 46
        word meaning deficit, 46
    social-emotional characteristics, 45–46
        behavior void of creativity, flexibility, and elaboration, 45
        intact self-esteem, 45
        lack of self-confidence factors, 45
        lack of visual cues for communication, 45
        lack of visual cues for modeling, 45
Vzgotsky, 66, 67. (*see also* Cultural systems and cognitive learning styles)
    interpersonal, social process of mediation, 67
    internalization of culture means, 67
    social relational boundaries and proximal development, 67

W

Whole child, 13, 167, 170, 172
Withdrawal or isolation, 9